the Omnivore's Dilemma

THE SECRETS BEHIND WHAT YOU EAT

MICHAEL POLLAN

NEW YORK TIMES BESTSELLING AUTHOR

adapted by Richie Chevat

DIAL BOOKS FOR YOUNG READERS AN IMPRINT OF PENGUIN BOOKS (USA) LLC

DIAL BOOKS FOR YOUNG READERS
Published by the Penguin Group
Penguin Group (USA) LLC
375 Hudson Street
New York, New York 10014

USA / Canada / UK / Ireland / Australia / New Zealand / India / South Africa / China
penguin.com
A Penguin Random House Company

Library of Congress Cataloging-in-Publication Data
Chevat, Richie.
The omnivore's dilemma : the secrets behind what you eat/by Michael Pollan;
adapted by Richie Chevat.—Young readers ed.
p.   cm.
ISBN 978-1-101-99382-8 (HC)
ISBN 978-1-101-99383-5 (PB)
1. Food supply—Juvenile literature. 2. Food chains
(Ecology)—Juvenile literature. I. Pollan, Michael. Omnivore's dilemma.
II. Title. III. Title: Secrets behind what you eat.
HD9000.5.C506 2009
338.10973—dc22
2009009283

Printed in the USA

7 9 10 8 6

Book design by Jasmin Rubero
Text set in Granjon LT Std

For Judith and Isaac

TABLE OF CONTENTS

PART IV
THE DO-IT-YOURSELF MEAL:
HUNTED, GATHERED, AND GARDENED FOOD

PREFACE

This book just might change your life.

I know: That sounds a little over-the-top, doesn't it? I would never make such a bold claim except that, in the years since *The Omnivore's Dilemma* was first published in 2006, thousands of readers have told me exactly that—sometimes in letters and emails, other times in person (including complete strangers on the street): "Your book changed my life." I'm always surprised to hear it, because that certainly wasn't my goal when I sat down to write the book, and changing people's lives sounds like a big responsibility. So I usually gulp and then say something like, "In a good way, I hope."

But I'm always curious to find out what they mean, so I often ask them to tell me exactly how they've changed since reading the book. The answers are very different, often surprising, and usually extremely gratifying.

Some people tell me that they lost weight after reading the

book, and then they pull out snapshots of their larger former selves. Apparently what they learned in the book about how fast food is made convinced them to stop eating it, and the pounds began to fall off. (Even though this is definitely not a diet book.) Other people tell me that they read *The Omnivore's Dilemma* and decided to change their career (!) and become a farmer. (Big gulp.) "How's it working out for you?" I ask, a little nervously, since farming is a tough way to making a living. They usually tell me that the work is incredibly hard but also incredibly satisfying, and that they wouldn't dream of doing anything else with their lives. (Phew.)

Many people tell me that the book changed the way they think about eating—and that now they spend a lot more time deciding what to put in their mouths. The book has made them aware of how their food choices affect the environment, or animals, or their own health, and they want to start "voting with their forks" (an idea I'll explain later). For young people, that can mean encouraging their parents to shop differently— to buy organic or local food, for example. Parents are used to their kids making all sorts of demands about food—usually for the latest sugary cereal or energy drink, and so they're pleasantly surprised when their kids start asking for organic vegetables or for eggs from small farms where the chickens live outdoors and eat a natural diet.

Then there are the vegetarians and the meat eaters, whose

reactions to the book could not be more different. I've heard from lots of readers who say that, after reading about the way animals are treated in factory farms, they felt they could no longer eat meat and decided to become vegetarians. (Even though the book is not an argument against eating meat.) So I figured that one of the impacts of the book was to inspire vegetarianism—until I began hearing from some *vegetarians*, whose reactions *really* surprised me.

Here's a typical letter from a vegetarian high-schooler: "I haven't eaten a bite of meat since I was six. But after reading your book I've decided to start eating meat again. I never knew there were farms, like Polyface in Virginia, where the animals are treated so well and get to lead such happy lives. I want to support those kinds of farms, so now I eat that kind of humanely raised meat when I can. Instead of calling myself a vegetarian, now I call myself a 'conscious carnivore.'"

The fact that carnivores and vegetarians responded in two totally different ways to the same information tells me that the book is doing its job. That job is simply to get us to think about something that hardly ever crosses our minds: where our food comes from and how it gets to us. So I really like the idea that two people could read the same book and come to such radically different conclusions. I didn't write *The Omnivore's Dilemma* to convince you to eat one kind of food or another. My aim was to give you the information you need to make good choices. What's a "good choice"? That's simple: It's one that allows you to be true to your values—to what you most care about.

The fact is, our food choices are some of the most important choices we get to make in life. The way we eat has a bigger effect on our health and the health of the planet than any other activity. Four of the top ten diseases that kill Americans are the result of a bad diet. What you put on your plate changes nature more than anything else you do. If that sounds over-the-top, think about it: Farming has changed the landscape more than any other human activity. Agriculture has also determined which species of animals are thriving (cows, chickens, and pigs—the ones we eat) and which are in trouble (wolves and the other predators that want to eat the ones *we* want to eat). And though you're probably well aware of how the fossil fuel your family uses to heat your home or power your car contributes to climate change, did you know that the farming and food industry produces even more greenhouse gases than all forms of transportation put together? That's what I mean when I say that the way you eat affects the world more than anything else you do.

This might sound like a big responsibility, and it is—but it's also a great opportunity, especially for people your age. Why? Because although you won't be able to vote in elections until you're eighteen, you can vote with your fork now—by choosing to eat foods that reflect your values, and to avoid ones that don't. Best of all, you can vote this way not just once, but three times a day.

Does this sort of voting make a difference? Without a doubt. Consider the changes we've seen in just the last few years. When *The Omnivore's Dilemma* was published in 2006, there were four thousand farmers' markets in America; now there are more than eight thousand. In 2006, organic food was a fifteen-billion-dollar industry; now it's a thirty-five-billion-dollar industry. The market for sustainably raised meat, milk, and eggs has exploded in the last decade. A new generation of young people are starting small sustainable farms. (One of the most popular internships for college students today is working on an organic farm.) Since Michelle Obama planted an organic vegetable garden on the grounds of the White House, the number of Americans growing vegetables at home has soared, to about 35 percent of all families. And a whole range of food and farming issues that have never been on the public's radar are now being debated across the country and in Washington, D.C.

One of the most exciting developments we've seen in the last decade or so is the rise of a "food movement" in America—a movement to change the way we produce and consume food, so that farmers, food workers, animals, the land, and the environment are all treated with greater respect. There's a lot we can all do to push the food system in this direction, but it begins with informing yourself about what's at stake, and then voting—with your fork now, and then in a few years with your ballot—for the kind of world you'd like to live in. This book is an invitation to think about both the problems of how we produce food today and some of the inspiring solutions people are coming up with to build a better food system for everyone and everything it touches. Welcome to the conversation.

Michael Pollan, 2015

INTRODUCTION

Before I began working on this book, I never gave much thought to where my food came from. I didn't spend much time worrying about what I should and shouldn't eat. Food came from the supermarket and as long as it tasted good, I ate it.

Until, that is, I had the chance to peer behind the curtain of the modern American food chain. This came in 1998. I was working on an article about genetically modified food—food created by changing plant DNA in the laboratory. My reporting took me to the Magic Valley in Idaho, where most of the french fries you've ever eaten begin their life as Russet Burbank potatoes. There I visited a farm like no farm I'd ever seen or imagined.

It was fifteen thousand acres, divided into 135-acre crop circles. Each circle resembled the green face of a tremendous clock with a slowly rotating second hand. That sweeping second hand was the irrigation machine, a pipe more than a thousand feet long that delivered a steady rain of water, fertilizer, and pesticide to the potato plants. The whole farm was managed from a bank of computer monitors in a control room. Sitting in that room, the farmer could, at the flick of a switch, douse his crops with water or whatever chemical he thought they needed.

One of these chemicals was a pesticide called Monitor, used to control bugs. The chemical is so toxic to the nervous system that no one is allowed in the field for five days after it is sprayed. Even if the irrigation machine breaks during that time, farmers won't send a worker out to fix it because the chemical is so dangerous. They'd rather let that whole 135-acres crop of potatoes dry up and die.

That wasn't all. During the growing season, some pesticides get inside the potato plant so that they will kill any bug that takes a bite. But these pesticides mean people can't eat the potatoes while they're growing, either. After the harvest, the potatoes are stored for six months in a gigantic shed. Here the chemicals gradually fade until the potatoes are safe to eat. Only then can they be turned into french fries.

That's how we grow potatoes?
I had no idea.

A BURGER WITH YOUR FRIES?

A few years later, while working on another story, I found myself driving down Interstate 5, the big highway that runs between San Francisco and Los Angeles. I was on my way to visit a farmer in California's Central Valley. It was one of those gorgeous autumn days when the hills of California are gold. Out of nowhere, a really nasty smell assaulted my nostrils—the stench of a gas station restroom sorely in need of attention. But I could see nothing that might explain the smell—all around me were the same blue skies and golden hills.

And then, very suddenly, the golden hills turned jet-black on both sides of the highway: black with tens of thousands of cattle crowded onto a carpet of manure that stretched as far as the eye could see. I was driving through a feedlot, with tens of thousands of animals bellying up to a concrete trough that ran along the side of the highway for what seemed like miles. Behind them rose two vast pyramids, one yellow, the other black: a pile of corn and a pile of manure. The cattle, I realized, were spending their days transforming the stuff of one pile into the stuff of the other.

This is where our meat comes from?

I had no idea.

Suddenly that "happy meal" of hamburger and fries

looked a lot less happy. Between the feedlot and the potato farm, I realized just how little I knew about the way our food is produced. The picture in my head, of small family farms with white picket fences and red barns and happy animals on green pastures, was seriously out-of-date.

THE OMNIVORE'S DILEMMA

Now I had a big problem. I went from never thinking about where my food came from to thinking about it all the time. I started worrying about what I should and shouldn't eat. Just because food was in the supermarket, did that mean it was good to eat?

The more I studied and read about food the more I realized I was suffering from a form of the omnivore's dilemma. This is a big name for a very old problem. Human beings are omnivores. That means we eat plants, meat, mushrooms—just about anything. But because we are omnivores we have very little built-in instinct that tells us which foods are good for us and which aren't. That's the dilemma—we can eat anything, but how do we know what to eat?

The omnivore's dilemma has been around a long time. But today we have a very modern form of this dilemma. We have a thousand choices of food in our supermarkets, but we don't really know where our food comes from. As I discovered, just finding out how our potatoes are grown might scare you off french fries for the rest of your life.

In the past, people knew about food because they grew it or hunted it themselves. They learned about food from their parents and grandparents. They cooked and ate the same foods people in their part of the world had always eaten. Modern Americans don't have strong food traditions. Instead we have dozens of different "experts" who give us lots of different advice about what to eat and what not to eat.

It's one thing to be crazy about food because you like to eat. But I found I was going crazy from worrying about food. So I set out to try to solve the modern omnivore's dilemma. I decided to become a food detective, to find out where our food comes from and what exactly it is we are eating. My detective work became the book you now hold in your hands.

FOUR MEALS

As a food detective, I had to go back to the beginning, to the farms and fields where our food is grown. Then I followed it each step of the way, and watched what happened to our food on its way to our stomachs. Each step was another link in a chain—a food chain.

A food chain is a system for growing, making, and delivering food. In this book, I follow four different food chains. Each one has its own section. They are:

Industrial

This is where most of our food comes from today. This chain starts in a giant field, usually in the Midwest, where a single crop is grown—corn, or perhaps soybeans—and ends up in a supermarket or fast-food restaurant.

Industrial Organic

This food is grown on large industrial farms, but with only natural fertilizers, and natural bug and weed control. It is sold in the same way as industrial food.

Local Sustainable

This is food grown on small farms that raise lots of different kinds of crops and animals. The food from the farm doesn't need to be processed, and it travels a short distance—to a farmers' market, for example— before it reaches your table.

Hunter-Gatherer

This is the oldest type of food chain there is. It's hardly a chain at all, really. It is made up simply of you, hunting, growing, or finding your food.

All these food chains end the same way—with a meal. And so I thought it important to end each section of the book with a meal, whether it was a fast-food hamburger eaten in a speeding car, or a meal I made myself from start to finish.

THE PLEASURES OF EATING

When I was ten years old, I started my own "farm" in a patch of our backyard. From that age until now, I have always had a vegetable garden, even if only a small one. The feeling of being connected to food is very important to me. It's an experience that I think most of us are missing today. We're so confused about food that we've forgotten what food really is—the bounty of the earth and the power of the sun captured by plants and animals.

There were parts of this book that were difficult to write, because the facts were so unpleasant. Some of those facts might make you lose your appetite. But the point of this book is not to scare you or make you afraid of food. I think we enjoy food much more if we take a little time to know what it is we're putting in our mouths. Then we can really appreciate the truly wonderful gifts that plants and animals have given us. To me, that's the point of this book, to help you rediscover the pleasures of food and learn to enjoy your meals in a new way.

THE MEAL:

Source: McDonald's
Eaten: In the car

MENU:
Classic cheeseburger
Large fries
Large Coke (32 oz.)

PART ONE

The Industrial Meal:

Food from Corn

1
How Corn Took Over America

A FIELD OF CORN

The average supermarket doesn't seem much like a field of corn.

Take a look around one. What do you see? There's a large, air-conditioned room. There are long aisles and shelves piled high with boxes and cans. There are paper goods and diapers and magazines. But that's not all. Look again. Somewhere, behind the brightly colored packaging, underneath the labels covered with information, there is a mountain of corn.

You may not be able to see it, but it's there.

I'm not talking about the corn in the produce section. That's easy to recognize. In the spring and summer, the green ears of corn sit out in plain view with all the other fruits and vegetables. You can see a stack of ears next to the eggplants, onions, apples, bananas, and potatoes. But that's not a mountain of corn, is it?

Keep looking. Go through produce to the back of the supermarket and you'll find the meats. There's corn here too, but it's a little harder to see. Where is it? Here's a hint: What did the cows and pigs and chickens eat before they became cuts of meat? Mainly corn.

Go a little further now. There's still a lot of corn hiding in this supermarket. How about those long aisles of soft drinks? Made from corn. That freezer case stuffed with TV dinners? Mostly corn. Those donuts and cookies and chips? They're made with a whole lot of corn.

Supermarkets look like they contain a huge variety of food. The shelves are stuffed with thousands of different items. There are dozens of different soups and salad dressings, cases stuffed with frozen dinners and ice cream and meat. The range of food choices is amazing.

Yet if you look a little closer, you begin to discover:

It's All Corn.

Well, maybe not *all* corn, but there's still an awful lot of it hiding here—a lot more than you suspect. We think of our supermarkets as offering a huge variety of food. Yet most of that huge variety comes from one single plant. How can this be?

Corn is what feeds the steer that becomes your steak.

Corn feeds the chicken and the pig.

Corn feeds the catfish raised in a fish farm.

Corn-fed chickens laid the eggs.

Corn feeds the dairy cows that produce the milk, cheese, and ice cream.

See those chicken nuggets in the freezer case? They are really corn wrapped up in more corn. The chicken was fed corn. The batter is made from corn flour. The starch that holds it together is corn starch. The oil it was fried in was corn oil.

But that's not all. Read the label on any bag of chips, candy bar, or frozen snack. How many ingredients do you recognize? *Maltodextrin? Monosodium glutamate? Ascorbic acid? What are those things?* What about *lecithin and mono-, di-,* and *triglycerides*? They are all made from corn. The golden food coloring? Made from corn. Even the citric acid that keeps the nugget "fresh" is made from corn.

If you wash down your chicken nuggets with

HIDDEN CORN

Ever look at the ingredient list on a food label and wonder about those strange names? All of these common ingredients and hundreds more are made from corn:

modified starch

unmodified starch

glucose syrup

maltodextrin

ascorbic acid

crystalline fructose

lactic acid

MSG

caramel color

xanthan gum

almost any soft drink, you are drinking corn with your corn. Since the 1980s almost all sodas and most of the fruit drinks sold in the supermarket are sweetened with something called high-fructose corn syrup.

Read the label on any processed food, and corn is what you'll find. Corn is in the non-dairy creamer and the Cheez Whiz, the frozen yogurt and the TV dinner, the canned fruit and the ketchup. It's in the candy, the cake mixes, the mayonnaise, mustard, hot dogs and bologna, the salad dressings and even in some vitamins. (Yes, it's in a Twinkie too.)

There are some forty-five thousand items in the average American supermarket and more than a quarter of them now contain corn. This goes for the non-food items as well— everything from toothpaste and cosmetics to disposable diapers, trash bags, and even batteries.

Corn is in places you would never think to look. It's in the wax that coats the other vegetables in the produce section. It goes into the coating that makes the cover of a magazine shine. It's even part of the supermarket building, because the wallboard, the flooring, and many other building materials are made with corn.

CARBON FROM CORN

You are what you eat, it's often said. If this is true, then what we are today is mostly corn. This isn't just me being dramatic—it's something that scientists have been able to prove. How do they do this? By tracing the element carbon as it goes from the atmosphere into plants, then into our food, and finally, into us.

You may have heard the expression that humans are a carbon-based life-form. (This always seems to come up in science fiction movies, but it's true.) Like hydrogen and oxygen, carbon is an element, one of the basic building blocks of matter. All the molecules that make up our cells—carbohydrates, proteins, and fats—contain the element carbon.

All of the carbon in our bodies was originally floating in the air, as part of a carbon dioxide molecule. Plants take the carbon out of carbon dioxide and use it to make food—*carbo*hydrates. They do this through a process called photosynthesis.

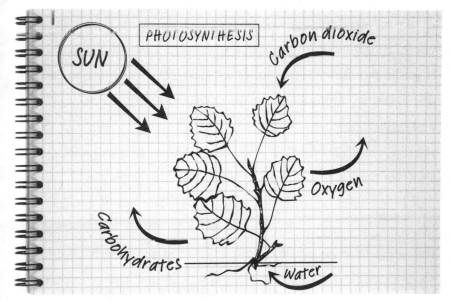

All food begins with the process of photosynthesis.

In photosynthesis, plants use the energy of the sun (*photo* means light) to *synthesize* (make) food.

All of our food, in fact almost all life on earth, can be traced back to photosynthesis in plants. It's more than a figure of speech to say that plants create life out of thin air.

So the plants take carbon and make it into food. Then we eat the plants, or we eat animals that have eaten the plants. That's how the carbon winds up in our cells. But not all carbon is the same. Corn uses slightly different types of carbon than other plants. So by looking at the type of carbon in our cells, scientists can tell how much corn we have been eating.

Todd Dawson, a biologist at the University of California, Berkeley, has done exactly that kind of research. He says that when you look at the carbon in the average American's cells, "we look like corn chips with legs."

Americans don't think of themselves as corn eaters. Our bread is made from wheat flour. We don't eat a lot of corn on the cob. When we think of serious corn eaters, we often think of people in Mexico. About 40 percent of their calories come directly from corn, mostly in the form of corn tortillas. Yet Americans have *more* corn in our diet than Mexicans. It's just that the corn we eat wears many different disguises.

How did corn take over America? It's really a tremendous success story—for corn, anyway. Corn has managed to become the most widely planted crop in America—more than 80 million acres of farmland are planted with corn every year. Today it covers more acres of the country than any other living species, including human beings. It has pushed other plants and animals off the American farm. It has even managed to push a lot of farmers off the farm. (I'll explain that one later.) Corn is now one of the most successful plants on earth.

It's important to remember that while humans use plants and other animals, it's not a one-way street. Plants and animals don't just sit around waiting for human beings to use them—they use us, too. The ones that can adapt use our farms and cities to spread and multiply. Corn became king of the farm and the supermarket because it adapted itself easily to the needs of farmers and food makers. It had qualities that human beings prized. Those qualities allowed it to spread and grow until it worked its way into every corner of our lives—and every cell in our bodies.

THE RISE OF MAIZE

When Columbus returned to Spain after his first voyage he described many wonderful things he had seen to Queen Isabella. One of his discoveries was a towering grass with an ear as thick as a man's arm, to which grains were "affixed in a wondrous manner and in form and size like garden peas, white when young." That grass was called maize, but today we know it as corn.

CORN OR MAIZE?

Maize is the other name for what Americans call corn. It is the name the Spanish learned from the Native Americans who grew it. In England and much of the world, the plant is still called maize.

CORN was the English word for any sort of grain, even a grain of salt. (That's where the term "corned beef" comes from.) The English who settled in North America called the plant Indian corn, meaning Indian grain. Today, in the United States and Canada, corn has become so important, it has taken over the word. Corn is just corn, and all those other grains have to stick to their own names.

Corn began as a wild grass called teosinte. (*Teosinte* means "mother of corn" in the Native American language Nahuatl.) Teosinte still grows wild in some places in Central America, but if you saw it, you might not recognize it as the mother of corn. Teosinte ears are no bigger than your thumb. They are not covered in thick husks. The kernels are tiny seeds. Yet long before Columbus arrived, that wild grass had managed to evolve into maize and spread across North America.

Corn spread because it could adapt to the needs of human beings. Of course, it needed human help. Humans selected bigger ears with fatter kernels and planted those seeds. By the year 700, Indians as far away as New England and Canada farmed maize. Corn had begun its march to world domination, but it still had a long way to go.

After Columbus, the Native Americans were conquered

by the Europeans. But maize, or corn, had no loyalties to the Maya and other people who had helped it spread. It was only concerned with its own survival. The Europeans presented a way for corn to spread even farther. The plant quickly adapted to the new humans and their needs.

The first thing corn did was push aside the European crops the new settlers brought with them. The European plants just couldn't compete. For example, wheat brought from Europe did not do as well as the native maize. A seed of wheat might, with luck, yield 50 new grains of wheat. A single planted corn seed could yield 150 to 300 fat kernels. Corn won that contest easily.

Corn continued quickly to win over the new settlers by being very useful. It could supply them with a ready-to-eat vegetable, a storable grain, a source of fiber, an animal feed, and heating fuel. Corn could be eaten fresh off the cob or dried on the stalk, stored over the winter and ground into flour. Corn could also be mashed and fermented to make beer or whiskey.

No part of the big grass went to waste. The husks could be woven into rugs and twine. The leaves and stalks made good feed for livestock. The shelled cobs could even be stacked by the outhouse and used as a rough substitute for toilet paper!

In the competition for king of the crops, corn left the European plants in the dust. Settlers who stuck to the Old World crops often perished. The colonists who recognized

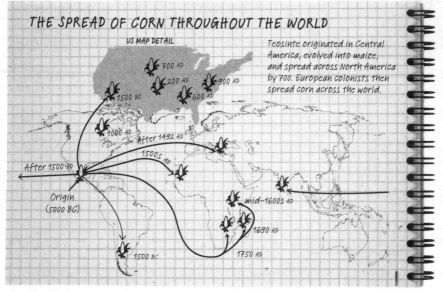

THE SPREAD OF CORN THROUGHOUT THE WORLD

US MAP DETAIL

Teosinte originated in Central America, evolved into maize, and spread across North America by 700. European colonists then spread corn across the world.

700 AD
200 AD
900 AD
1500 BC
600 AD
1000 AD
After 1492 AD
1500s AD
After 1500 AD
Origin (5000 BC)
mid-1600s AD
1690 AD
1500 BC
1750 AD

Sources: *The Natural History Museum, London, and Smith, C. Wayne (Ed.) Corn: Origin, History, Technology and Production. John Wiley & Sons.*

corn's usefulness did well. And of course, one thing the successful farmers did was plant more corn, helping maize to build its kingdom. Corn helped the colonists and the colonists helped corn.

Corn made itself useful in one other important way. It turned out that corn was an excellent way to store and trade wealth. Dried corn is easy to transport and almost indestructible. The farmer can take any surplus to market and sell or trade it. In the new colonies corn often took the place of money.

Corn allowed farming settlements to become trading settlements. Corn made the slave trade possible. Traders in Africa paid for slaves with corn and then fed slaves corn when they were brought here. Corn was the perfect plant for the growing economy of the colonies. And just as important, the new colonists gave corn a way to get to the rest of the world.

M. POLLAN, FOOD DETECTIVE

Once I realized how much of our food is made from corn, I began to look at supermarkets differently. Instead of a giant variety of food, I saw corn hiding in every aisle. Now, I have nothing against corn. There's nothing more delicious than a roasted ear of fresh sweet corn. But I didn't understand why there had to be corn in *everything* we eat. Who decided that corn would be our main food? How did that hap-

WHY CORN NEEDS PEOPLE

Wild teosinte does not look like modern corn. It does not have fat ears with hundreds of kernels wrapped in a thick husk. Instead, it has a single row of triangular seeds growing on a single stalk. Its kernels are covered in a hard shell. The seeds are spread by animals.

Some time several thousand years ago, teosinte mutated or changed. The mutation made its seeds grow on a cob, covered by a husk. Now its seeds could not come loose by themselves. Luckily, a creature came along that knew how to pick those husks, take out the seeds, and plant them. That creature was us. Humans took the ears off the plant, separated the kernels, ate some and planted others.

Teosinte gave up its independence, but it gained an ally who helped it spread across the globe. Ever since, corn and human beings have been joined together. The plant cannot live without us. Can we live without the plant?

TEOSINTE   MODERN CORN

pen? Where did all this corn come from and how did it take over our supermarket?

So I decided to find out. And like any good detective, I realized I had to start at the very beginning, which in this case meant a field of corn in Iowa. I began with that field and tried to trace the corn as it traveled across the country, first to my supermarket and then to my stomach. I watched it being turned into meat, milk, and eggs by cows and chickens. I watched as it was torn apart and rebuilt into all the different foods and products listed on all those labels.

What I discovered was a vast industry—a giant agriculture business or *agribusiness*. This industry doesn't look much like farming the way most people imagine it. It's more like a series of factories that turn raw materials into food products. It's a giant food chain, the one that supplies most of the food Americans eat today.

A food chain in nature helps us understand who eats what (or whom). But the food chain that feeds most Americans is anything but natural. The *industrial* food chain that supplies our supermarkets stretches thousands of miles and has dozens of different links. It's a chain that's powered by oil and gasoline and controlled by giant corporations. It's a chain that separates us from our food and keeps us from knowing what it really is we're eating.

Most of all, it's a food chain built around one plant. Somehow, that small wild grass that started in the hills of

Central America has become the star of the biggest, most expensive food chain in the history of the world. But if corn is the star of this story, is it the hero or is it the bad guy? Before I could decide, I needed to get to know it better. And so I went to see it where it lives, in the vast cornfields of the Midwest.

2

The Farm

ONE FARMER, 140 EATERS

It was the first week of May and I was at the wheel of a clattering 1975 International Harvester tractor, driving through an Iowa cornfield. The tractor was dragging a spidery machine called an eight-row planter, which dropped corn seeds into the earth. Driving over that field was like trying to steer a boat through a sea of dark chocolate. The hard part was keeping the thing on a straight line. If you mess up, your rows will wobble, overlapping or spreading apart. Your neighbors will laugh and, worst of all, you will not be able to plant as much corn.

The tractor I was driving belonged to George Naylor, a big man with a moon face and a scraggly gray beard. He sat next to me as I drove and tried to shout instructions over the diesel roar. He had on the farmer's usual baseball cap, a yellow shirt,

and overalls—the stripy blue kind worn by railroad workers. The field was part of Naylor's farm, 470 acres in Greene
County, Iowa. Naylor had been working the farm for more
than thirty years, since he took it over from his father in the
mid-1970s.

This part of Iowa has some of the richest topsoil in the
world, a layer nearly two feet thick. It was laid down over ten
thousand years ago by retreating glaciers. Tall-grass prairie
grew here until the mid-1800s, when the sod was first broken
by the settler's plow. George's grandfather moved his family
to Iowa from Derbyshire, England, in the 1880s. The sight
of such soil, curling behind the blade of his plow, must have
made him feel happy and confident. It's gorgeous stuff, black
gold as deep as you can dig, as far as you can see.

THE FAR END OF THE FOOD CHAIN

Back in 1919, when the Naylors bought this land, farming
was very different and so was the Naylor farm. All sorts of
crops grew here: corn, but also fruits and other vegetables, as
well as oats, hay, and alfalfa to feed the pigs, cattle, chickens,
and horses. (Horses were the tractors of that time.) Back then
one out of every four Americans lived on a farm. The average
farmer grew enough food to feed twelve other Americans.

Less than a century later the picture is very different. Corn
has muscled out most of the other plants and animals. The

sheep, chickens, pigs, and horses are gone. So are most of the fruits and vegetables. George Naylor grows only two crops on his 470 acres—corn and soybeans. Corn has even pushed most of the people off the farm. Out of 300 million Americans, only 2 million are still farmers. That means the average American farmer today grows enough food to feed 140 other people.

The 140 people who depend on George Naylor for their food are all strangers. Like me, they live at the far end of a food chain that is long and complicated. George Naylor doesn't know the people he is feeding and they don't know him.

I came to the Naylor farm as an unelected representative of the 140 people he feeds. I was curious to learn whom, and what, I'd find at the far end of the food chain that keeps me alive. Of course, I had no way of knowing if it was George or some other farmer who grows the corn that feeds the steer that becomes my steak. That's the nature of the industrial food chain. But I knew that a Midwest cornfield just like George Naylor's is the place most of our food comes from.

I PLANT CORN

The day I showed up at the farm was supposed to be the only dry one all week, and George was trying to get his last 160 acres of corn planted. A week or two later he'd start in on the soybeans. The soybean has become the second major crop in

photo courtesy of George Naylor

George Naylor loads his truck with corn from his storage bin, which he'll then tow to the grain elevator in town.

the industrial food chain, taking turns each year in the field with corn. It now finds its way into two-thirds of all processed foods.

For most of the afternoon I sat on a rough cushion George had made for me from crumpled seed bags. After a while he let me take the wheel. We drove back and forth across the field, a half a mile in each direction. Every pass across this field, which is almost perfectly flat, represents another acre of corn planted.

The corn seed we were planting looked like regular kernels of corn, but it was actually something called Pioneer Hi-Bred 34H31. You and I think of corn as corn, but farmers like Naylor know there are dozens of varieties, most created by large agribusiness companies. That's one of the reasons corn has succeeded so well. It's relatively easy for humans to breed new types of corn to fit our needs. But what's good for corn (and agribusiness) isn't always good for farmers. That's the case with the new types of corn seed.

Back when George's grandfather started farming, farmers grew their own seed. That's the way farmers had always gotten their seed—they just kept some of their crop to be planted for the next season. Then in the 1930s seed companies came up with a new kind of corn seed—hybrid corn. A *hybrid* is a plant or animal whose parents have different traits. For example, you might take a type of corn that resists disease and cross it with another type of corn that produces a lot of ears. The result is a hybrid—a disease-resistant plant that produces a lot of corn. Sounds good, right?

The catch is that hybrid corn does not "come true." The first crop planted from hybrid corn seed will all be identical. The plants will have all the good traits the seed company promised. But the "children" of that crop will be mixed. Some plants will be like their hybrid parents, but most will not. The only way to make sure your plants produce the same amount of corn—that they have the same yield as the original hybrid—is to buy new seed every year from a seed company.

Hybrid corn *quadrupled* the yields of farmers, from about twenty bushels per acre to about eighty bushels per acre.

This was the beginning of a major change in the way farmers operated and the way we get our food. In a way it was the beginning of the industrial food chain.

HOW BIG IS A BUSHEL?
One bushel of corn is 56 pounds of kernels. That's about the size of an extra-large bag of dog food.

The secret of modern corn hybrids is that they can be planted very close together. Before hybrids, a farmer could plant eight thousand corn plants in an acre. Today, George can grow *thirty* thousand plants in an acre. Hybrids have been bred for thicker stalks and stronger root systems, the better to stand upright in a crowd. This also makes it possible to harvest them with large machines. Basically, the plants live in a city of corn, crowded together in neat rows.

New hybrids have increased farm yields to about 180 bushels per acre. One bushel holds 56 pounds of kernels, so 180 bushels is slightly more than 10,000 pounds of food per acre. The field George and I planted that day would produce 1.8 million pounds of corn. Not bad for a day's work sitting down, I thought to myself.

FRANKENSEEDS?

When farmers first planted hybrid corn in the 1930s their yields doubled or tripled. But if they planted seed from that first crop, yields dropped again, since the second generation of corn was not identical to the first. The only way to get the higher yields was to buy seed from seed companies. Soon, the only way for a farmer to compete was to buy hybrid seed every year. Even if farmers face hard times, the seed companies continue to make money year after year, selling farmers something they used to grow themselves.

Today the seed companies have taken things a step further. Genetically modified corn seed (or GMO, for genetically modified organism) promises even higher yields than hybrid seed. GMO corn is not bred the old-fashioned way, by crossing corn plants. It is created in a laboratory by adding genes to corn DNA. The new genes don't come from corn plants. They might come from a bacteria or some other organism. So with human help, corn can now take genes from other plants and animals. This opens up a whole new world of possibilities for the plant and its breeders.

These new GMO seeds could be a bonanza for the seed companies. No one can own the species called "corn." It is part of the natural world, the common property of all humanity. But with GMOs, a company can own a patent on a living organism. When Monsanto, or some other corporation, invents a new type of corn, it belongs to them and they can charge farmers for the right to grow it. But many farmers like George Naylor refuse to grow GMO crops. They believe that GMOs are a reckless experiment with the natural order of things.

CORN VS. EVERYONE

When George Naylor's grandfather was farming, the typical Iowa farm was home to many different plant and animal species. At the top of the list were horses, because every farm needed working animals. After horses were cattle, chickens, and then corn. After corn came hogs, apples, hay, oats, potatoes, and cherries. Many Iowa farms also grew wheat, plums, grapes, and pears. This *diversity*, with many different types of crops, allowed the farmer to get by if prices fell for any one crop.

The arrival of high-yield corn changed all that. It changed the very landscape of Iowa, as corn drove out the other plants and animals and even many of the people.

1920 — DIVERSITY LOST — 2002

These lists show the number of crops and livestock produced for sale on Iowa farms in 1920 and 2002.

1920			2002
Horse	Plums	Barley	Corn
Cattle	Grapes	Raspberries	Soybeans
Chicken	Ducks	Turkeys	Hay
Corn	Geese	Watermelon	Cattle
Hogs	Strawberries	Gooseberries	Horses
Apples	Pears	Sweet Corn	Hogs
Oats	Mules	Apricots	Oats
Potatoes	Sheep	Tomatoes	Sheep
Cherries	Peaches	Cabbage	
Wheat	Bees	Popcorn	

Source: Leopold Center for Sustainable Agriculture, Iowa State University; USDA.

As yields grew and farmers grew more corn, prices dropped. Suddenly it was cheaper to feed corn to cattle, instead of raising them on hay or grass. People also found it cheaper to feed corn to chickens and hogs. A new business emerged—cattle, pigs, and chickens started being stuffed full of corn in large factory-type operations called feedlots. So the animals disappeared from the farm, and with them the pastures and hay fields and fences. (The horses began to disappear when farmers started buying tractors.)

In the place of the pastures, the farmers planted more corn (and sometimes soybeans). Now the corn began to push out people too. A farm of corn and soybeans doesn't require nearly as much human labor as the old-fashioned farm full of

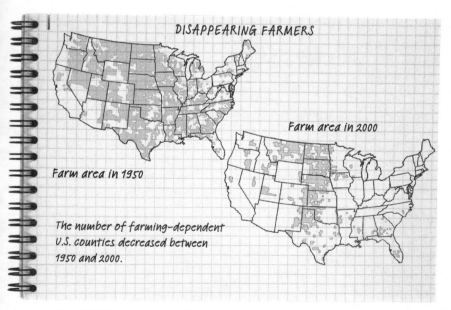

DISAPPEARING FARMERS

Farm area in 2000

Farm area in 1950

The number of farming-dependent U.S. counties decreased between 1950 and 2000.

Source: USDA Economic Research Service.

different kinds of crops. Bigger tractors and machines, chemical weed killers, and artificial fertilizer made it easier for one farmer to handle more acres.

"Growing corn is just riding tractors and spraying," Naylor told me. It only takes a few weeks of work over a year to raise five hundred acres of industrial corn. So the farms have gotten bigger, but fewer people live on them.

When Naylor's grandfather arrived in America the population of Greene County was near its peak: 16,467 people. In the 2006 census data it had fallen to below 10,000. The town of Churdan in the center of the county is like a ghost town. The barbershop, a food market, and the local movie theater have all closed in recent years. The middle school has so few students left it can no longer field a baseball team. It takes four local high schools to field a single football team: the Jefferson-Scranton-Paton-Churdan Rams.

Just about the only business left standing in Churdan is the grain elevator, the tall structure where corn is stored before it is shipped elsewhere. The elevator stands at the far end of town like a windowless concrete skyscraper. It still makes money because, people or no people, the corn keeps coming, more of it every year.

3
From Farm to Factory

TURNING BOMBS INTO FERTILIZER

It may seem that I've given corn too much credit. After all, corn is just a plant. How could a plant take over our food chain and push out almost every other species? Well, it had some help—from the U.S. government.

At the heart of the industrial food chain are huge businesses, *agri*-businesses. The same businesses that create new seeds provide farmers with the tools and fertilizer they need to grow lots of corn. Agribusinesses also need cheap corn from which they make processed food and hundreds of other products. To get the corn flowing and keep it flowing, agribusiness depends on government regulations and taxpayer money.

The government started seriously helping corn back in 1947. That was when a huge weapons plant in Muscle Shoals, Alabama, switched over to making chemical fertilizer. How can a weapons plant make fertilizer? Because ammonium nitrate, the main ingredient in many explosives, happens to be an excellent source of nitrogen. And nitrogen is one of the main ingredients in fertilizer.

After World War II, the government found itself with a tremendous surplus of ammonium nitrate. There was a debate about what the government should do with the leftover bomb material. One idea was to spray it on forests to help out the timber industry. But scientists in the Department of Agriculture had a better idea: Spread the ammonium nitrate on farmland as fertilizer. And so the government helped launch the chemical fertil-

PLANTS AND NITROGEN

Plants and all living organisms need the element nitrogen. Without nitrogen, cells cannot make proteins or DNA.

For thousands of years, farmers added nitrogen to their soil, even before they knew what nitrogen was. They fertilized their crops with manure from their animals. They also rotated crops. That means they never grew corn in a field more than two years in a row. Then they would switch that field to soybeans or some other legume. Legumes such as beans add nitrogen to the soil with the help of friendly bacteria that live on their roots.

Then in 1909 a chemist discovered a way to take nitrogen out of the air. This nitrogen could be used for fertilizer. However, making nitrogen this way takes enormous amounts of energy, energy that we mainly get from burning fossil fuels. Not only that, it uses a lot of hydrogen that also comes from gas and oil. With chemical fertilizer, farming went from being solar powered to being powered by oil, coal, and gas.

izer industry. (It also helped start the pesticide industry, since insect killers are based on poison gases developed for the war.)

Chemical fertilizer was needed to grow hybrid corn because it is a very hungry crop. The richest acre of Iowa soil could never feed thirty thousand hungry corn plants year after year without added fertilizer. Though hybrids were introduced in the thirties, it wasn't until farmers started using chemical fertilizers in the 1950s that corn yields really exploded.

THERE GOES THE SUN

When George Naylor's father spread his first load of ammonium nitrate fertilizer, the ecology of his farm underwent a quiet revolution. Until then, the farm's nitrogen had been recycled in a natural loop. Legumes used the sun's energy to fix nitrogen in the soil. Other plants used the nitrogen to grow. Animals ate the plants and the farmer recycled the nitrogen by spreading the animals' manure on the soil.

But now the Naylors didn't need to produce their own nitrogen—they went out and bought it. The nitrogen for the fields would no longer be made with the sun's energy but with fossil fuels. Farming was no longer an ecological loop—it was more like a factory. The farmer bought raw materials (seed and fertilizer) and turned it into a finished product—corn.

Since there was no need for legumes to fix nitrogen, farmers could plant corn in every field, every year. Animals and their pastures could be eliminated. Farming became much simpler. Like a factory, the industrial farm produces just one product (or at most, two).

And like most factories, the industrial farm is powered with fossil fuels. There's the natural gas in the fertilizer and the fossil fuel energy it takes to make the pesticides, the diesel used by the tractors, and the fuel needed to harvest, dry, and transport the corn. Add it all

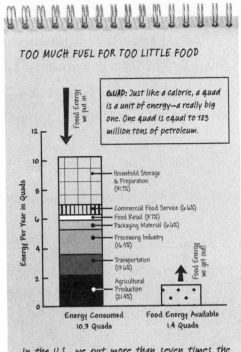

TOO MUCH FUEL FOR TOO LITTLE FOOD

Fossil Energy we put in

QUAD: Just like a calorie, a quad is a unit of energy—a really big one. One quad is equal to 183 million tons of petroleum.

Energy Per Year in Quads

Household Storage & Preparation (31.7%)
Commercial Food Service (6.6%)
Food Retail (3.7%)
Packaging Material (6.6%)
Processing Industry (16.4%)
Transportation (13.6%)
Agricultural Production (21.4%)

Food Energy we get out!

Energy Consumed
10.3 Quads

Food Energy Available
1.4 Quads

In the U.S., we put more than seven times the amount of energy into growing, transporting, and storing food than we get out of the food itself.

Source: University of Michigan Center for Sustainable Systems.

up and you find that every bushel of corn from an industrial farm requires about half a gallon of oil to grow. That's around seventy-five gallons of oil per acre of corn. (Some estimates are much higher.)

Here's another way to look at it. Calories, like the calories in food, are units of energy. On the industrial farm, it takes about ten calories of fossil fuel energy to produce one calorie of food energy. That means the industrial farm is using up more energy than it is producing. This is the opposite of what happened before chemical fertilizers. Back then, the Naylor farm produced more than two calories of food energy for every calorie of fossil fuel energy invested. In terms of energy, the modern farm is a losing proposition. It's too bad we can't simply drink the petroleum directly—it would be more efficient.

The factory farm produces more food much faster than the old solar-based farm. But the system only works as long as fossil fuel energy is cheap.

NITROGEN POLLUTION

Hybrid corn eats up a lot of nitrogen, but farmers still feed it far more than it can possibly eat. In fact, farmers waste most of the fertilizer they buy. Many farmers put down extra just to play it safe. "They say you only need a hundred pounds per acre. I'm putting on closer to one hundred eighty," Naylor explained to me, a bit sheepishly. "It's a form of yield insurance."

But what happens to the eighty pounds of man-made nitrogen that Naylor's corn plants don't take up? Some of it evaporates into the air, where it creates acid rain. Some of it turns into nitrous oxide, a gas that increases global warming.

Some of the extra fertilizer seeps down to the groundwater. Because of this, the Naylors don't drink the well water on their farm. When I went to pour myself a glass of water in the kitchen, George's wife, Peggy, made sure I used a special faucet connected to a water filter system.

As for the rest of the extra nitrogen, the spring rains wash it off Naylor's fields, carrying it into drainage ditches. Eventually it spills into the Raccoon River. From there it flows into the Des Moines River, and down the Mississippi to the Gulf of Mexico. There, in a strange twist of nature, the fertilizer winds up poisoning the ocean. The flood of extra nitrogen causes a wild growth of algae, and the algae take up all the oxygen in the water, smothering the fish. The nitrogen

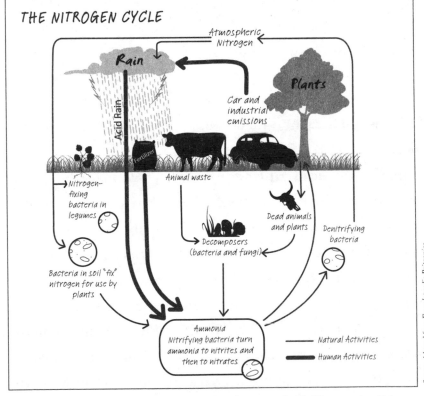

Nitrogen, the most abundant element in the atmosphere, is necessary for life. The process by which nitrogen moves from the air to the soil and back again is called the nitrogen cycle.

runoff has created a "hypoxic," or dead, zone in the Gulf that is as big as the state of New Jersey—and still growing.

RICH FIELDS, POOR FARMERS

The industrial food chain makes some people very rich. Big agribusiness companies take in billions of dollars in profit. Yet one person who is not getting rich from the mountain of corn is the American farmer. George Naylor is all but going broke—and he's doing better than many of his neighbors. His farm might feed 140 people, but it doesn't support the four who live on it. They have a garden and some laying hens but don't grow most of their own food. The farm doesn't produce enough income to pay their bills. The family only gets by because of the paycheck George's wife, Peggy, brings home from her job—and because of a subsidy check from the U.S. government.

If the American farmer is more productive than ever before, how come so many farmers are going broke? One morning, after George had his crop planted, I sat down with him at his kitchen table and we talked about the problem. The answer is a little complicated, but it boils down to this: The price of corn is kept low by government policies. The low price means there's plenty of cheap corn for the industrial food chain. It means cheap animal feed to produce cheap meat and cheap high-fructose corn syrup for soft drinks. It means corn can stay king of the supermarket. But it also makes it hard for the average farmer to stay in business, even with government payments.

In the United States the price of corn is usually below what it costs to grow it. For example, when I visited George Naylor in 2005, it cost him about $2.50 to grow a bushel of corn. That cost includes things like fertilizer, seed, pesticide, and gas for the tractor and combine. But that year, the price the grain elevator co-op paid for a bushel of corn was only about $1.45. At that price Naylor would have lost more than a dollar on every bushel of corn.

With prices like that, how can Naylor and the other corn farmers stay in business? Because the government pays them part of the difference. In some years nearly half the income of America's corn farmers comes from government checks. It is these government checks, or *subsidies,* that keep corn and soybean prices low. Yet the payments are never quite enough to cover expenses.

SUBSIDY FACTS

In the twelve years between 1995 and 2006,

- $177.6 billion were paid in farm subsidies.
- Taxpayers have spent $56 billion on corn subsidies paid to over 1.5 million recipients, making it the top crop for federal assistance.
- Ten percent of all recipients collected 74 percent the subsidies, amounting to $130.6 billion.
- Recipients in the top 10 percent averaged $36,290 in annual payments between 1995 and 2006. The bottom 80 percent of the recipients saw only $731 on average per year.
- The single top subsidy recipient received $554 million over this time period.

That's why Peggy Naylor has to have a job off the farm. That's also why a lot of farmers go out of business or just give up and retire.

I asked George Naylor why he doesn't grow something besides corn, and he laughed. "What am I going to grow here, broccoli? Lettuce?" The grain elevator is the only buyer in town, and the elevator only pays for corn and soybeans. The government will give payments to farmers for all the corn they can produce, but not for growing vegetables or fruit. Besides, Naylor has the equipment to plant corn and soybeans, he doesn't have the equipment to grow that lettuce or broccoli—or anything else.

George Naylor finds himself in the same trap as all the other corn and soybean farmers in America. When prices fall, the only way they can stay in business is to find a way to grow even more corn or soy. One way is to boost yield per acre. That means using more chemical fertilizer or maybe trying new hybrid or GMO seeds. Another way is to rent more farmland, maybe from your neighbor who has given up. After all, if you already have the tractor and machinery, it doesn't cost much more to farm another 100 acres, or another 500.

This means bigger and bigger farms, worked by fewer farmers. It means more fertilizer pollution. And it means even more corn on top of the bulging mountain of corn. And that's the catch. As farmers produce more corn, the price falls even more! Then the only thing an industrial farmer like

George Naylor can do is try to grow even more corn. It's a vicious circle. Prices go lower, but the mountain of corn gets higher and higher.

THE HIGH PRICE OF CHEAP CORN

Okay, so farmers like George Naylor are having a hard time. Everyone agrees that's a bad thing. But isn't this system still doing what it's supposed to do? Doesn't it produce cheap food for the American people? The problem is that government policies don't really give us cheap food. It only gives us the kinds of cheap food made from corn and soy. Your soft drink or hamburger may be cheaper, but that's because taxpayers have already paid for part of it. And that corn

THE ETHANOL BOOM

In 2006, with rising fuel prices and fears of global warming growing, the U.S. government looked around for alternatives to gas and oil, and what did they find? Why, corn, of course! Suddenly, corn (in the form of ethanol) was the solution to our energy problems. Ethanol is a kind of alcohol that can be added to gasoline and burned in cars and trucks. It is made from plants such as corn and sugarcane.

Luckily, there was a government-subsidized mountain of corn ready to become car fuel. In 2008, as gasoline prices shot up, demand for ethanol rose. This drove up prices for corn. Since then, gas prices have come back down and so has the price of corn.

Is corn a good source of alternative fuel? It takes a lot of energy to turn corn into ethanol. In fact, making ethanol may use more energy than it produces. Many environmentalists think it's better to run cars on electricity from renewable sources or ethanol made from non-food crops like grass.

is only cheap if you don't count all the hidden costs, like the cost of pollution from chemical fertilizers.

U.S. farm policy wasn't always like this. Before the 1970s, government policy was designed to support small farmers, not agribusiness. Instead of trying to keep corn prices low, government farm policy was aimed at keeping food prices— and farmers' income—stable.

Remember the law of supply and demand. If there is a lot of grain on the market, sellers have to compete with each other for customers. They lower their prices to try to sell their grain. If there is a shortage of grain, people will pay more for it. Then farmers can charge more for their crops.

Starting in the 1930s, during the Great Depression, the government began a policy to keep prices from rising *or* falling too much. That would protect consumers from having to pay too much for food. The policy would also protect farmers from going bankrupt if prices fell too much.

This is how it worked: In times when prices were low, the government gave farmers loans so they could store, rather than have to sell, their crops. It bought some grain to keep it off the market. It also paid some farmers *not* to grow grain. When prices were higher, farmers sold their grain and repaid the government. If prices were too high, the government sold some of the grain from its storehouses. That put extra grain on the market and brought the price down. This system worked pretty well for almost forty years.

AGRIBUSINESS, GOVERNMENT, AND CORN

Beginning in the early 1970s this system was thrown out the window. Now farm policy was aimed at one thing: keeping corn prices as low as possible. The government told farmers it would pay them for all the corn they could grow. To be exact—instead of the government buying all the extra corn, or loaning farmers' money so they could store it, it just paid farmers part of the cost of growing it. So all the corn the farmers grew was put on the market, driving the price down. Farmers planted even more, corn prices began falling, and, with a few interruptions, they have been falling ever since.

Why did government policy change to favor growing more and more corn? Did corn somehow sneak into Washington and change the laws? No, even King Corn couldn't do that. Instead, one of corn's best friends did it. Big agribusiness corporations, the same ones that need cheap corn for their mills, helped write the very laws that set farm policy.

This is a farm policy that is not designed to help farmers. Lower corn prices drive farmers out of business. Small family farms get replaced with larger industrial farms. Meanwhile agribusinesses like Cargill and Archer Daniels Midland (ADM) and food companies like Coca-Cola and McDonald's make billions thanks to cheap corn and soy. This policy makes it cheaper to buy a corn-sweetened soft drink than whole vegetables, fruits, and grains. But most of all, this policy helps corn to take over our land, our food industry, and even our bodies.

4
THE GRAIN ELEVATOR

FOOD ON THE GROUND

One wet spring afternoon I visited the grain elevator in Farnhamville, Iowa. That's where George Naylor hauls his corn each October. The sky was a soft gray, and it was drizzling lightly. My car rumbled across the railroad tracks.

Grain elevators are tall, hollow concrete tubes, like silos. They are the tallest buildings by far in this part of Iowa. You can see them for miles. But what stood out on this gray day was a bright yellow pyramid the size of a circus tent pitched near the base of the elevator. It was an immense pile of corn— left out in the rain.

The year before, farmers in the Midwest had had a bumper corn crop. It was too much for the elevators to handle, so some was just dumped on the ground. Even now, seven months later, there was still a huge pile. As I walked around it, I saw golden kernels everywhere, ground into the mud by tires and boots. Most of this grain is headed for factory farms and processing plants, so no one worries much about keeping it clean. Even so, it was hard not to feel that something was deeply wrong at the sight of so much food left out in the rain.

The next afternoon I met a Mexican American crop scientist named Ricardo Salvador, a professor at Iowa State University. He told me he'd had a similar reaction the first time he'd seen kernels littering Iowa roads in October. Farmers haul their corn to town in big open wagons that scatter a light rain of corn behind them. Salvador said the sight of so much corn on the ground made him feel sick. In Mexico, for thousands of years corn was honored as a source of life. Even today, he said, you do not let corn lie on the ground. To do so would be considered almost sinful.

Salvador's reaction, like mine, came about because we were looking at corn the old-fashioned way, as a food. But the businesses that run the grain elevators and the industrial food chain do not look at corn as food. They look at it as a commodity, something to be bought and sold.

The corn at the grain elevator was not the same kind of corn you or I eat when we have corn on the cob. What George Naylor grows, and what was in the pile by the elevator, is a type called "number 2 field corn." These kernels are hard to eat, but if you soak them in water for several hours you'll find they taste like lightly corn-flavored starch. It is not a food for human beings. It is the raw material out of which the industrial food chain makes beef or chicken or high-fructose corn syrup or maltodextrin.

CORN THE COMMODITY

Before the railroads crossed America, corn was bought and sold in burlap sacks. More often than not the sacks bore the name of the farm where the corn had been grown. You could follow a sack from a farm in Iowa to the mill in Manhattan, where it was ground into meal, or to the dairy in Brooklyn, where it was fed to a cow. This made a big difference. Consumers knew who was growing their food. They knew exactly what it was and where it came from.

With the coming of the railroads and the grain elevator, the sacks suddenly became a problem. It is a lot easier to break the corn down into kernels and pump it, like a liquid, into the grain elevators and into the railroad cars. The sacks, and the names of the farms, had to go. Corn from hundreds of different farms was now mixed all together in a great golden river. The river of corn would flow from the farms to buyers anywhere in the world. Since the buyer couldn't know whose corn they were purchasing, the Chicago Board of Trade made up a category called number 2 field corn. Any batch of number 2 corn was guaranteed to be as good as any other number 2 field corn.

THE RIVER OF CORN

At the height of the harvest the grain elevator in Farnhamville runs twenty-four hours a day, seven days a week. When George Naylor delivers his truckload of corn, it is weighed and graded and his account is credited with that day's price per bushel. At that point it is no longer George Naylor's corn—it becomes part of the vast river of corn flowing out of the Midwest toward your supermarket.

I watched a pile of corn pour into a railroad hopper car painted with Cargill's blue and yellow logo. That car was joined to a train more than a mile long, holding 440,000 bushels of corn. Yet that number is a tiny fraction of all the corn produced in the United States. American farmers produce thirteen *billion* bushels of corn a year. (That's up from four billion bushels in 1970.)

The supply of corn is usually far greater than the demand for corn, so new uses must be found for it all the time. People have to consume it in new ways, in new kinds of processed food. Animals that never ate corn before must be taught to eat it. We have to turn it into ethanol fuel for our cars. We have to get other nations to import it.

My plan when I came to Iowa was to somehow follow George Naylor's corn on its path to our plates and into our bodies. I should have known that tracing a single bushel of industrial corn is as impossible as tracing a bucket of water after it's been

© istockphoto.com/Gaussian Blur

Grain elevators are tall, hollow silos where farmers like George Naylor unload their corn harvest each year.

poured into a river. Making matters still more difficult, the golden river of corn is controlled by a tiny number of corporations. It has been estimated that Cargill and ADM together buy somewhere near a third of all the corn grown in America.

These two companies guide corn's path every step of the way. They sell the pesticides and fertilizer to the farmers. They operate most of America's grain elevators. They ship most of the corn exported to other countries. They mill the corn into its different parts to be used in processed food. They feed the corn to livestock and then slaughter the corn-fattened animals. Oh, yes—don't forget that they also help write many of the rules that govern this whole game.

Yet in spite of their size and power, Cargill and ADM are almost invisible. Neither company sells products directly to consumers, so they don't advertise. They work in secret and seldom cooperate with journalists. Both companies refused to let me follow the corn river as it passed through their elevators, pipes, freighters, feedlots, mills, and laboratories.

NINETY THOUSAND KERNELS

Let's imagine a bushel of number 2 field corn. One bushel holds about ninety thousand kernels. Those kernels could come from dozens of different farms. Some might be George Naylor's Pioneer Hi-Bred 34H31. Some might be his neighbor's genetically modified variety, called 33P67. Some might be kernels grown with atrazine, an herbicide (weed killer) now banned in Europe but widely used in the U.S. Those might be mixed with kernels grown with another herbicide, metolachlor. In the industrial food chain it doesn't really matter. It's all number 2 corn.

Where do those ninety thousand kernels wind up? Since all number 2 corn is treated as though it is exactly the same, we don't have to follow Naylor's kernels. We just have to follow the main branches of the river of corn as it flows and divides through the industrial food chain.

As you can see, most of those kernels wind up being fed to animals. Much of that goes to feeding America's 100 million beef cattle. And the place they are fed is the American factory farm.

The factory farms take the raw material, corn, and turn

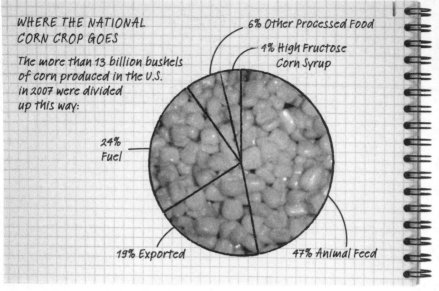

WHERE THE NATIONAL
CORN CROP GOES

The more than 13 billion bushels
of corn produced in the U.S.
in 2007 were divided
up this way:

6% Other Processed Food

1% High Fructose
Corn Syrup

24%
Fuel

19% Exported

47% Animal Feed

Source: USDA Economic Research Service.

it into another product—meat. If you count all the chickens, pigs, and fish, there are hundreds of millions of food animals raised on factory farms every year. These animals once were raised on family farms and ranches. Now they are gathered together in great eating camps, where they consume the mounting pile of surplus corn.

One of the strangest parts of the industrial food chain is the way it forces some animals to eat corn. And the saddest example of this might be what it means for cows. The cow is by nature not a corn eater. Getting cows to eat a corn diet takes a heroic effort on the part of the factory farm. But the river of surplus corn is waiting and so the cows must be forced to consume it and turn it into beef you and I can buy.

Enter the corn-fed American steer.

5
The Feedlot—
Turning Corn into Meat

CITY OF COWS

I was speeding down a ramrod-straight road in Finney County, Kansas, when the empty, dull tan prairie suddenly turned black. The gently rolling sea of grass became a grid of steel fences as far as the eye could see. (In Kansas, that is *really* far.) I had made it to my destination—Poky Feeders, a feedlot and home to thirty-seven thousand head of cattle.

The feedlot appeared suddenly, but the stench of the place had been rising for more than a mile. I soon learned why. At first I thought the cattle were standing or lying in a grayish mud. Then it dawned on me—that wasn't mud at all. It was manure.

An endless series of cattle pens stretched to the horizon, each one home to a hundred or so animals. The cattle pens,

photo courtesy of PETA

Most cattle today are raised in densely packed, city-like "Concentrated Animal Feeding Operations" like this one.

filled with animals and their waste, are built around a corn mill. Twelve hours a day, seven days a week, the mill noisily turns America's river of corn into cattle feed.

I'd traveled to Poky early one January with the crazy idea of visiting a particular resident. I was looking for a young black steer with three white blazes on his face, the same one I'd met the previous fall on a ranch in South Dakota, five hundred miles due north of here. In fact, the steer belonged to me. I'd purchased him as an eight-month-old calf from the Blair Ranch for $598. I was paying Poky Feeders $1.60 a day for his room and board (all the corn he could eat).

My idea was to follow my steer as he traveled through the meat-making branch of the industrial food chain. And so I had followed him here.

CAFO—CONCENTRATED ANIMAL FEEDING OPERATION

The old-fashioned way of raising cattle, like the old-fashioned way of growing corn, was on the small family farm. Cattle were raised in pastures, eating grass and hay—the food they naturally eat. But as corn took over the family farm, cows and other animals were pushed out.

Cattle are now raised in densely packed animal cities like Poky's. These places are called CAFOs—Concentrated Animal Feeding Operations. Farmers gave up raising cattle because, as strange as it might seem, it costs a farmer more to grow feed corn than it costs a CAFO to buy it. (Thanks to those government subsidies.) Eating meat used to be a special occasion in most American homes. Thanks to CAFOs, meat is now so cheap that many of us eat it three times a day. Of course, the American taxpayers have already paid part of the cost by subsidizing corn.

But there are other costs involved in raising cattle this way, costs that shoppers don't see when they buy a steak at the supermarket. On the old-fashioned farm, there is really no such thing as waste. Animal manure goes back into the fields as fertilizer. But the waste from CAFOs is a huge source of very toxic pollution. Tons of animal manure are produced with no good way of disposing of it. The feed-lots are also breeding grounds for new and deadly bacteria.

Some of these bacteria are finding their way into our food.

And there is another cost to raising cattle on CAFOs, one that's even harder to see. These animals have evolved to eat grass. But in a CAFO they are forced to eat corn—at considerable cost to their health, to the health of the land, and ultimately to the health of us, their eaters.

STEER NUMBER 534

I first met steer number 534 on the Blair Ranch—fifty-five hundred acres of rolling short-grass prairie a few miles outside Sturgis, South Dakota. In that part of the prairie, you can still make out ruts dug by stagecoaches and cattle drives of the 1800s. In November, when I visited, the ground was covered with a thick coat of yellow and gold grass. Sprinkled across the fields were moving black dots: Angus cows and calves, grazing.

Ed and Rich Blair run what's called a "cow-calf" operation. Their business is the first stage in the production of a hamburger. It is also the stage least changed by the modern industrial food chain. Beef cattle still get born on thousands of independently owned ranches like theirs.

Steer number 534 spent his first six months in these pastures alongside his mother, a cow named 9534. The number means she was the thirty-fourth cow born in 1995. His mother never met his father, an Angus by the name of Gar Precision

1680. Like all beef cattle, 534 is the product of artificial insemination.

Born on March 13, 2001, in the birthing shed across the road, 534 and his mother were turned out to pasture just as soon as the eighty-pound calf could stand up. Within a few weeks the calf began adding to his diet of mother's milk. He chose from a salad bar of grasses: western wheatgrass, little bluestem, buffalo grass, green needlegrass.

Apart from the Saturday in April when he was branded and castrated, one could imagine 534 looking back on those six months as the good old days. No one can really know what a cow feels. But we can say with confidence that a calf grazing on grass is doing what he is supremely well suited to do. Yet, after a few months at Poky my steer will never have the opportunity to eat green grass again.

COWS AND GRASS—A PARTNERSHIP

Cows have evolved over millions of years to eat grass. It's not a one-sided deal. At the same time, grasses have evolved over millions of years to be eaten by cows. This partnership is one of nature's wonders.

When a cow eats grass, it doesn't kill the plant. Grasses have evolved so that they can survive being eaten very well. (As long as the cows give them a chance to recover.) In return for being chewed on, the plants get help from the cows. The cow protects the grass habitat by eating young trees and shrubs that might compete with grasses. The animal also spreads grass seed, plants it with his hooves, and then fertilizes it with his manure.

Only certain animals, including cows, sheep, goats, and bison, can make a meal out of grass. They can do this because they have a specialized second stomach called a rumen. (That's why these animals are called *ruminants*.) The rumen is like a twenty-five-gallon fermentation tank. Here is where the cow gets some help. Inside that tank lives a type of bacteria that dines on grass. The bacteria break down the cell walls of the grass and allow the cows to get at the protein and carbohydrates within.

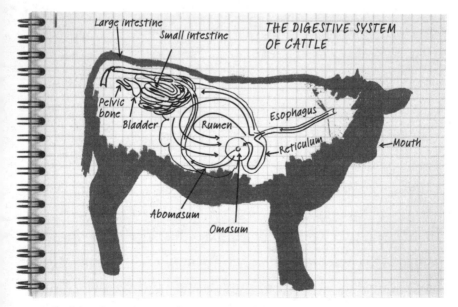

Cattle have four separate stomach compartments, while other farm animals such as chickens and pigs have only one.

On the plains of the American west, where steer 534 was born, bison and the prairie grasses lived together in partnership for thousands of years. (I guess we should include the bacteria in that partnership, also.) It was a natural, solar-powered loop. The plants used the sun's energy to make food. The bison (with the help of bacteria) ate the grass and in return planted it, fertilized it, and defended its territory. It was a successful ecological system.

A rumen has evolved into the perfect organ for digesting grass. But it is not good at digesting corn. So then why is steer number 534 forced to eat corn insead of grass? The answer is one word: speed. Cattle raised on grass simply take longer to grow than cattle raised on corn. "In my grandfather's time, cows were four or five years old at slaughter," Rich Blair explained to me. "In the fifties, when my father was ranching, it was two or three years old. Now we get there at fourteen to sixteen months." What gets a steer from 80 to 1,100 pounds in fourteen months is tremendous amounts of corn, food supplements, and drugs. Fast food indeed.

COW CHOW

In October, two weeks before I made his acquaintance, steer number 534 was weaned from his mother. Weaning is the hardest time on a ranch for animals and ranchers alike. Cows separated from their calves will mope and bellow for days.

The calves are prone to getting sick. Calves are weaned for a couple of reasons. First, it frees their mothers to have more calves. Second, it gets the calves, now five or six hundred pounds, ready for life on the feedlot.

The calves are rounded up and herded into a "backgrounding" pen. They will spend a couple of months there before boarding the truck for Poky Feeders. Think of backgrounding as a training school for feedlot life: The animals are, for the first time in their lives, confined to a pen. They are "bunk broken"—taught to eat from a trough. And they must gradually get used to eating what is for them a new and unnatural diet. Here is where they first eat corn.

It was in the backgrounding pen that I first met 534. Rather,

© Marcus Mam

This is Steer #534. I purchased him as a calf so I could follow him as he traveled through the meat-making part of the industrial food chain.

it's where I picked him out. I had told the Blairs I wanted to follow one of their steers from birth to slaughterhouse. Ed Blair suggested, half jokingly, that I might as well buy one. Then I could have the whole beef-making experience. He told me how to pick out a good calf: one with a broad straight back and thick shoulders. Basically you're looking for a sturdy frame on which to hang a lot of meat.

I also wanted a calf with a face I could easily spot in a crowd, so I could easily find him again. I went out to the pen and gazed over the sea of ninety black Angus cattle. Almost at once, steer number 534 moseyed over to the fence and made cye contact with me. He had a wide, stout frame and three easy-to-spot white marks on his face. Here was my boy.

NEW HOME, NEW DIET

Steer 534 and I traveled from the ranch to the feedlot (in separate vehicles) the first week of January. It felt a lot like going from the country to the big city. A feedlot is not a very pleasant city, however. It is crowded and filthy and stinking, with open sewers, unpaved roads, and choking air thick with dust.

At the center of the feedlot stands the feed mill. That is where three meals a day for thirty-seven thousand animals are designed and mixed by computer. A million pounds of feed pass through the mill each day. Every hour of every day a tractor trailer pulls up to the loading dock to deliver another fifty tons of corn. The driver opens a valve in the belly of the truck and a golden stream of grain begins to flow down a chute into the bowels of the mill.

Around to the other side of the building, tanker trucks pump in thousands of gallons of liquefied fat, usually beef fat from a nearby slaughterhouse. There's also the protein supplement, a sticky brown goop made of molasses and urea. (Urea is a form of synthetic nitrogen made from natural gas, similar to the fertilizer spread on George Naylor's fields.)

In a shed attached to the mill sit vats of liquid vitamins. Beside them are fifty-pound sacks of antibiotic drugs. Along with alfalfa hay and silage (stems and leaves of corn plants), all these ingredients will be automatically blended together to make the feed for the cattle. Three times a day a parade of dump trucks fills up with this feed and carries it to the cattle pens.

Before being put on this strange diet, new arrivals to the feedlot are treated to a few days of fresh long-stemmed hay. (They don't eat on the long ride and can lose up to one hundred pounds. The hay gives them a chance to get adjusted.) Over the next several weeks they'll gradually step up to a daily ration of thirty-two pounds of feed, including twenty-four pounds of corn. That would be enough corn to fill a paper grocery bag.

CATTLE EATING CATTLE

Feedlots are beef factories. Their goal is to turn corn into beef. But corn isn't the only thing the cattle are fed. You might be as shocked as I was to learn that they are also fed parts of other cattle. That's right, these herbivores, natural plant eaters, are fed meat.

For years, leftover beef scraps were ground up and put into cattle feed. After all, it was protein, and cattle need protein to grow. Then people in England began dying of a sickness called mad cow disease. Mad cow is a brain disease that is always fatal. It is spread by eating the brains of infected animals. Ground-up cattle brains were put into cattle feed and some of those cows got mad cow disease. Human beings who ate infected beef also got the disease, although there were no human cases reported in the United States.

The government banned the practice in 1997, but there are some exceptions. As I already noted, beef tallow (fat) is one of the ingredients that cows at Poky will eat. Where does the tallow come from? It comes from other cows that have been sent to the slaughterhouse. Though Poky doesn't do it,

POSSIBLE INGREDIENTS IN CATTLE FEED
Chicken manure, cattle manure, chocolate, stale pastry, cement dust, molasses, candy, urea, hooves, feathers, meat scraps, fish meal, pasta, peanut skins, brewery wastes, cardboard, corn silage, pesticides

the rules also permit feedlots to feed cattle protein from other kinds of animals. Feather meal and chicken litter (that is, bedding, feces, and discarded bits of feed from chicken farms) are accepted cattle feeds, as are chicken, fish, and pig meal. Some public health experts worry that other diseases like mad cow could start to appear because of this practice.

SICK FROM CORN

Compared to all the other things we feed cattle these days, corn seems positively wholesome. Yet feeding corn to cattle goes against the natural order almost as much feeding them beef. During my day at Poky I spent a few hours with Dr. Mel Metzin, the staff veterinarian. Dr. Mel, as he's known at Poky, runs a team of eight cowboys. Their job is to ride the yard's dusty streets, spotting sick animals and bringing them into Poky's three "hospitals" for treatment. From Dr. Mel I learned more than any beef eater might want to know about the life of the factory farm steer.

Basically, almost all of the cattle in the feedlot are sick. And it's their corn-based diet that makes them ill. "They're made to eat forage," Dr. Metzin explained, "and we're making them eat grain." (*Forage* means grass.)

The most serious illness is bloat. Remember, there are bacteria in the animal's rumen and they produce a lot of gas. Usually cattle belch a lot to release the gas. But a corn diet

IS CORN-FED BEEF HEALTHY?

Advertisers use the phrase "corn-fed" as though it is something old-fashioned and good. Yet it is neither very old, nor very good, not for the cows and not for us. It's true that cattle fed corn get fat quickly. Also, their meat becomes "marbled." That's what it's called when veins of white fat run through the red meat. Marbled meat is tasty and considered higher quality by the government grading system. Yet this corn-fed meat is actually less healthy for us.

Corn-fed beef contains more saturated fat than the meat of grass-fed animals. Too much saturated fat has been linked to heart disease and other health problems. Corn-fed beef also has less of the kind of fats that are healthy for us, a kind called omega-3 fatty acids. That is the same kind of "good" fat found in salmon and other fish. The higher the ratio of omega-6 to omega-3, the less healthful the meat. Grass-fed beef generally has lower amounts of "bad" fats and higher "good" fats. Just as it is not healthy for cattle to eat corn, it is not healthy for us to eat corn-fed cattle.

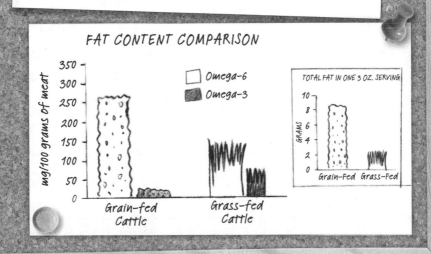

FAT CONTENT COMPARISON

Sources: Journal of Animal Science, Journal of Food Quality, and eatwild.com.

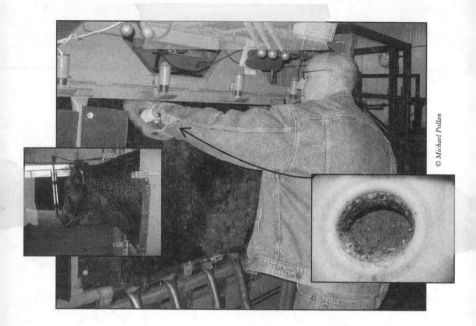

© Michael Pollan

causes a condition that keeps the gas from escaping. This is called bloat. The gases in the rumen get trapped and the rumen inflates like a balloon until it presses against its lungs. To save the animal, a vet must force a hose down the animal's throat to release the gas. Otherwise, the pressure will choke the animal to death.

A corn diet also gives cattle acidosis (too much acid in the rumen). Human stomachs are naturally highly acid. A rumen, however, is naturally neutral or non-acid. Feeding corn to a steer changes the chemistry of the rumen, making it acid and causing a kind of heartburn that in some cases can kill the animal, but usually just makes him sick. Cattle with acidosis stop eating, pant and drool, paw and scratch their bellies, and eat dirt. This can so weaken the animal that it can develop a long list of other diseases like diarrhea, ulcers, liver disease, pneumonia, and feedlot polio.

ANTIBIOTICS FOR ANIMALS

Cattle rarely live on feedlot diets for more than 150 days, which might be about as much as their systems can stand. Over time the acids eat away at the rumen wall, allowing bacteria to enter the animal's bloodstream. These microbes wind up in the liver. Between 15 percent and 30 percent of feedlot cattle have damaged livers.

CORN-FED BACTERIA

Some of the bacteria that live in the guts of cattle find their way into our hamburgers and steaks. If those bugs come from a grass-fed cattle, they grow up in a low-acid rumen. When they hit the acid in our stomachs, they die.

However, the rumens of corn-fed cattle are nearly as acidic as our stomachs. New types of bacteria have evolved to live in those acid-filled rumens. Those new bacteria don't get killed by the acids in our stomachs.

E. coli 0157:H7 is one of these new bacteria. It was unknown before the year 1980. It thrives in feedlot cattle and 40 percent of them carry it in their gut. Perhaps 70,000 Americans are infected with E. coli 0157:H7 every year, though most of them recover without going to a hospital. However, a handful get very sick and die.

Dr. Mel told me that in some pens the figure runs as high as 70 percent.

What keeps a feedlot animal healthy—or healthy enough—are antibiotics. Most of the antibiotics sold in America today are for animal feed, not for humans. Without these drugs cattle could not survive. The only reason they need the drugs is because they are being raised on factory farms and fed corn. The problem is that in response to antibiotics, bacteria can mutate or change. They can develop into new types of bacteria that the drugs don't affect. By giving antibiotics to the millions of cattle in the U.S. we are actually breeding new superbacteria that can't be killed by antibiotics.

I asked Dr. Mel what would happen if drugs were banned from cattle feed. "We'd have a high death rate," he told me. "We just couldn't feed them as hard. Hell, if you gave them lots of grass and space, I wouldn't have a job."

MY STEER

I found my steer, number 534, in pen 63. Pen 63 is about the size of a hockey rink, with a concrete feed bunk along the road, and a fresh water trough out back. My first impression was that his home wasn't too bad. It was far enough from the feed mill to be fairly quiet and it had a view of what I thought was a pond. Then I noticed the brown scum. The body of water is what is known as a manure lagoon.

I asked the feedlot manager why they didn't just use the liquid manure as fertilizer on neighboring farms. The farmers don't want it, he explained. The nitrogen and phosphorus levels are so high that it would kill the crops. (He didn't tell me that feedlot wastes also contain toxic chemicals and drugs that end up in waterways downstream.) On a farm, manure would be a source of fertility. At a CAFO like Poky it becomes a toxic waste.

I climbed over the railing and joined the ninety steers, which retreated a few lumbering steps. I couldn't find number 534 at first. And then I spotted him—the three white blazes on his face—way off in the back. As I gingerly stepped toward him the shuffling mass of black cowhide between us parted, and there stood 534 and I, staring dumbly at each other. I had worn the same orange sweater I'd worn at the ranch in South Dakota, hoping that maybe he would recognize me. There was no sign that he did. I told myself not to take it personally. After all, 534 and his pen mates were bred for their meat, not for their memories.

I noticed that his eyes were a little bloodshot. That was probably from all the feedlot dust, which wasn't really dust but dried-up cow manure. Aside from that, it was hard to tell how he was getting on. I don't know enough about cattle to tell you if he was bored or miserable. On the other hand, I would not say he looked happy.

MEAT MACHINE?

My steer had certainly grown. He'd put on a couple of hundred pounds since I'd seen him last, which of course was the whole point of the feedlot. Dr. Mel complimented me on his size and shape. "That's a handsome-looking beef you got there," he said. (Aw, shucks.)

That is one way of looking at a steer like 534—the feedlot way, the industrial way. To the industrial food chain, cattle are just machines for turning number 2 field corn into cuts of beef. So number 534 was doing a good job as a meat machine. Yet standing there, I realized once again that number 534, despite his name, was not a machine. Number 534 was a living, breathing organism. My health is directly related to his health (or to the health of other steers just like him). We live in the same habitat as the animals we eat. Whatever happens to them, happens to us.

While I stood in pen 63 a dump truck pulled up alongside the feed bunk

TURNING CORN INTO MEAT

Compared to other food animals, cattle are very bad at turning grain into meat. Every day until his slaughter 534 will convert thirty-two pounds of feed into four pounds of new weight—new muscle, fat, and bone. That's seven pounds of grain for one pound of cow. A chicken, on the other hand can turn about three pounds of corn into one pound of chicken. That is why chicken costs less than beef.

7 pounds of corn = 1 pound of beef
6.5 pounds of corn = 1 pound of pork
2.6 pounds of corn = 1 pound of chicken

and released a golden stream of feed. The black mass of cow-hide moved toward the trough for lunch. The $1.60 a day I was paying for my steer's meal may seem cheap—but it doesn't include all the costs of the industrial farm, not by a long shot. It doesn't include the billions the government spends to subsidize corn. It doesn't include the cost to the environment from manure, pesticide, and fertilizer pollution. It doesn't include the cost to our health from new superbacteria.

I stood alongside 534 as he lowered his big head into the stream of grain. At that moment I couldn't imagine ever wanting to eat one of these animals. Hungry was the last thing I felt. Yet after enough time goes by, and the stink of that place is gone from my nostrils, I will probably eat feedlot beef again. Most people can eat feedlot meat because they just don't know where it comes from. For me, it will take a lot of forgetting.

6
Processed Food

SPLITTING THE KERNEL

Do you eat a lot of corn? Looking at it one way, each American eats only about a bushel of corn per year. But that number only includes the corn that *looks* like corn—corn on the cob, or corn out of a can, or corn chips.

But if you count *all* the corn we eat, directly and indirectly the average American eats a *ton of corn* every year. We don't recognize it as corn, though, because it's been turned into something else. Almost half is eaten by animals and turned into beef, chicken, fish, or pork. One-tenth of the U.S. corn crop is turned into processed food.

To make processed food, corn is first broken down into different parts. Those parts are put back together in new ways to make the sweetener in your soft drink or the starch in your hamburger roll. All of this happens in a factory called a "wet mill." (The old sort of mill, which simply grinds grain into flour, or meal, is a "dry" mill.) To follow the industrial food chain, I had to follow the river of corn through a wet mill.

There are twenty-five major wet mills in the United States, most of them owned by two corporations, Cargill and Archer Daniels Midland. George Naylor's corn probably went to Cargill's mill in Iowa City. ADM runs a giant plant in Decatur, Illinois. Both of those companies refused to let me tour their plants.

Luckily, I was allowed to visit a smaller mill at Iowa State University in Ames, Iowa. Iowa State really should be called the University of Corn. Corn is the hero of many of the sculptures and murals on campus. (The soybean, Iowa's second-largest crop, gets its share of attention too.) The school's wet mill is part of something called the Center for Crops Utilization Research. Larry Johnson, the center's director, was more than happy to show me around.

INDUSTRIAL DIGESTION

Johnson described the wet mill as kind of an industrial digestive system. The mill itself is a maze of stainless steel pipes, valves, filters, and tanks. Corn travels through the maze and is broken down through a series of steps including grinding (like the teeth) and soaking in acid (like the stomach). By the time it reaches the end, the corn is reduced to simple molecules, mostly sugars. Soybeans go through a similar process.

The first step in the "digestion" of corn is to split the kernel into its different parts:

- The yellow skin.
- The germ, the tiny dark part nearest the cob. That's the part that holds a tiny embryo of a corn plant.
- The endosperm. The biggest part of the kernel, filled with carbohydrates.

When a shipment of corn arrives at the mill, it is soaked for thirty-six hours in a slightly acid bath. This swells the kernels and loosens the skin. After the soak, the swollen kernels are ground in a mill. "By now the germ is rubbery and it pops right off," Johnson explained.

The germ is then squeezed for corn oil. Corn oil can be used as a cooking or salad oil. Some of it is hydrogenated. That means hydrogen is forced into the oil molecules. This makes the oil stay solid at room temperature and so it can be used for margarine. Doctors used to think margarine was healthier for you than butter and would not cause heart disease. Now researchers think these hydrogenated trans fats in margarine are actually worse for our hearts

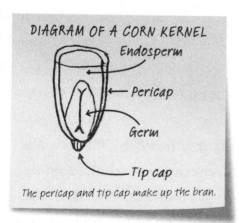

DIAGRAM OF A CORN KERNEL

Endosperm

Pericap

Germ

Tip cap

The pericap and tip cap make up the bran.

than butter. Trans fats are also used in processed snacks, baked goods, and many other processed foods.

Once the germ has been removed for oil, the kernels are crushed. That makes a white mush of protein and starch called "mill starch." The mill starch can be used in animal feed.

STARCH INTO SUGAR

What's left after that is a white liquid that's poured out onto a stainless steel table. It dries to a fine, superwhite powder—cornstarch. Cornstarch was wet milling's first product back in the 1840s. At first the starch was mainly used for laundry—to make shirts stiff. Then cooks and food companies began adding cornstarch to as many recipes as they could. The starch was cheap and had a nice white color that people thought was "pure."

By 1866, the mill owners had learned how to break down cornstarch into a kind of sugar called glucose. The glucose corn syrup wasn't as sweet as sugar, but it was cheap. Ever since, corn sweeteners have been the industry's most important product.

The big breakthrough came in the 1960s. That's when Japanese chemists discovered an enzyme that could transform glucose into the much sweeter sugar molecule called fructose. High-fructose corn syrup was born. It's a blend of 55 percent

Made from CORN

FROM THE CENTER FOR CROPS UTILIZATION RESEARCH, IOWA STATE UNIVERSITY

WHOLE CORN PRODUCTS

COB AND KERNEL

FOOD:
Baby corn
Canned corn
Frozen packaged

INDUSTRIAL:
Decorative items
(pod, Indian corn)

COB OR STOVER

INDUSTRIAL:
Dust absorbant
Construction board
Cosmetic powders

WHOLE KERNEL PRODUCTS

FOOD:
Popcorn
Snack food
Soup mixes

FEED:
Livestock feed
Wild animal feed

ALKALI COOKED

FOOD:
Tortilla flours
Corn chips
Taco shells

WET-MILLED CORN

STARCH PRODUCTS

STEEP WATER

INDUSTRIAL/FEED:
Steep water (feed)
Antibiotics
Chemicals
Pharmaceuticals
Yeast culture

GERM:
(Same as dry-milled germ)

GLUTEN

FEED:
Cattle feed
Poultry feed

MODIFIED STARCH

FOOD:
Baby foods
Bakery products
Chewing gum
Puddings, custards
Salad dressings
Candies
Condiments
Icings and glazes
Instant tea
Low-calorie sweeteners
Nougats
Pan coatings

INDUSTRIAL:
Book-binding agents
Pastes, glues
Candles
Ceramics
Insecticides
Fiberglass
Leather products
Fireworks
Poster paints
Sandpaper
Wallpaper, shade cloth

PHARMACEUTICAL
COSMETICS:
Antibiotic products
Aspirin
Powdered cosmetics
Disinfectants
Surgical dressings

NATIVE STARCH

FOOD:
Brewed beverages
Chocolate drinks
Meat products
Prepared mustards
Precooked, frozen
  meals
Powdered sugar
Canned vegetables
Candies

INDUSTRIAL:
Abrasive papers
Dry-cell batteries
Briquettes
Detergents, cleaners
Paper color carriers
Paper products
Cork products
Crayon, chalk binders
Dispersion agents

FRACTIONED PRODUCTS

DRY-MILLED CORN

GRITS/CONES

FOOD:
Breakfast cereals
Breads, bakery
   products
Fermented beverages
Pet foods
Corn bread

INDUSTRIAL:
Wallpaper paste
Floor wax
Hand soap

FLOUR

FOOD:
Baby foods
Baking mixes
Batters
Desserts
Pie fillings
Gravies and sauces

INDUSTRIAL:
Explosives
Paper products
Drilling fluids
Label adhesives
Edge paste
Pharmaceuticals

HOMINY FEED

FEED:
Livestock feed

GERM

MEAL

INDUSTRIAL FEED:
Livestock feed
Amino acids
Fur cleaner

OIL

PHARMACEUTICAL/
FOOD:
Vitamin carriers
Cooking oil
Margarine
Mayonnaise
Potato chips

INDUSTRIAL:
Linoleum
Printing inks
Rubber substitutes
Rust preservatives
Soaps
Tanning agents
Textiles

SWEETENERS

FRUCTOSE

FOOD:
Bakery products
Canned fruit
Canned juices
Condiments
Soft drinks
Wine products

FERMENTATION

FOOD/FEED:
Alcoholic
   beverages
Flavor enhancers
Soft drinks
Amino acids

INDUSTRIAL/FUEL:
Industrial alcohols
Engine fuel
Fuel octane
   enhancers
Plastics
Solvents

GLUCOSE

FOOD/
PHARMACEUTICAL:
Baby foods
Medicinal syrups
Cheese spreads
Non-dairy creamers
Cordials and liquers
Prepared egg
   products
Extracts
Flavors
Fruit juice drinks
Frozen seafood
Peanut butter

INDUSTRIAL:
Chemicals
Dyes and inks
Explosives
Leather tanning
Shoe polish
Rayon
Theatrical makeup
Tobacco products

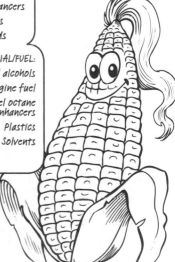

fructose and 45 percent glucose that tastes exactly as sweet as table sugar. Today it is the most valuable food product refined from corn.

High-fructose corn syrup, or HFCS, is by far the biggest food output of the country's wet mills. But there are hundreds of other food ingredients created from the remaining cornstarch. Some is made into other sugars like maltodextrin, which can be used to make instant pudding or gravy. Some is fermented to become ethanol. Some of the fermented starch is used to make plastic. At the end there's almost nothing left. Even the dirty water from the process is used to make animal feed.

The wet mill is like a giant steel beast, with a maze of pipes and machines inside. At one end it eats millions of bushels of corn fed to it every day by the trainload. At the other end of the beast are hundreds of spigots, large and small. Out of each spigot flows a different product made from corn, called "fractions" by the food industry. Many of these fractions, the sugars and starches, the alcohols and acids, the emulsifiers and stabilizers with the strange names, will be made into food. They are put together to make cereal or snack food or chicken nuggets or TV dinners or just about anything else you can imagine and ingest. In fact, you would be hard-pressed to find a processed food today that isn't made from corn or soybeans.

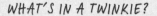

WHAT'S IN A TWINKIE?

Hostess bakes 500 million Twinkies each year, a task requiring 8 million pounds of sugar, 7 million pounds of flour and 1 million eggs. Even with all that sugar, flour and eggs, corn is still the raw material that shows up most often on the Twinkie ingredients list. The highlighted ingredients below are made from corn, the italicized ones from soybeans.

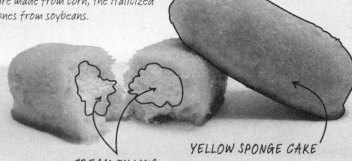

YELLOW SPONGE CAKE

CREAM FILLING

INGREDIENTS: ENRICHED BLEACHED WHEAT FLOUR [FLOUR, REDUCED IRON, "B" VITAMINS (NIACIN, THIAMINE MONONITRATE (B1), RIBOFLAVIN (B2), FOLIC ACID)], **CORN SYRUP**, **HIGH FRUCTOSE CORN SYRUP**, WATER, *PARTIALLY HYDROGENATED VEGETABLE AND/OR ANIMAL SHORTENING (SOYBEAN, COTTONSEED AND/OR CANOLA OIL, BEEF FAT), WHOLE EGGS, **DEXTROSE**. CONTAINS 2% OR LESS OF: **MODIFIED CORN STARCH**, **GLUCOSE**, LEAVENINGS (SODIUM ACID PYROPHOSPHATE, BAKING SODA, MONOCALCIUM PHOSPHATE), SWEET DAIRY WHEY, *SOY PROTEIN ISOLATE*, CALCIUM AND SODIUM CASEINATE, SALT, MONO AND DIGLYCERIDES, **POLYSORBATE 60**, *SOY LECITHIN, SOY FLOUR*, **CORNSTARCH**, CELLULOSE GUM, *SODIUM STEAROYL LACTYLATE*, NATURAL AND ARTIFICIAL FLAVORS, SORBIC ACID (TO RETAIN FRESHNESS), YELLOW 5, RED 40. CONTAINS WHEAT, EGG, MILK AND *SOYBEANS*. MAY CONTAIN PEANUTS.

Source: Adapted from Twinkie, Deconstructed, by Steve Ettlinger and www.hostesscakes.com

CEREAL SECRETS

A few years ago I had the chance to visit one of the places where new foods are invented. I was given a tour of the research and development laboratory for General Mills, the sixth-largest food company in the world. The lab is called the Bell Institute and it is housed in a group of buildings on the outskirts of Minneapolis. Here nine hundred food scientists spend their days designing the future of food.

Much of their work is top secret, but nowhere more so than in the cereals area. Deep in the heart of the Bell Institute is a maze of windowless rooms called, rather grandly, the Institute of Cereal Technology. The secrecy surrounding cereals like Lucky Charms seemed silly, and I said so. But an executive

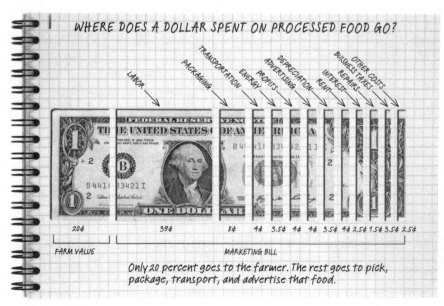

WHERE DOES A DOLLAR SPENT ON PROCESSED FOOD GO?

LABOR 20¢ · PACKAGING / TRANSPORTATION / ENERGY 39¢ · PROFITS 8¢ · ADVERTISING 4¢ · DEPRECIATION 3.5¢ · RENT 4¢ · INTEREST 4¢ · REPAIRS 3.5¢ · BUSINESS TAXES 4¢ · OTHER COSTS 2.5¢ 1.5¢ 3.5¢ 2.5¢

FARM VALUE   MARKETING BILL

Only 20 percent goes to the farmer. The rest goes to pick, package, transport, and advertise that food.

Source: USDA.

explained to me that recipes can't be patented or copyrighted—which means that once you introduce a new cereal, anyone can put out another one just like it. All you can hope for is to have the market to yourself for a few months to establish your brand. That's why companies keep their new cereals top secret.

In the interests of secrecy, the food scientists would not talk to me about current projects. But they would talk about past failures, like the cereal in the shape of little bowling pins and balls. "The kids loved it," the product's inventor told me, "but the mothers didn't like the idea of kids bowling their breakfast across the table." Which is why bowling pins never showed up in your cereal bowl.

Breakfast cereal is a great example of why companies love to make processed foods. A box of cereal contains four cents worth of corn (or some other grain). Yet that box will sell for close to four dollars. Cereals generate higher profits for General Mills than any other food. In the same way, McDonald's makes much more by selling you a chicken nugget than a piece of recognizable chicken.

The farmer, on the other hand, makes more money from whole foods than processed foods. For example, for every dollar a consumer spends to buy eggs, forty cents finds its way back to the farmer. But for every dollar a consumer spends on HFCS, say in a soft drink, farmers get only four cents. Companies like ADM and Coca-Cola and General Mills capture most of the rest. That's why George Naylor told me more than once: "There's money to be made in food, unless you're trying to grow it."

CAN YOU EAT MORE, PLEASE?

It seems that food corporations have got it made. The U.S. government helps pay for their raw materials. They make more money from selling food than farmers. But they have one big problem that limits their sales: the size of the human stomach.

Unlike many other products—CDs, say, or books—there's a natural limit to how much food we each can consume without exploding. Try as we might, the average person can eat only about fifteen hundred pounds of food a year. The demand for food rises only as fast as the population grows. In the U.S., that's around 1 percent per year.

This leaves food companies like General Mills with two choices. They can figure out how to get people to spend more money for the same amount of food. Or they can get us to eat more food than we need. Which do they choose? Why both, of course.

Processing food allows companies to charge more for it. Consumers will only pay so much for an ear of corn. But they can be convinced to pay a lot more for the same corn if it has been turned into a funny shape, sweetened, and brightly colored. The industry calls this "adding value."

Added value can be anything. It might be the convenience

of a dinner you just pop in the microwave. Or it might be a feeling like "this food product is good for me." Or it might be that a food is fun to eat—like ridged potato chips or cereal bars. That's why food companies spend so much on advertising—to convince us they really have added value to the corn and soybeans.

They also try to convince us that their corn or chickens or apples are better (and worth more) than those of another company. They don't want us to buy just any old chicken, but Tyson chicken or Perdue. They don't want us to buy any old oat cereal—they want us to buy Cheerios.

Companies can also try to convince us that their food is healthier, even a sort of medicine. We're used to having vitamins and minerals added to our food. (Of course, manufacturers wouldn't need to add them if they hadn't been *removed* during processing.) And some manufacturers are going even further than adding vitamins. One company, called Tree Top, has developed a "low-moisture, naturally sweetened apple piece infused with a red-wine extract." Natural chemicals in red wine called flavonoids are thought to fight cancer. So Tree Top has added value to an apple by injecting it with flavonoids from red wine.

It seems that an old-fashioned apple just isn't enough anymore. We need an apple that fights cancer! We need orange juice with calcium that builds strong bones. We need cereal that keeps us from having a heart attack.

FOOD THAT DOESN'T FEED

The latest invention to come from the wet mill and the lab is something called resistant starch. This new corn "fraction" has food makers very excited because—it can't be digested! That's right, it's a food that your body can't use. Since the body can't break down resistant starch, it slips through the digestive track. It's the ultimate diet food—food with no calories. It's food that isn't really food.

You would think this would be a bad thing. Imagine the advertisement: "Our food doesn't feed you!" But for food companies, it's an excellent invention. They have finally overcome the natural limit of what the human body will eat. You could eat this stuff twenty-four hours a day, like a human-size corn processing plant!

Maybe this fake food is corn's final victory. It has succeeded up until now by being useful to humans. Now it is about to succeed by being of no use at all.

EAT UP!

Resistant starch can be added to many common manufactured foods, including bread, pizza crust, pastries, salad dressing, ice cream, and pasta.

7
Fat from Corn

CAN YOU EAT MORE, PLEASE? PART II

So food companies have been very successful at getting us to pay more for the same food. What about their other money-making scheme, to get us to buy (and eat) more food than we need? How has that worked out? Well, let's see . . .

Three of every five Americans are overweight; one of every five is obese. Among kids, it's almost as bad. Seventeen percent of kids age six through nineteen are obese. This is a giant public health problem, costing the health care system an estimated $90 billion a year. The disease formerly known as adult-onset diabetes has had to be renamed Type II diabetes since it now occurs so frequently in children, and the Centers for Disease Control estimates that one in three American children born in 2000 will develop it. Diabetes can mean blindness, amputation, and early death. Because of diabetes

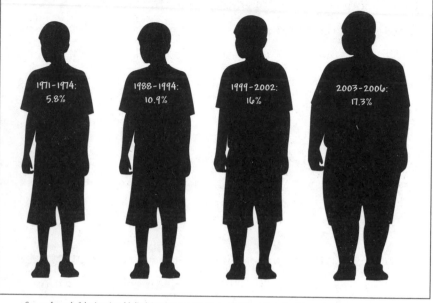

CHILDHOOD OBESITY ON THE RISE
National Health and Nutrition Examination survey results from 1976 to 2006 show an alarming increase in the percentage of obese children ages 6–19.

1971–1974:
5.8%

1988–1994:
10.9%

1999–2002:
16%

2003–2006:
17.3%

Sources: Journal of the American Medical Association and the Centers for Disease Control and Prevention.

and all the other health problems caused by obesity, kids in the U.S. today may turn out to be the first group of Americans with life spans that are shorter than their parents'. To put it simply, Americans are getting fatter and it's killing us.

You hear plenty of explanations for our expanding waist-line. We sit all day at desks in school or at work, then sit around all night watching television. We play video games instead of sports. Fast-food advertising encourages us to eat supersized meals. It is actually cheaper to eat high-calorie, fatty, processed foods than whole foods. All these explanations are true, but they don't tell the whole story.

EXTRA CALORIES

Behind our epidemic of obesity lies this simple fact: When food is abundant and cheap, people will eat more of it. Since 1977, an American's average daily intake of calories has jumped by more than 10 percent. Since we aren't exercising more, the calories end up being stored away in fat cells in our bodies. Where did all those cheap calories come from? If you've read this far, you already know the answer—most of them come from cheap corn.

Since 1970, farmers in the United States have managed to produce 500 additional calories per person every day. (The average person needs about 2,000 calories a day, but that number varies greatly depending on your age, size, and amount of exercise.) Where are those extra calories going? Some are sold overseas. Some are turned into ethanol for our cars. But a lot of them are going into us.

An awful lot of those extra corn calories are being eaten as high-fructose corn syrup. Not surprisingly, HFCS is the leading source of sweetness in our diet.

A LOT OF SYRUP
Every year approximately 500 million bushels of corn are turned into high-fructose corn syrup. One bushel of corn yields 33 pounds of HFCS. That makes more than 16 billion pounds of HFCS a year—about the same weight as 1.5 million elephants.

A SWEET DEAL

In 1985, the average American consumed 45 pounds of HFCS a year. In 2006, it was 58 pounds. You might think that it has replaced other sweeteners in the American diet, but that isn't so. In addition to the extra HFCS, Americans are eating more old-fashioned cane sugar too. In fact, since 1985 our consumption of all sugars—cane, beet, HFCS, glucose, honey, maple syrup, whatever—has climbed from 126 pounds to 139 pounds per person. That's what makes HFCS such a "sweet deal" for the food industry; since we like sweet things, adding it to our food increases the amount we eat.

Read the food labels in your kitchen and you'll find that HFCS is everywhere. It's not just in our soft drinks and snack foods, but in the ketchup and mustard, the breads and cereals, the relishes and crackers, the hot dogs and hams.

But it is in soft drinks that we consume most of our fifty-eight pounds of high-fructose corn syrup. We can trace this back to the year 1980—an important year in the history of corn. That was the year corn first became an ingredient in Coca-Cola. By 1984, Coca-Cola and Pepsi had switched over entirely from sugar to high-fructose corn syrup. Why? Because HFCS was a few cents cheaper than sugar and consumers couldn't taste the difference.

The soft drink makers could have just switched one sugar for another. That would not have led us to drink more. But

Could it be
another schmear
campaign?

Lately, high fructose corn syrup has had its name dragged through the media. Truth is, it's nutritionally the same as table sugar. Has the same number of calories, too. Even registered dietitians agree that you can keep enjoying the foods and beverages you love, just do it in moderation. To get the facts, visit our website. We welcome a healthy discussion.

www.SweetSurprise.com

© 2008 Corn Refiners Association

Lately the companies that make HFCS have been fighting back. Their trade group, the Corn Refiners Association, has been running ads on television and in newspaper suggesting that corn syrup has been unfairly criticized, and that it is no worse for us than sugar. They may be right about that, but the problem with HFCS is not that it is worse for us than sugar, but that it is everywhere in the food supply—in products that never used to be sweetened at all.

that wasn't all they did. They began to increase the size of a bottle of soda.

HFCS was so cheap that Pepsi and Coke could have cut the price of each bottle they sold. But they had a much better idea: They would supersize their sodas. Since corn sweetener was now so cheap, why not get people to pay just a few pennies more for a bigger bottle? Drop the price per ounce, but sell a lot more ounces.

Did you ever see an old-fashioned Coke bottle, from around 1950? It looks tiny, because it only held eight ounces. Today the standard size of a Coke or Pepsi is twenty ounces.

SUPERSIZE!

Soda makers don't deserve credit for the invention of super-sizing. That belongs to a man named David Wallerstein. In the 1950s Wallerstein worked for a chain of movie theaters in Texas. Movie theaters make most of their profits from their snack counters, not from ticket sales. It was Wallerstein's job to figure out how to sell more soda and popcorn. Wallerstein tried everything he could think of but found he simply could not get customers to buy more than one soda and one bag of popcorn. He thought he knew why: Going for seconds makes people feel piggish.

Wallerstein discovered that people would buy more pop-corn and soda—a lot more—as long as it came in a single giant serving. Thus was born the two-quart bucket of popcorn and the sixty-four-ounce Big Gulp. In 1968, Wallerstein went to work for McDonald's, but try as he might, he couldn't con-vince Ray Kroc, the company's founder, to try supersizing.

"If people want more fries," Kroc told him, "they can buy two bags." Wallerstein explained that McDonald's custom-ers wanted more but didn't want to buy a second bag. "They don't want to look like gluttons."

Finally Kroc gave in and approved supersized portions, and what followed was a dramatic rise in sales. People had been holding back because they didn't want to seem greedy. Now Wallerstein and McDonald's had figured out a way to make them feel okay about eating more. After all, it was still just one serving, even if it was twice the size. They had discovered the secret to expanding the (supposedly) fixed human stomach.

One might think that people would stop eating and drinking these huge portions as soon as they felt full, but it turns out hunger doesn't work that way. Researchers have found that people (and animals) will eat up to 30 percent more if they are given larger portions.

SUPERSIZED SERVINGS*

Calories in a serving of McDonald's french fries

1960—200
1970—320
Mid-1990s—450
Late 1990s—540
2001—610
2009—500

Although McDonald's ceased to call their servings "supersized" in 2004, a large soda is still at a hefty 32 oz.—that's about 310 calories, 16 percent of an average person's recommended daily calories. 7-Eleven convenience stores still offer a 64-oz. Double Gulp, which weighs in at an incredible 800 calories. So after two and a half Double Gulps, you've consumed a entire day's worth of calories in sweet, liquefied corn.

*based on calories in Coca-Cola Classic and an RDA of 2,000 calories.

Our eating habits were formed over millions of years of evolution. Early humans, who lived by hunting and gathering, didn't always have enough food. Our bodies tell us to eat more when we have the chance, because hunger might be just around the corner. The problem is that with the mountain of cheap corn, hunger never comes (at least not for most Americans).

In the same way, our built-in instincts tell us to eat lots of sugar and fat. Humans, like most other warm-blooded creatures, have a built-in sweet tooth. The taste of sweet or fat tells our body we're eating an energy-rich food. Our instinct is to eat as much as we can, in case we can't find food tomorrow. Yet in nature we would never find a fruit with anywhere near the amount of fructose in a soda. We would never find a piece of animal flesh with as much fat as a chicken nugget.

You begin to see why processing foods is such a good way of getting people to eat more. The fast-food chains have been able to build foods that push our evolutionary buttons. Huge amounts of sweets and fats fool our instincts and we wind up eating much more than we should. Animal experiments prove this is so. Rats presented with solutions of pure sugar or tubs of pure lard will gorge themselves sick.

CHEAP FAT

Surprisingly, the health problems of eating too much hit poor people hardest. That's because if you count the calories, foods loaded with sugar and fat are the cheapest foods in the market. A recent study showed this was true. In a typical supermarket, one dollar could buy 1,200 calories of potato chips and cookies. The same dollar could only buy 250 calories of carrots and other whole vegetables.

On the beverage aisle, you can buy 875 calories of soda for a dollar. But a dollar will only buy you 170 calories of fruit juice from concentrate. These numbers show why people with limited money to spend on food spend it on the cheapest calories they can find. It makes even more sense when you realize that those cheap calories reward our instincts for fat and sugar.

King Corn shoved the other plants and animals off the farm. Now it is winning out in the supermarket too. It is so cheap and comes in so many different forms, the other foods just can't compete.

As we have seen, it has had a lot of help. The U.S. government (spending taxpayer dollars) helps pay farmers to grow corn and soybeans, but not to grow carrots. That means the government helped pay for your soft drink or cookies, but it won't help pay for green vegetables. One part of the government puts out food pyramids telling you to eat more fruits and vegetables and fewer sweets. Meanwhile another part of the government is making it cheaper for you to eat more sweets. The government says it wants you to eat healthy, then it makes sure that the cheapest calories in the supermarket are the unhealthiest. Talk about mixed messages!

The processed food industry has brought us corn in a thousand different forms. It's given us cheap corn sweeteners and hundreds of extra calories a day. It's managed to confuse our instincts, to get us to eat more food than we need. All of this is part of a bigger problem, and not a new problem either. It's the problem of figuring out what we should and shouldn't eat.

It boils down to this: As creatures who can eat many different things, how do we know what's good to eat and what's not? That's the omnivore's dilemma and it's growing bigger every day.

8
The Omnivore's Dilemma

IS THAT FOOD?

For some animals, there is no dilemma at dinnertime. The koala eats eucalyptus leaves. Period. To the koala, eucalyptus leaves=food. The monarch butterfly only eats milkweed. There's no choice to make. Everything else in nature is not food.

The koala gets all the nutrients it needs from eucalyptus leaves. The monarch gets everything it needs from milkweed leaves. But, unlike koalas and monarch butterflies, omnivores not only can

OMNIVORE, CARNIVORE, HERBIVORE

Human beings are omnivores. Omne in Latin means all or everything, Vore comes from the Latin vorare, which means to eat or devour.

Carnivores, like lions and sharks, eat only meat. Carne is Latin for meat.

Herbivores, like cows, eat only plants. Herbe in Latin means grass or green plant.

eat different foods, we *need* to eat a variety of foods to stay healthy. For example, we need vitamin C, which is only found in plants. But we also need vitamin B-12, which is only found in animals. Ultimately, our omnivore's dilemma is rooted in our nature as human beings—but we've made our choices much harder than they used to be.

The industrial food chain has brought the world to our supermarkets. Today we can buy just about any sort of food from anywhere in the globe, in any season. We can buy kiwis from New Zealand and grapes from Chile. We can buy fresh tomatoes in the middle of the winter, flown in from Israel or Holland or Mexico. Add that to the thousands of new processed foods—about 17,000 each year—and we have an incredible amount of food choices (even if most of them are made from corn). With all this variety and the constant stream of messages from the food industry and the media, how can we ever make up our minds?

THE MODERN OMNIVORE

Over thousands of years, human beings built a culture of food that helped us figure out what to eat and what to avoid. We learned what was safe to eat and what could kill us. We learned how to find and cook local foods. These rules and habits made eating a lot easier. When it was time to eat, people didn't have to think about it much. They ate what their parents and grandparents had eaten.

If you lived in Mexico you ate rice, beans, and corn tortillas. If you lived in West Africa you ate cassava, yams, beans, and millet. What you ate also depended on the season. You ate apples in the fall and leafy greens in the spring. In most places people ate small portions of meat, though not at every meal. By following simple rules like these, people solved the omnivore's dilemma.

Today, the modern omnivore has almost no culture to fall back on. Standing in our giant supermarkets, we feel more lost than someone standing in a forest ten thousand years ago. We no longer know for sure which foods are good for us and which aren't. Thanks to the food indus-

YOU'RE EATING WHAT?

Why are there are so many more rats and humans in the world than koalas? Because the koalas' food supply is limited to one thing—eucalyptus leaves. Koalas can only live where there are eucalyptus trees. And if the eucalyptus trees die because of drought or disease, that's it for the koala.

But the rat and the human can live just about anywhere on earth. When their familiar foods are in short supply, there's always another they can try. The list of things human beings have eaten or will eat is pretty much endless. It includes: bugs, worms, dirt, fungi, lichens, seaweed, rotten fish; the roots, shoots, stems, bark, buds, flowers, seeds, and fruits of plants; and every imaginable part of every imaginable animal. (Not to mention haggis, granola, and Chicken McNuggets.)

try, we don't even know what it is we're eating. Sometimes it even seems like we've forgotten *why* we eat.

Modern Americans have lost the solution to the omnivore's dilemma and today the problem is bigger than it has ever been. But it's not an unsolvable problem. We need to recover the skills and knowledge people used to have.

TASTE AND THE TONGUE

Traditionally, "maps" of tastebuds show areas where the four different tastes—sweet, bitter, salty, and sour—are detected on the tongue. New research, however, has not only uncovered a fifth taste called "umami" (which means "savory" in Japanese), but suggests that tastebuds may be more complicated. Certain cells may be dedicated to detecting one taste but found all over the tongue, or certain areas may just be more sensitive to particular flavors. There's also some evidence that men and women taste flavor differently—and that some lucky supertasters experience more intense flavors because they have more tastebuds than the average person.

THE OMNIVORE'S BRAIN

The first thing we should remember is that our bodies have evolved to help us solve the omnivore's dilemma. For example, we have different teeth for different jobs. We can bite like a carnivore, or chew like an herbivore, depending on the dish. Our digestive tract is also good at digesting different types of foods.

The omnivore's dilemma is one reason our brains are so large. The koala doesn't need a lot of brainpower to figure out what to eat. As it happens, the koala's brain is *so* small it doesn't even fill up its skull. Zoologists think the koala once ate a more varied diet than it does now. As it evolved toward eating just one food, it didn't need to think as much. Over generations, unused organs tend to shrink. In other words, as the koala's diet shrank, so did its brain.

Humans, on the other hand, need a lot of brainpower to safely choose an omnivore's diet. We can't rely on instinct like the koala does. For us, choosing food is a problem that has to be solved with our brains and our senses.

To help it make food decisions, our brain developed taste preferences. We think of taste as something that helps us to enjoy food, but our sense of taste evolved to help us screen foods. Our tastebuds divide food into two groups: sweet foods that are good to eat and bitter foods that might harm us.

Sweetness is a sign that a food is a rich source of carbohydrate energy. We don't have to be taught to like sweet foods—we are born liking them. A sweet tooth is part of our omnivore's brain. It is an instinct that evolved to help us through times of food shortage. It says: Eat as much of this sweet high-energy food as you can because you never know when you're going to find some again. This built-in sweet tooth is so strong that we will keep eating sweets even after we are no longer hungry. Our instinct doesn't realize that in modern times there are always sweet foods available to us. We don't have to go hunting and gathering to get more—all we have to do is walk to the refrigerator.

THE BITTER AND THE SWEET

We are also born with a built-in signal that tells us to stop eating certain foods. That's the taste we call bitter. Many plant toxins (poisons) are bitter. Avoiding bitter foods is a good way to avoid these toxins. Pregnant women are very sensitive to bitter tastes. This instinct probably developed to protect the developing fetus against even the mild toxins found in foods like broccoli. But this is not a good excuse to stop eating broccoli. It turns out that some of the bitterest plants contain valuable nutrients, even useful medicines. We can't only rely on our sense of taste when we choose what we eat. (Besides, many people like the taste of broccoli.)

The bark of the willow tree is extremely bitter, but early humans learned to make tea from it anyway. Why? Because willow bark contains salicylic acid, a pain reliever. (It's the active ingredient in aspirin.) Our

THAT'S DISGUSTING!

Humans are great omnivores. But there are some things that we just won't eat, things that all human beings find disgusting. The list of disgusting things includes corpses, decaying flesh, and animal waste. (Curiously, the one bodily fluid of other people that doesn't disgust us is the one produced by the human alone: tears. Consider the only type of used tissue you'd be willing to share.) The disgust we feel about these items is probably genetic—part of the inborn instinct that tells us what we should eat and what we shouldn't eat. Disgust is an important feeling for omnivores, since it keeps us from eating rotten meat or other items that carry disease and bacteria.

food choices are not just dictated by instinct. We can learn to eat bitter foods if they are good for us. We sometimes even decide that we like them.

One way we have overcome the bitterness of some plants is by cooking. Acorns are very bitter. But Native Americans figured out a way to turn them into a rich food by grinding, soaking, and roasting them. The roots of the cassava, a plant in Africa, contain the poison cyanide. This keeps most animals from eating them. But once again, humans figured out a way to safely eat cassava, by pounding and then cooking it. And humans had the cassava roots all to themselves, since pigs, porcupines, and other animals wouldn't touch them.

Once it was discovered, cooking became one of the most important tools of the human omnivore. Cooking vastly increased the number of plants and animals we could eat. In fact, cooking probably was a turning point in human evolution. Anthropologists think early primates (pre-humans) learned to use fire and cook about 1.9 million years ago. That was around the same time the human brain grew larger and our teeth and jaws grew smaller.

RATS!

Rats are also omnivores. But unlike us, rats can't pass lessons or food habits down to their many, many children. When it comes to the omnivore's dilemma, each rat is on its own.

Rats solve the omnivore's dilemma by testing new food. If a rat finds something new to eat, it will nibble a very tiny bit and wait to see what happens. Most poisons in nature are not that strong. A tiny amount will make the rat sick but not kill it. If the rat doesn't get sick, then it knows it can eat the whole thing—a knowledge it retains for the rest of its life. This ability to learn is what makes poisoning rats so difficult.

Luckily, we don't have to use the rat method for solving the omnivore's dilemma. And in fact, over thousands of years, people in every corner of the globe built a large body of food knowledge. Through experience, they learned what combinations of local foods made them healthy. They learned which foods to avoid. They learned how to cook and prepare those foods and passed all this knowledge on to their children. You grew up knowing what to eat and how to cook it.

The culture of food didn't just solve the omnivore's dilemma. It was also an important glue that bound people together. It was part of the identity of a tribe or a nation. People hold on to their national foods, even after they move to other countries. Visit any neighborhood where there are immigrants, and you'll see shops that sell food from the home country—pastas from Italy, kielbasa sausages from Poland, curry spices from India.

National food cultures are more than just a list of foods. They are a set of manners, customs, and rules that cover everything from the correct size of a serving to the order of dishes served at a meal. Some of these rules have clear health benefits. If you live in Japan and eat raw fish (sushi), then it makes sense to eat it with spicy wasabi. Raw fish can contain bacteria, and wasabi kills bacteria. The people who developed the custom of eating sushi with wasabi didn't even know there was such a thing as bacteria. But somehow they figured out that eating wasabi kept them healthier.

People in Central America cook corn with lime and serve it with beans. It turns out there are important health reasons for doing these things. Corn contains niacin, an important vitamin. The way to unlock the niacin in corn is to cook it with an alkali like lime. And eating corn and beans together supplies all the amino acids humans need.

FOOD FADS

We have never had a national food culture in the United States. There's really no such thing as "American food." (Fast-food hamburgers don't count.) We have few rules about what to eat, when to eat, and how to eat. We don't have any strong food traditions to guide us, so we seek food advice from "experts." This may be one reason we have so many diet fads in this country.

One of the earliest of these so-called experts was Dr. John Harvey Kellogg. Yes, that's the same Kellogg whose name is on Kellogg's Corn Flakes and other cereals. Kellogg was a doctor

A staunch ally of modern medicine

IN THIS day of preventive medicine, Kellogg's ALL-BRAN is a valuable aid to the profession. It not only relieves constipation, but prevents it. Promotes regular, natural elimination of the intestinal tract.

Physicians know they can rely upon Kellogg's because it is 100% bran. Because it provides the "roughage" or bulk so necessary to correct faulty elimination —in a quantity no part-bran product can possibly carry.

Kellogg's ALL-BRAN is a prescription patients like to take. Children love it. Cooked and krumbled by a special process, Kellogg's has a delicious nut-like flavor. Delightful as a breakfast cereal —there are many other appetizing ways to serve it.

Sold by all grocers. Served everywhere. Made by Kellogg in Battle Creek, Michigan.

Kellogg's

the original ALL-BRAN—ready-to-eat

The earliest so-called "food expert" was Dr. John Harvey Kellogg, who prescribed all-grape diets and hourly enemas before going on to launch the cereal company.

A scene from the Swedish treatment room at Kellogg's health spa, the Battle Creek Sanitarium, circa 1900.

photo courtesy of the Willard Library

who ran a "sanitarium," or health clinic, in Battle Creek, Michigan. Large numbers of wealthy people traveled there and followed Kellogg's nutty ideas about diet and health. Some of his advice included all-grape diets and almost hourly enemas. (An enema is a cleansing of the bowel in which . . . Oh, never mind.) He followed the enemas with doses of yogurt, applied to the digestive tract from both ends. (Half was eaten and the other half was . . . Well, you can figure it out.)

Around the same time, millions of Americans got caught up in the fad called "Fletcherizing." This involved chewing each bite of food as many as one hundred times. It was named after its inventor, a man named Horace Fletcher, also known as the Great Masticator.

It's easy to make fun of the people who paid good money to

follow his advice. But are we really so much smarter today? Food fads still come and go with alarming speed: A scientific study, a new government guideline, a lone crackpot with a medical degree can change our nation's diet overnight. In 2002, one article in the *New York Times Magazine* said that carbs make you fat. Suddenly millions of Americans gave up bread and other carbohydrates and started eating mainly meat. Fifty years from now that diet might seem as crazy as Kellogg's enemas.

THE NO-FAD FRENCH

Relying on experts or magazine articles is a very new way of solving the omnivore's dilemma. But there are still lots of countries where people solve it the old-fashioned way. They eat traditional foods, following customs that haven't changed for hundreds of years. And amazingly, in those countries where people pick their foods based on custom and taste, the people are actually healthier than we are. They have lower rates of diet-related illness such as heart disease.

Take the French, for example. They eat by and large as they have for generations. They drink wine, eat cheese, cook with butter, and eat red meat. Oh yes, they also eat bread without worrying about it! Yet their rates of heart disease and obesity are lower than the health-crazy Americans'. How can that be? Maybe because *how* we eat is just as important as *what* we eat.

French culture includes a set of customs or rules about how to eat. For example, the French eat small portions and don't go back for seconds. They don't snack—you'll almost never see a French person eating while driving or walking down the street. They seldom eat alone. Instead they eat with family or friends, and their meals are long, leisurely affairs. In other words, the French culture of food allows the French to enjoy their food and be healthy at the same time.

Because we have no such food culture in America, almost every question about eating is up for grabs. Fats or carbs? Three square meals or little snacks all day? Raw or cooked? Organic or industrial? Vegetarian or vegan? We seem to have even forgotten what real food looks and tastes like. Instead we make "meals" of protein bars and shakes. Then we consume these non-foods alone in our cars. Is it any wonder Americans suffer from so many eating disorders?

A GLOBAL DILEMMA?

Traditional food culture is under attack in France and in many other countries. One reason is the spread of global industrial food companies like McDonald's. In countries big and small, lifestyles are changing as people adjust to modern jobs and a global marketplace. Will the omnivore's dilemma grow in these countries as it has grown in the U.S.? Or will we learn from these traditional food cultures before they disappear?

MARKETING NEW MEALS

And so for us, the omnivore's dilemma becomes bigger and bigger. We can't rely on taste to choose among processed foods. We can't just eat foods that we enjoy. We have no stable food culture to guide us, handed down over generations. We are told instead to rely on science. Science (and the industrial food system) will tell us which foods are good for us and which are not. But the "science" keeps changing with every new study.

This situation suits the food industry just fine. The more anxious we are about eating, the more likely we are to listen to claims from food marketers. Food companies make more money if they can get us to change our eating habits and buy their processed foods. They spend billions to create a constant stream of these new foods and then spend billions more to get us to buy them.

Some of these foods are marketed as being healthy. Others are sold under the banner of "convenience." Many are not meant to be eaten at a dinner table. The protein bar or Pop-Tart is designed to be consumed in the car on the way to school or to work. Campbell's has even designed a microwavable soup that can be eaten in a car.

About 47 percent of American families say they still eat together every night. But research shows that many of those "family dinners" are in fact something quite new. In many houses now, each member of the family prepares something different to eat. Mom might cook something vegetarian, while the kids take a pepperoni pizza from the freezer and zap it. They don't all gather at the table at the same time.

By the time Dad sits down, with his own low-carb meal, the kids may have gotten up. Is that a family dinner? Not in my opinion.

What difference does it make if families don't eat together? Well, let me answer that question with another question. Is eating just a task that we have to get done as fast and "conveniently" as possible? Is it something we do only because we have to, like taking medicine or brushing our teeth? Looking at food that way robs us of one of life's greatest pleasures. We should not only enjoy and appreciate our food, we should enjoy making it and eating it in the company of others. Food is not just fuel. It's also about family and friends and community.

Yet in spite of this, as part of my research I decided to have one of these alone-but-together meals. My family and I were going to share our separate processed meals, from a fast-food restaurant at the end of the industrial food chain. We were going to solve the omnivore's dilemma the way millions of Americans do every day. We were going to McDonald's.

9
My Fast-Food Meal

FAST FOOD

Every food chain ends in a meal. When it came time to eat my industrial food chain meal, since it was impossible to follow Naylor's corn or steer 534 directly to my plate, I had a lot of choices. I could have bought a meal from KFC or Pizza Hut or Applebee's, or from hundreds of other fast-food outlets. I could have bought a bunch of prepared foods and heated them up (I don't want to say *cooked*) at home. In the end I decided to buy a meal at a McDonald's and eat it in a moving car. Somehow it seemed like the thing to do.

My eleven-year-old son, Isaac, was more than happy to join me at McDonald's. He doesn't get there often, so it's a treat. (For most American children today, it is no longer such a treat: One in three American kids eats fast food every single day.) Judith, my wife, wasn't quite as happy. She's careful about what she eats. To her, having a fast-food lunch meant giving up a "real meal."

Isaac pointed out that she could order one of McDonald's new "premium salads" with the Paul Newman dressing. I read in the business pages that these salads are a big hit, but even if they weren't, they'd probably stay on the menu. Marketers know that a salad or veggie burger in a fast-food chain gives kids something to say to overcome parents' objections. "But Mom, you can get the salad . . ."

Which is exactly what Judith did: order the Cobb salad with Caesar dressing. At $3.99, it was the most expensive item on the menu. I ordered a classic cheeseburger, large fries, and a large Coke. Large turns out to be a full thirty-two ounces (a quart of soda!). Of course, thanks to the magical economics of supersizing, it cost only thirty cents more than the sixteen-ounce "small." Isaac went with Chicken McNuggets, plus a double-thick vanilla shake, and a large order of fries. He also ordered a new dessert treat consisting of freeze-dried pellets of ice cream.

We would be eating alone together. That each of us ordered something different is one of the wonders of the industrial food chain. Marketers break the family down into its various groups (parents, kids, moms, dads) and sell something slightly different to each group. That way we each have a reason to go to McDonald's. The total for the three of us came to fourteen dollars, and was packed up and ready to go in four minutes.

Before I left the register I picked up a handout printed in tiny type that was called "A Full Serving of Nutrition Facts: Choose the Best Meal for You."

CHICKEN OR NUGGETS?

We could have slipped into a booth, but it was such a nice day we decided to put the top down on the convertible and eat our lunch in the car. Both the food and the car have been designed for eating on the road. These days 19 percent of American meals are eaten in a car. In fact, we could have ordered, paid for, and picked up the food without opening the car door.

Our car has cup hold-

CHEMICAL NUGGETS

Among the chemicals added to a chicken nugget are sodium aluminum phosphate, monocalcium phosphate, sodium acid pyrophosphate, and calcium lactate. Those are antioxidants that keep the fat in the nugget from spoiling. Something called dimethylpolysiloxene is an antifoaming agent. It is added to keep foam from forming when the nugget is fried. Dimethylpolysiloxene is a suspected cause of cancer.

Then there is also something called tertiary butylhydroquinone, or TBHQ. This chemical is made from petroleum and is either sprayed directly on the nugget or the inside of the box it comes in. Its job is to "help preserve freshness." TBHQ is a form of butane (lighter fluid). Eating a single gram of TBHQ can cause "nausea, vomiting, ringing in the ears, delirium, a sense of suffocation, and collapse." Ingesting five grams of TBHQ can kill you. But the government allows food makers to spray a tiny amount of this on your food to preserve it.

ers, front seat and rear, and, except for the salad, all the food could be eaten with one hand. Indeed, this is the genius of the chicken nugget. Now it is just as easy to eat chicken in a car as a hamburger. No doubt the food scientists at McDonald's are right now hard at work on the one-handed salad. By the way, the car was running on gas mixed with ethanol. So while we were eating corn, the car was eating corn too.

I ate a lot of McDonald's as a kid. This was back when you still had to order a second little burger or sack of fries if you wanted more. The chicken nugget had not yet been invented. I loved everything about fast food. The individual portions were all wrapped up like presents and I didn't have to share with my three sisters. I loved the combination of flavors when I bit into a burger—the soft, sweet roll, the crunchy pickle, the tasty moistness of the meat.

Fast food has a flavor all its own. That flavor has little to do with the flavors of hamburgers or french fries you might make at home. It's flavor created from chemicals in a laboratory. These "fast food" flavors make a lot of fast-food meals taste the same. Even Chicken McNuggets have the same fast-food taste as the hamburgers or french fries, though they're technically chicken, not potato or beef.

Isaac announced that his white-meat McNuggets, a new McDonald's recipe, were tasty. When I asked Isaac if the new nuggets tasted more like chicken than the old ones, he seemed surprised by the question. "No, they taste like what they are, which is nuggets." He then dropped on me a withering two-syllable "duh." In his mind, at least, there is no real link between a nugget and a chicken except the name. No doubt a lot of you feel the same.

Isaac passed one up to the front for Judith and me to sample. It looked and smelled pretty good, with a nice crust and a bright white inside that looked sort of like chicken breast meat. Yet all I could really taste was salt and that all-purpose fast-food flavor. Maybe there was a hint of chicken in there somewhere, but not much.

Later I looked at the flyer I had grabbed to see exactly what goes into a nugget. Of the thirty-eight ingredients it takes to make a McNugget, I counted thirteen that can come from corn. Among them are the corn-fed chicken itself; modified cornstarch; mono-, tri-, and diglycerides; dextrose; lecithin; yellow corn flour; regular cornstarch; vegetable shortening; partially hydrogenated corn oil.

NUGGET KNOWLEDGE

In 1983, Tyson invented the chicken nugget at the request of McDonald's, which was looking for a hands-free chicken product.

In 1992, chicken surpassed beef as the most popular meat in America

6 Chicken McNuggets contain nearly twice as much fat as a regular hamburger

As of 2004, McDonald's sold about 4.8 billion individual nuggets per year

According to the handout, McNuggets also contain several completely synthetic ingredients, items that come not from a corn or soybean field but from a petroleum refinery or chemical plant. These chemicals are what make modern processed foods possible. They keep the food from going bad or looking strange after months in the freezer or on the road.

WHERE'S THE BEEF?

Compared to Isaac's nuggets, my cheeseburger is a fairly simple food product. According to the McDonald's handout, the cheeseburger contains only six ingredients: a 100 percent beef patty, a bun, two American cheese slices, ketchup, mustard, pickles, onions, and "grill seasoning," whatever that is. It tasted pretty good too, though what I mainly tasted were the ketchup, mustard, pickles, and onions. By itself, the gray patty had hardly any flavor.

Eating it, I had to remind myself that the burger came from an actual cow. (Probably an old burned-out dairy cow, which is where most fast-food beef comes from.) Part of the appeal of hamburgers and nuggets is that their boneless forms allow us to forget we're eating animals. I'd been on the feedlot at Poky only a few months earlier, yet I had trouble connecting that place to my cheeseburger. I could not taste or smell the feed corn or the petroleum or the antibiotics or the hormones—or the feedlot manure, even though I knew they were there.

By the time it reaches us, industrial food has been processed so much it no longer seems like something made from plants and animals. Where did my cheeseburger come from? It came from McDonald's. As far as industrial food companies are concerned, that's all we need to know. But it's just not so. My cheeseburger came from slaughterhouses and factory farms in towns like Garden City, Kansas, from ranches in Sturgis, South Dakota, from food science laboratories in Oak Brook, Illinois, from flavor companies on the New Jersey Turnpike, from processing plants owned by ADM and Cargill, from grain elevators in towns like Farnhamville, and, at the end of that long and twisted trail, from a field of corn and soybeans farmed by George Naylor in Churdan, Iowa.

How much corn did Judith, Isaac, and I consume in our McDonald's meal?

Add it up:

> Hamburger: corn fed to a cow = 2 pounds corn
> 6 nuggets: corn fed to a chicken = ½ pound
> High fructose corn syrup in 3 drinks = 1 pound
> Subtotal: 3 1/2 pounds of corn.

There's more corn in the meal, but it's harder to measure. There are corn products everywhere. For example, there's more corn sweetener in my cheeseburger. The bun and the ketchup both contain HFCS. It's in the salad dressing too, and the sauces for the nuggets, not to mention Isaac's dessert. (Of the sixty menu items listed in the McDonald's handout, forty-five contain HFCS.)

The nugget is made with corn products called binders and emulsifiers and fillers. Isaac's shake contains milk from corn-fed animals. Judith's salad contains cheese and eggs from corn-fed animals. The salad's grilled chicken breast is injected with a "flavor solution" that's also full of corn products. In fact, the majority of calories in the "healthy" salad come from corn. And the french fries? You would think those are mostly potatoes. Yet half of the 500 calories in a large order of fries come from the oil they're fried in. That means the source of those calories is not a potato farm but a field of corn or soybeans.

CORN EATERS 'R' US

Some time later I found another way to figure out just how much corn we had eaten that day. Scientists can use a machine called a spectrometer to look at the carbon in food and tell how much of it came from corn. I asked Todd Dawson, a biologist at the University of California, Berkeley, to run a McDonald's meal through his spectrometer.

Dawson and his colleague Stefania Mambelli prepared a graph that showed roughly how much of the carbon in the various McDonald's menu items came from corn. In order from most corny to least, this is how the laboratory measured our meal:

Soda (100 percent corn)
Milk shake (78 percent)
Salad dressing (65 percent)
Chicken nuggets (56 percent)
Cheeseburger (52 percent)
French fries (23 percent)

What looks like a meal with lots of variety turns out to be mainly corn. But so what? Why should it matter that we have become a race of corn eaters such as the world has never seen? Is this a bad thing? The answer all depends on where you stand.

If where you stand is in agribusiness, processing cheap corn into forty-five different McDonald's items is a great thing. It is a way for agribusinesses to sell us more food than we need and so a way for them to make more money. We may not be expanding the number of eaters in America, but we've expanded how much food they eat, which is almost as good. Judith, Isaac, and I together consumed a total of 4,510 calories at our lunch, which is about two-thirds of what the three of us should eat in a day. We had certainly done our parts in chomping through the corn surplus. (We had also consumed a lot of petroleum, and not just because we were in a car. To grow and process those 4,510 food calories took at least ten times as many calories of fossil energy,

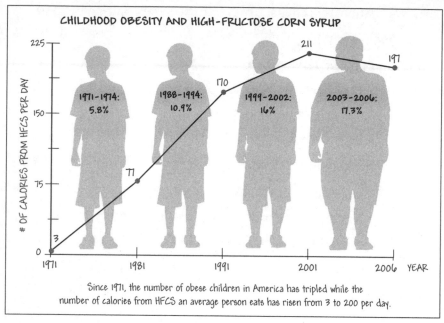

CHILDHOOD OBESITY AND HIGH-FRUCTOSE CORN SYRUP

1971–1974: 5.8%
1988–1994: 10.9%
1999–2002: 16%
2003–2006: 17.3%

Since 1971, the number of obese children in America has tripled while the number of calories from HFCS an average person eats has risen from 3 to 200 per day.

Source: See page 77, also USDA Economic Research Service.

something like 1.3 gallons of oil.)

Corn-based food does offer cheap calories, if you don't count the billions the government spends to support cheap corn. For people with low incomes, this might seem like a good thing. In the long run, however, these cheap calories come with a high price tag: obesity, Type II diabetes, heart disease.

For poor people in other countries, America's industrial food chain is a complete disaster. If you eat corn directly (as Mexicans and many Africans do) you consume all the energy in that corn, but when you feed that corn to a steer or a chicken, 90 percent of its energy is lost. It is used up to make bones or feathers or fur, or just to keep the steer or chicken alive. This is why vegetarians say we should all eat "low on the food chain." Every step up the chain reduces the amount of food energy by a factor of ten. Processing food also burns energy. All of this means that the amount of food energy lost in the making of a Chicken McNugget could feed a great many more children than just Isaac.

And how does this corn-based food chain look to the corn farmer? As you've seen, the industrial food chain has been an economic disaster for the farmers who grow the food in it. Growing corn and nothing but corn has also damaged the soil of our farmlands, polluted the water, and threatened the health of all the creatures downstream. And of course it means that billions of animals are doomed to live out their lives on factory farms.

Yet there is one winner in all of this—corn itself. Of all the species that have adapted to thrive in a world dominated by humans, surely no other has done better than *Zea mays*. Imagine an Iowa farm with corn, corn, corn as far as the eye can see, ten-foot stalks in perfect thirty-inch rows to the horizon. That farm is just a small part of an eighty-million-plus-acre corn lawn rolling across the continent. If the corn could, it would laugh at us, the humans eating and drinking it as fast as they can. You have to wonder why we Americans don't worship this plant as the Aztecs did. Like they once did, we make great sacrifices to it.

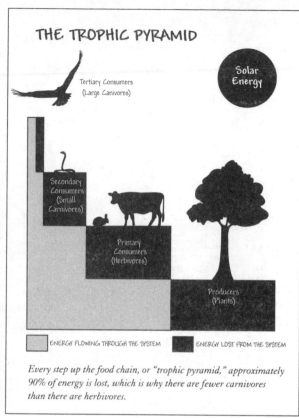

THE TROPHIC PYRAMID

Solar Energy

Tertiary Consumers
(Large Canivores)

Secondary
Consumers
(Small
Carnivores)

Primary
Consumers
(Herbivores)

Producers
(Plants)

ENERGY FLOWING THROUGH THE SYSTEM

ENERGY LOST FROM THE SYSTEM

Every step up the food chain, or "trophic pyramid," approximately 90% of energy is lost, which is why there are fewer carnivores than there are herbivores.

Adapted from Encyclopaedia Britannica

These were my thoughts as we sped down the highway putting away our fast-food lunch. What is it about fast food? Not only is it served in a flash, but more often than not it's eaten that way too. We finished our meal in under ten minutes. From the packaging to the taste, fast food is designed to be eaten quickly. Real food is a pleasure to eat. You want to take your time and enjoy every bite. There's no point in taking your time with fast food. After a few bites, you forget what you're eating. It's not exactly food, but a kind of food substitute. So you eat more and eat more quickly, bite after bite, until you feel not satisfied, exactly, but simply, regrettably, full.

THE MEAL:

Source: Whole Foods
Eaten: At home in Berkeley, CA

MENU:

Mains: Roasted organic chicken ("Rosie" from Petaluma Poultry), roasted organic veggies (yellow potatoes, purple kale, and red winter squash from Cal-Organics)

Sides: Steamed organic asparagus (from Argentina), spring mix salad (from Earthbound Farms)

Dessert: Organic ice cream (from Stonyfield Farms), organic black-berries (from Mexico)

© Alisha Niehaus

PART TWO

The Industrial Organic Meal

10
Big Organic

ONCE UPON A TIME

I'm certainly not the only one who has learned the truth about the industrial food chain. In recent years, more and more Americans have discovered the same sad facts. A lot of them are trying to get away from the kingdom of corn and processed foods by buying organic food. And in my part of the world, there is no greater temple to all things organic, natural, and unprocessed than my local Whole Foods supermarket.

I confess that I really enjoy shopping at Whole Foods. It has some of the same feeling as browsing a good bookstore. Maybe that's because at Whole Foods I spend a lot of my time reading—not books, but labels. Every food item in the store seems to have a little story attached to it.

Take the "range-fed" sirloin steak in the meat case.

There's a flyer on the counter that says once upon a time the steak was part of a steer that spent its days "living in beautiful places." Among the places the steer got to visit were "high-mountain meadows," "thick aspen groves," and "miles of sagebrush-filled flats." Now, a steak like that has got to taste better than one without a story. You can bet it will cost more too.

These food stories are showing up everywhere. On a recent shopping trip I filled my shopping cart with:

- Eggs "from cage-free vegetarian hens"
- Milk from cows that live "free from unnecessary fear and distress"
- Wild salmon caught by Native Americans in Yakutat, Alaska (population 833)
- "Heirloom" tomatoes from Capay Valley Farm ($4.99 a pound), "one of the early pioneers of the organic movement"

The organic chicken I picked even had a name: Rosie. Rosie was a "free-range chicken" from Petaluma Poultry.

Almost all of the labels featured the word *organic*. Forty years ago there was no such category as "organic" food. Today it is a $20-billion business—the fastest growing part of the food industry. The word *organic* has become a kind of shorthand for food that is healthier or more natural or chemical-free. Yet as I had learned, "organic" has different meanings. Now I had more questions than answers. For example, can there be such a thing as an organic TV dinner? What about an organic Twinkie? Exactly how different is "organic" food from industrial food? I was about to find out.

THE BIRTH OF ORGANIC FOOD

Once upon a time all food was "organic." It was grown without the help of fossil fuels, pesticides, or chemical fertilizers. As we have seen, that all began to change about fifty years ago, with the growth of the industrial food chain.

One of the first to notice this change was a man named J. I. Rodale. In 1940 he started a magazine called *Organic Gardening and Farming*. In his magazine, Rodale wrote about the health benefits of growing food without synthetic chemicals—"organically."

But the idea of organic food did not really catch on until 1969. That year marked the height of the counterculture of the 1960s. Civil rights and anti-war protests rocked the country. Young people were rebelling against a society they thought was violent, corrupt, and immoral. Some "dropped out" to join communes, groups of people living and working on farms.

One part of this counterculture was the environmental movement. It was spurred in part by a 1962 book called *Silent Spring* by a woman named Rachel Carson. In it, she warned of the dangers of pesticides like DDT. Events in the news in

1969 also made people aware of the dangers of pollution. A giant oil spill off Santa Barbara blackened California's coastline. A river in Cleveland was so full of filth that it caught fire.

Suddenly people started using the word *ecology* and talking about cleaning up the planet. The first Earth Day was held in April 1970. And the idea of organic food began to catch on. Eating whole wheat bread and whole grains like brown rice became a symbol of the new movement. Processed food like white bread was called "plastic food." The first organic food co-ops were founded. Neighbors would get together once a week and order organic vegetables from farmers. They had to agree on what to order. Often they bought whatever the local farmers had to offer.

To the young people who founded those first co-ops, the word *organic* meant more than a method of farming. It meant living in harmony with nature instead of trying to control it. It meant being free from the control of big corporations. Growing organic food was a way to live their principles and not just talk about them.

Most of those food co-ops are gone now. Many of them have been driven out of business by national "organic" supermarket chains like Whole Foods. Today in the average supermarket there's a selection of organic fruits and vegetables flown in from all over the world. You can buy your organics at any time of the year, no matter the season. And you don't have to get a dozen other people to agree on what to buy.

INDUSTRIAL ORGANIC

But if you look a little closer you'll see that something has been left behind. The organic food in stores like Whole Foods is organic because it is grown without chemical fertilizers or pesticides. Yet much of it is also industrial. Most organic vegetables in the U.S. are grown in large monoculture farms (farms growing only one crop), far from the people who eat it. Most of it is processed and sold by the same industrial food chain as the corn from George Naylor's farm. Because this food chain has elements of both, I call it "industrial organic."

For example, some organic milk comes from cows on small farms. But most organic milk comes from factory farms. The cows on these "farms" spend their time in a fenced lot eating

© Michael Pollan

A field of organic leafy greens being grown for Cascadian Farms.

organic grain except for the three times a day they are hooked up to milking machines. Likewise, organic beef is often raised in "organic feedlots." The cows are fed corn just like the cows at Poky, but their feed is organic.

The government rules about organic food allow companies to make organic high-fructose corn syrup—words I never expected to see combined. This organic HFCS could come in useful when making "organic" processed foods, like organic soda or organic TV dinners. I found one such TV dinner that included thirty-one ingredients, from guar and xanthan gum to "natural grill flavor." Several of the ingredients were synthetic additives that are permitted under federal organic rules.

HIPPIE FOOD

The TV dinner was made by a company called Cascadian Farm. The story of Cascadian tells you a lot about the growth of the organic food movement and how it has changed.

Cascadian started as a kind of hippie commune in 1972, founded by a fellow named Gene Kahn and his friends. Like other young people at the time, Kahn had the idea of getting back to the land and changing the American food system. Today Cascadian is owned by General Mills, and Kahn is a General Mills vice president. Cascadian doesn't even grow its own food anymore. Instead the company buys produce from large (organic) industrial farms, many of them monocultures.

On the Cascadian package there's a picture of a pretty little farm—the original commune. The place still exists, but it's just

I bought and ate this TV dinner made by Cascadian Farms. Once a hippie commune in Washington State, Cascadian is now an industrial organic brand owned by food giant General Mills.

for show. (I guess so they can take photos of it.) One overcast morning Gene Kahn himself drove me out to see it, about seventy-five miles northeast of Seattle. We followed the twists of the Skagit River in his new forest-green Lexus. (His vanity license plates say "Organic.")

Kahn is a boyish-looking man in his fifties. He spoke without regret about the compromises he's made along the path from organic farmer to agribusiness executive. He explained that part of the idea behind Cascadian was to get folks to eat whole foods instead of processed foods. They wanted people to be able to buy their food from local farmers instead of from big corporations. But somewhere along the way, Kahn decided that it was impossible to make all of those changes. So he decided to focus on how food was grown.

"You have a choice of getting sad about all that or moving

on," he told me. "We tried hard to build a cooperative community and a local food system, but at the end of the day it wasn't successful. This is just lunch for most people. Just lunch."

BIG ORGANIC BREAKDOWN

These large corportations own the following organic companies.

COCA-COLA: Honest Tea, Odwalla

DEAN: Horizon, White Wave/Silk

DANONE: Stonyfield Farms

GENERAL MILLS: Cascadian Farm, Muir Glen

HAIN CELESTIAL (Allied with HEINZ and CARGILL): SunSpire Spectrum Organics, Garden of Eatin', Imagine/Rice Dream/Soy Dream, Celestial Seasonings

KELLOGG: Bear Naked, Kashi, Morningstar Farms/Natural Touch

KRAFT: Boca Foods, Back to Nature

PEPSI: Naked Juice

UNILEVER: Ben & Jerry's

MAJOR INDEPENDENTS*

Amy's Kitchen

Clif Bar

Newman's Own

Applegate Farms

Eden Foods

*Most of these companies have refused buyout offers from larger companies

AGRIBUSINESS MOVES IN

So Kahn, like some other organic farmers, started following the model of the industrial food chain. Cascadian started "adding value" to some of its food, by freezing berries or making them into jam. Once they started processing food, they discovered they could make more money by buying produce from other farmers than by growing it themselves.

The demand for organic food really jumped in the year 1990, after the Alar food scare. Alar was a chemical conventional grow-ers sprayed on apples to help them ripen. In

1990 the Environmental Protection Agency found that Alar could cause cancer. Suddenly the demand for organic apples and all sorts of organic produce shot through the roof. People who had never thought about organic food started buying it.

Organic food companies saw their business boom overnight. Some, like Cascadian, borrowed money to increase their production. Having borrowed too much, when the rush to buy organic food slowed down, Gene Kahn was forced to sell control of Cascadian to Welch's. The hippie commune was now under the control of corporate America.

Other large agribusiness corporations started paying attention to organic food. It wasn't because they suddenly saw the error of their ways. They just recognized that a growing number of consumers wanted organic food, and they wanted a piece of that business. Gerber's, Heinz, Dole, ConAgra, and ADM all bought organic brands or started their own.

GROWING BY THE RULES

Now all sorts of foods with labels like "natural" and "organic" began to show up in supermarkets. Those words had become great marketing tools. But what exactly did they mean? In 1990 Congress passed a law telling the Department of Agriculture (the USDA) to decide on some rules for organic food. What followed was a great debate to determine the future of the organic industry.

On one side of the fight were the agribusiness corporations, which had just jumped onto the organic food bandwagon. They fought to define organic as loosely as possible. For example, they wanted the right to call genetically modified food (GMO) organic. They also wanted to be able to fertilize their "organic" fields with sewage sludge. At first the USDA went along. In 1997 it proposed a very loose set of rules that gave agribusiness everything it wanted. In response there was a huge outcry from small organic farmers and the public. A flood of protest forced the USDA back to the drawing board.

USDA ORGANIC LABELING STANDARDS

"100% Organic" products contain only certified organic ingredients.
"Organic" products must contain at least 95% organic ingredients.
"Made with organic ingredients": At least 70% of ingredients must be organic.

Products with less than 70% organic ingredients can list specific organic ingredients on the packaging.

AND: There are no restrictions on use of other labeling claims such as "no drugs or growth hormones used," "free range," or "sustainably harvested."

One big question was whether there could be such a thing as organic processed food. Gene Kahn sat on the board that set the new standards. He argued that the rules for organics had to allow synthetic additives and preservatives. Without synthetics, processed foods like TV dinners just can't be manufactured. Many people from the old organic movement argued that to put synthetics in a processed food and then call it organic was a fraud. They said there could be no such thing as a truly organic Twinkie or TV dinner. In the end, Kahn's side won out. That's why there are now "organic" processed foods, although still no organic Twinkie.

These new rules cleared the way for a huge growth in the organic food market. "If we had lost on synthetics," Gene Kahn told me, "we'd be out of business."

DOWN ON THE INDUSTRIAL ORGANIC FARM

I guess I missed the old Cascadian, the one on the package. Or at least, I missed the idea of it. This just didn't fit my picture of what an organic farm should look like.

Get over it, Gene Kahn told me. Just because a farm is big doesn't mean it isn't organic. The important thing, he would argue, is that behind every organic TV dinner or chicken stands acres of land that will no longer be doused with chemicals. I could see his point. This is clearly a great thing for the environment and the public health. So I decided to go see some industrial organic farms for myself.

Kahn sent me to visit a large organic farm operation called Greenways, in California's Central Valley. That's where they grow vegetables for Cascadian Farm frozen dinners.

Greenways Organic is really 2,000 acres of organic farmland tucked into a 24,000-acre conventional farm. That gave me a chance to compare the two types of farming side by side. Even up close it's almost impossible to tell them apart. The crops, the machines, the crews, and the fields look the same. The big difference is one you can't see. For every chemical that is put on the conventional fields, Greenways finds a substitute for the organic fields.

In place of petrochemical fertilizers, Greenways's organic acres are fed with compost from a nearby horse farm and by poultry manure. Instead of toxic pesticides, crops are sprayed with natural substances, like BT, a pesticide made from a common soil bacteria.

ORGANIC WEEDING

Organic farming rules do not allow chemical weed killers, so Greenways has to use other methods to fight weeds. Even before the crops are planted, the fields are watered to get any weed seeds to grow. A tractor then plows the field to kill them. This is repeated several times. Later, when the crops are high, farmworkers use propane torches to burn the weeds by hand. The result of all this hard work is fields that look just as clean as if chemical weed killers had been used.

No chemicals means no toxic runoff into rivers and oceans. But it turns out that plowing the land over and over damages the soil almost as much as chemical weed killers do. It kills off the nitrogen-fixing bacteria that make the soil fertile. It releases a lot of nitrogen into the air. Because of this damage, industrial organic farmers have to add a lot of nitrogen fertilizer to their fields. Where do they get it? From compost, manures, or fish meal.

Most of the organic food sold in America comes from farms like Greenways. Supermarket chains like Whole Foods or Walmart are not set up to do business with dozens of small family-owned farms. It takes too much time and money to coordinate. It makes much more sense (for them) to buy from large suppliers like Cascadian. And for the same reason, it's much easier for Cascadian to buy its produce from large farms like Greenways.

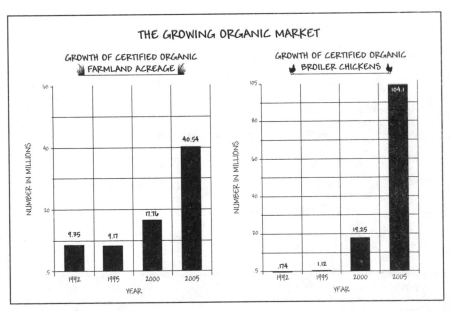

Demand for certified organic produce and meat has increased dramatically since the early 1990s—although organic items make up only about 3.5% of the total U.S. food supply in 2009.

Sources: USDA and the Organic Trade Association.

To meet the demands of their customers, Greenways has to farm on an industrial scale. It must plant one or two crop varieties that ripen at the same time. It must plant foods that can survive shipment across the country. It must buy fertilizer from someone else instead of getting it from animals on the farm.

Again, Gene Kahn and many other people think this is just fine. After all, because of companies like his, thousands of acres of American farmland are now chemical-free. Organic food can now be found in most supermarkets. Surely that is a very good thing.

LET US SELL YOU LETTUCE

I learned more about the industrial organic system when I visited Earthbound Farm. Earthbound grows 80 percent of the organic lettuce sold in America. You may have seen some of it in plastic boxes in your supermarket. You could argue that Earthbound represents industrial organic farming at its best.

Earthbound Farm grows 80% of the organic lettuce sold in America.

The company was started in the 1980s by Drew and Myra Goodman, two farmers who started with exactly no farming experience. They are childhood friends from New York City, who started dating when they both went to college in California. During a break before going to grad school, they started a roadside organic farm on a few rented acres, growing raspberries and baby salad greens. Every Sunday Myra would wash and bag a bunch of lettuce for their own use, a salad for each night of the week. They discovered that the whole-leaf lettuces stayed fresh right through to dinner the following Saturday. So began the pre-washed salad business in America.

Before the Goodmans, salad for most Americans meant iceberg lettuce. They introduced dozens of different salad mixes to mainstream America. Along the way, they changed the way lettuces were grown, harvested, cleaned, and packed. And today Earthbound is a company that takes in $400 million a year.

I met Myra Goodman, now a tanned, talkative forty-two-year-old, over lunch at the company's roadside stand in the Carmel Valley. Unlike Cascadian Farm, Earthbound still grows its own produce. Most of its farmland is an hour northeast of Carmel, in the Salinas Valley. That fertile valley is cooled by sea breezes, making it an ideal spot for growing lettuces nine months of the year. In winter, the company picks up and moves its operation, and many of its employees, south to Yuma, Arizona.

Myra explained that Earthbound Farm's growth exploded in 1993. That's when the Costco chain placed an order. "Costco was moving two thousand cases a week to start," Myra said, "and the order kept increasing." Other chains like Walmart, Lucky, and Albertsons soon followed. The Goodmans realized their days of washing lettuce in the living room were over.

"We didn't know how to farm on that scale," Drew told me, "and we needed a lot more land—fast." So the Goodmans entered into partnerships with growers who knew how to grow, harvest, pack, and distribute large quantities of produce. As part of the deal, the growers had to agree to change to organic farming methods.

If you include all the farmland growing fruits and vegetables for Earthbound it comes to a total of 25,000 organic acres. The Goodmans estimate that this has eliminated some 270,000 pounds of pesticide and 8 million pounds of petrochemical fertilizer that would otherwise have been applied to those fields.

THE SALAD FACTORY

The Earthbound Farm land looks like a giant patchwork of color: dark green, burgundy, pale green, blue green. Each color block is a different type of lettuce.

The lettuce is grown in raised beds. Each bed is eighty inches wide, and smooth and flat as a tabletop. Workers use a laser to make sure they are perfectly level. That's so that the custom-built harvester can snip each leaf at precisely the same point.

To control pests, one out of every seven beds is planted with

photo courtesy of Earthbound Farm

Earthbound Farm's lettuce-washing assembly line in San Juan Bautista, California.

flowers. The flowers attract lacewings and a type of fly that eats the lettuce-eating bugs. Pesticides, even the ones allowed by the USDA organic rules, are seldom sprayed.

The leaves are harvested with a machine that Earthbound designed. It moves down the rows, cutting the baby greens at the same point just above the crown. Spidery arms gently rake through the bed in advance of the blade, scaring off any mice that might find their way into the salad. The leaves are blown into plastic trays and the trays are loaded by hand into refrigerator trucks. From that point they will be refrigerated until they reach your supermarket.

Once filled, the trucks deliver their cargo of leaves to a processing plant. There the leaves are sorted, mixed, washed, dried, and packaged. The whole plant is kept at thirty-six degrees. Because of the refrigeration, the employees, most of them Mexicans, are dressed in full-length down coats. The plant washes and packs 2.5 million pounds of lettuce a week. That's a truly amazing amount of lettuce.

It also represents a truly amazing amount of energy. Think of the electricity bill to refrigerate a 200,000-square-foot plant. Think of the diesel fuel needed to truck all that salad to supermarkets across the country or to manufacture the plastic containers it's packed in. A one-pound box of pre-washed lettuce contains 80 calories of food energy. Growing, chilling, washing, packaging, and transporting that box of organic salad to a plate on the East Coast takes more than 4,600 calories of fossil fuel energy, or 57 calories of fossil fuel energy for every calorie of food.

What could be more healthy than eating a salad? It's basically a bunch of leaves, eaten raw. And organic salad has to be even better, right? Still, the idea of packing lettuce in plastic boxes and shipping it five days and three thousand miles away didn't *feel* very organic to me.

Like Gene Kahn, Drew and Myra Goodman make no apologies for the way they do business. Their company has done a world of good, for its land, its workers, the growers it works with, and its customers. But is this kind of organic the best we can do? Before I could make up my mind, I had to visit one more industrial organic farm. I was on my way to meet Rosie, the organic chicken.

11
More Big Organic

MEET ROSIE, THE FREE-RANGE CHICKEN

I visited Rosie the free-range organic chicken at her farm in Petaluma. Of course, this wasn't the same Rosie as the chicken I had bought at my Whole Foods market. Rosie is the brand name for a type of chicken raised by Petaluma Poultry. Like Earthbound Farm, Petaluma Poultry is a large industrial organic company.

When I got to Petaluma, I looked for a pretty little red barn, a cornfield, and farmhouse, like the ones on the Petaluma package. By now you'll have guessed that I couldn't find them.

Petaluma turns out to be more

Organic or not, factory farms typically keep at least 20,000 broiler chickens in huge sheds such as this one.

animal factory than farm. Rosie lives in a shed with twenty thousand other Rosies. Ah, you ask, what about the "free-range" words on Rosie's label? Doesn't that mean they can "freely range" outside? Not exactly. It's true there's a little door in each shed leading out to a narrow grassy yard. But here's the catch: The door remains firmly shut until the birds are at least five weeks old. By that time they are so used to the shed that none of them go outside. And then all of them are slaughtered two weeks later.

Rosie and all the other chickens raised at Petaluma are the same breed: Cornish Cross broilers. The Cornish Cross is a type of chicken bred for the industrial food chain. It is the fastest-growing chicken ever, turning corn into meat faster than any other bird. They go from egg to full size in just seven weeks. In fact, the birds grow so rapidly that their poor legs cannot keep up. Often, by seven weeks, Rosie can no longer walk.

IT'S A BIRD'S LIFE

The folks at Petaluma gave me a tour of the fully automated processing plant. The machinery there can turn a chicken from a clucking, feathered bird into a shrink-wrapped pack of parts in just ten minutes. After the tour the head of marketing drove me out to the chicken houses.

The sheds look more like a military barracks than a barn. They are long, low buildings with giant fans at either end. To go inside I had to put on a white hooded suit. Since the birds receive no antibiotics and they are all genetically alike, if one gets sick, they will all get sick. An infection could kill 20,000 birds overnight.

Twenty thousand is a lot of chickens. Inside the shed they formed a moving white carpet that stretched nearly the length of a football field. The air was warm and humid and smelled powerfully of ammonia from their droppings. The fumes caught in my throat.

Compared to conventional chickens, I was told, these organic birds have it pretty good. They get a few more square inches of living space per bird. (It was hard to see how they could be packed together much more tightly.) Because there are no hormones or antibiotics in their feed to speed growth, they get to live a few days longer.

I stepped back outside into the fresh air, grateful to escape the humidity and smell. Running along the entire length of each shed was a grassy yard maybe fifteen feet wide. USDA rules say an organic chicken should have "access to the outdoors." But as I've said, the birds never go outside, even when the doors are opened. This is no accident. The last thing Petaluma wants is for these birds to go outside and catch a cold.

MY ORGANIC INDUSTRIAL MEAL

After visiting Cascadian, Earthbound, and Petaluma, I decided it was time to make my industrial organic food chain meal. (There isn't any organic fast-food restaurant chain to visit, at least not yet.) I planned a simple Sunday night dinner and bought the food at my local Whole Foods supermarket.

I'd prepare roast chicken (Rosie) with roasted vegetables: yellow potatoes, purple kale, and red winter squash. All but one of them was grown by a company called Cal-Organic Farms. They pretty much share the organic vegetable market with Earthbound. On the side would be steamed asparagus and a spring mix salad from Earthbound Farm. Dessert would be even simpler: organic ice cream from Stonyfield Farm topped with fresh organic blackberries from Mexico.

I also bought one of those Cascadian Farm organic TV dinners. I had a hunch it probably wasn't quite ready for prime time (or at least for my wife). So I ate it myself for lunch, right in its microwaveable plastic bowl. Five minutes on high and it was good to go. As I peeled back the film from the bowl, I felt a little like a flight attendant serving meals. Indeed, the meal looked and tasted very much like airline food.

To be fair, one shouldn't compare an organic TV dinner to real food but to a conventional TV dinner, and by that standard Cascadian Farm has nothing to be ashamed of. Still, the chunks of white meat chicken had only a faint chicken taste. That probably came from the "natural chicken flavor" mentioned on the box. The "creamy rosemary dill sauce" was made without cream or milk. I'm betting it got its creaminess from xanthan gum or some other additive.

AIRLIFT ASPARAGUS

The dinner went much better, if I don't mind saying so myself. I roasted the bird in a pan surrounded by the potatoes and chunks of winter squash. After removing the chicken from the oven, I spread the crinkled leaves of kale on a cookie sheet, sprinkled them with olive oil and salt, and slid them into the hot oven to roast. After ten minutes or so, the kale was nicely crisped and the chicken was ready to carve.

The one vegetable I cooked that wasn't grown by Cal-

Organic or Earthbound was the asparagus. It had been grown in Argentina. It had been picked, packed, and chilled on Monday, flown by jet to Los Angeles Tuesday, trucked north and put on sale in Berkeley by Thursday, and steamed, by me, Sunday night.

That one bundle of asparagus presented its own little dilemma. How much fossil fuel was burned to keep it refrigerated and fly it to the U.S.? Should farmland in South America be used to grow expensive food for well-off North Americans? Should we even try to eat asparagus (or any vegetable) out of season?

Yet there are good arguments on the other side. My purchase helps the economy of Argentina. It also keeps some of that country's land free from pesticides or chemical fertilizer.

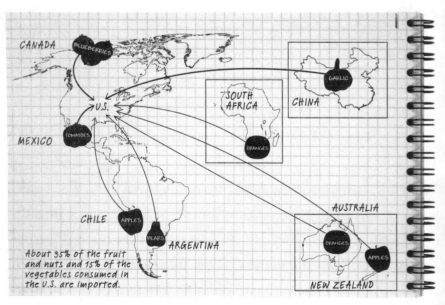

About 35% of the fruit and nuts and 15% of the vegetables consumed in the U.S. are imported.

Source: USDA Economic Research Service

This was all a lot of baggage for a few spears of asparagus to carry, I admit.

So how did it taste?

My jet-setting Argentine asparagus tasted like damp cardboard. After the first spear or two no one touched it. All the other vegetables and greens were much tastier—really good, in fact. Of course, we live in California, so they didn't have far to travel to our table. Whether they would have been quite so sweet and bright after a cross-country truck ride is doubtful.

I have to admit that the Earthbound greens, in their plastic bag, stayed crisp right up to the expiration date, a full eighteen days after leaving the field. This is partly due to the space-age technology used to pack them. But as the Goodmans had explained to me, organic greens just last longer. Since they're not pumped up on synthetic nitrogen, the cells of organic leaves grow more slowly. These slower-growing leaves develop thicker walls and take up less water, helping them stay fresher longer.

IS ORGANIC BETTER FOR YOU?

My industrial organic dinner certainly wasn't cheap, considering I made it from scratch. Rosie cost $15 ($2.99 a pound), the vegetables another $12 (thanks to that six-buck bunch of asparagus), and the dessert $7 (including $3 for a six-ounce box of blackberries). That comes to $34 to feed a family of three at home. (Though we did make a second meal from the leftovers.) That's a hefty price compared to the same meal from the industrial food chain. So why buy organic anyway? Is the extra cost worth it? What exactly are you paying for?

Does organic food taste better? I think the answer is probably, but not always. A freshly picked non-organic vegetable is bound to taste better than one that's been riding in a truck for three days. On the other hand, organic Rosie was a tasty bird, with more flavor than mass-market birds fed on a diet of antibiotics and animal by-products. Those "unnatural" feeds make chickens with mushier and blander meat.

Okay, so organic food sometimes tastes better. But is it better for you? I think the answer to this is also yes, but I can't prove it scientifically.

I know the dinner I prepared contained little or no pesticides. Those chemicals have been proven to cause cancer, damage nerve cells, and disrupt your endocrine system—your hormones. These poisons are routinely found in non-organic produce and meat. Yet I can't prove that the low levels of these poisons in food are enough to make you sick. The government says the levels are low enough that our systems can "tolerate" them.

Very little research has been done to determine the effects of low levels of these poisons. One problem is that the official tolerance levels are set for adults, not children. Since children are smaller and still growing, the danger for them is greater than for adults. Given what we do know about the dangers of these chemicals, it makes sense to keep them out of a kid's diet.

It was important to me that the organic ice cream came from cows that did not receive injections of growth hormone to boost their productivity. We don't know if these hormones are affecting kids who drink non-organic milk, but again, I think it's better to avoid them. Also, organic cows, like Rosie the organic chicken, are never fed corn that contains residues of atrazine, the herbicide commonly sprayed on American cornfields. The tiniest amount of this chemical (0.1 part per billion) has been shown to change the sex of frogs. There's been no study to show what it does to children.

So it seems to me I have two choices: I can wait for that study to be done or I can decide that it's better to be safe than sorry and buy foods without atrazine. As you may recall from chapter four, although the U.S. government allows atrazine spraying, the chemical is already banned in Europe.

IS IT HEALTH FOOD?

Okay, getting rid of poisons is a no-brainer. But there's still another question about organic food. Is it healthier for you? Does it contain more nutrients—vitamins, minerals, and natural substances—that our bodies need to stay healthy?

As far as the USDA is concerned, all carrots are created equal, organic and non-organic. Yet there is some real evidence that this is not so. In 2003, a study by University of California, Davis, researchers studied two crops of corn, strawberries, and blackberries. The plants were identical and grown in side-by-side plots. One set of plants was grown using organic methods. The other set was grown conventionally with chemical fertilizer, pesticides, and herbicides.

The study showed that the organic fruits and vegetables contained higher levels of vitamin C. They also had a wider range of natural chemicals called polyphenols. Polyphenols are a group of chemicals made by plants that seem to play an important role in human health. Some help prevent or fight cancer; others fight infections. You may have seen one of these polyphenols advertised on your ketchup bottle—one called lycopene. There are many others.

Why in the world should organically grown blackberries or corn contain more of these polyphenols? These compounds help plants to defend themselves against pests and diseases. Perhaps plants that are sprayed with man-made pesticides don't bother to produce much of their own.

The soils in industrial farms are often lifeless. Perhaps these dead soils don't supply all the raw ingredients plants need to make polyphenols. Artificial fertilizer may be enough to get plants to grow, yet still may not give a plant everything it needs to make enough lycopene or resveratrol (another one of the polyphenols).

Here is what we do know. We have evolved over millions

of years eating plants that today we would call "natural" or "organic." Those plants, growing in complex, living soils, produced polyphenols to protect themselves from pests and disease. Our bodies evolved to use those same compounds to protect us from disease. Yet in the last fifty years we have built a food system that strips many of those healthy compounds out of our foods.

Who knows what other healthy substances are in plants that we have yet to discover? The industrial food chain breaks all food down into a few simple elements. But what if our bodies need more than that? The evidence is starting to come in that this is the case.

DO PLANTS NEED ORGANIC FOOD?

The conventional food industry says fertility is a matter of three elements: nitrogen, phosphorus, and potassium. The symbols for these elements in the periodic table are N, P, and K. Every bag of fertilizer has three numbers on it, for example, 5-10-5. Those numbers represent the ratio of the NPK elements in that fertilizer. If you give plants these three elements, they will grow. But is that all plants need?

Natural, untreated soil is a very complex thing, filled with literally thousands of different substances. As dead organisms are decomposed or broken down, they too become part of the soil. So too do animal wastes. A normal patch of dirt will be teeming with life, from earthworms to bacteria to the microscopic threads of fungi. Soil that is treated with pesticides and herbicides becomes lifeless.

Artificial fertilizer is designed to deliver the NPK elements and nothing else. Yet we are beginning to learn that the health of plants—and therefore our health—depends on a much more complex set of nutrients.

EATING OIL

I hope I've made it clear that I think organic industrial food is a big improvement over the non-organic food chain. To grow the plants and animals that made up my meal, no pesticides found their way into any farmworker's bloodstream, no nitrogen runoff seeped into the watershed, no soils were poisoned, no antibiotics were wasted, no government subsidy checks were written. And yet . . .

FOOD MILES AND JET-SETTING CARROTS

The term "food miles" tells you how far your food has traveled from where it was originally grown to your supermarket. In the U.S., that's usually about 1,500 miles—or 27 times farther than it would travel to a local market. For example, while carrots at the farmers market are likely grown within 50 miles of your house, the carrots you find at the grocery store traveled around 1,800 miles (or about the distance between New York City and Denver.) Many of our fruits, vegetables, and meat also come from foreign countries—and in a typical TV dinner, at least five of the ingredients are shipped in from abroad.

The wages and working conditions of the farmworkers in an organic field aren't much different from those on non-organic factory farms. "Organic" factory farm chickens live only slightly better lives than non-organic factory chickens. In the end a CAFO is a CAFO, whether the cattle are fed organic corn or not. An organic label does not guarantee that cattle have spent any time in a real pasture, any more than "free-range" chickens really range freely.

To top it off, my industrial organic meal is nearly as drenched in fossil fuel as a non-organic meal. Asparagus traveling in a 747 from Argentina; blackberries trucked up from Mexico; a salad chilled to thirty-six degrees from the moment it was picked to the moment I walk it out the doors of my supermarket. That takes a lot of energy and a lot of fossil fuel. Organic farmers generally use less fuel to grow their crops. Yet most of the fuel burned by the food industry isn't used to *grow* food. Almost 80 percent of the fuel burned is used to process food and move it around. This is just as true for an organic bag of lettuce as a non-organic one.

The original organic food movement thought organic farming should be sustainable. That means it should be, as much as possible, a closed loop, recycling fertility and using renewable energy. The industrial organic food chain is anything but a closed, renewable loop. The food in our organic meal had floated to us on a sea of petroleum just as surely as the corn-based meal we'd had from McDonald's.

Well, at least we didn't eat it in the car.

A DIFFERENT KIND OF FOOD CHAIN

But I wasn't done searching for more responsible food. As part of my research I kept hearing about this incredible farmer in Virginia. His name was Joel Salatin and he and his family ran a 500-acre spread called Polyface Farm near the town of

Swoope. So I gave him a call. I wanted to interview him and I also wanted him to ship me some of his food so I could taste it myself. Well, I got my interview, but Salatin said he couldn't ship me any chicken or steak. I figured he meant he wasn't set up for shipping, so I offered him my FedEx account number.

"No, I don't think you understand. I don't believe it's sustainable—or 'organic,' if you will—to FedEx meat all around the country. I'm sorry, but I can't do it."

This man was serious.

He explained that just because we can ship organic lettuce from California, or organic apples from Chile, doesn't mean we *should* do it. Shipping food thousands of miles and burning up fossil fuels went against his whole philosophy as a farmer.

"I'm afraid if you want to try one of our chickens," he said, "you're going to have to drive down here to Swoope to pick it up."

It turns out there's another food chain in America, one that looks very different from the industrial farms I had been visiting. It's based on small family farms like Salatin's, which practice true sustainable farming. These farms aren't owned by big agribusiness corporations. They don't ship their vegetables and meat across the country or across the globe. In fact, they look more like the picture I had of an organic farm when I had started out. So I decided to take Joel Salatin up on the offer he'd extended when I told him about my book. I decided to go to Virginia to see his farm firsthand. My wife called it my Paris Hilton adventure. And she was right—I was about to do a lot of hard work I wasn't quite ready for. I was also about to find out how different an organic farm could be.

© Alisha Niehaus

THE MEAL:

Source: Polyface Farm
Eaten: at a friend's house in Charlottesville, VA

MENU:

Main: Brined and applewood smoked BBQ chicken

Sides: Roasted sweet corn, rocket salad

Dessert: Chocolate soufflé (made with Polyface eggs and Belgian chocolate)

Wine (from Virginia)

PART THREE

The Local Sustainable Meal:

Food from Grass

12
Polyface Farm

GREEN ACRES

Early in the afternoon on the first day of summer, I found myself sitting in the middle of a bright green pasture. The first day of summer is the longest day of the year. This day felt like the longest day of my life. I was more tired than I thought anyone could be.

I'd spent the afternoon making hay. After just a few hours in the June sun lifting and throwing fifty-pound bales, I hurt. We think of grass as soft and friendly stuff, but once it's been dried in the sun and shredded by machines, it becomes hay. And the ends of hay are like needles, sharp enough to draw blood. My forearms were dotted red with pinpricks and my lungs were filled with hay dust.

Joel Salatin had gone off to the barn with his grown son, Daniel. That left me a welcome moment in the pasture to rest before we started up again. It was Monday, the first day of the week I would spend on the farm. After just half a day I knew I would never again complain about any price a farmer wanted to charge me for food. If the work was this hard, one dollar for an egg seemed reasonable. Fifty dollars for a steak was a steal.

TIME TRAVEL?

The farm machinery had fallen silent, and I could hear the sounds of songbirds in the trees, and also the low clucking of hens. Up on the green, green hill rising to the west I could see a small herd of cattle grazing. The meadows were dotted

My first glimpse of the Salatins' Polyface Farm.

Joel Salatin the grass farmer with his cattle at Polyface Farm.

with contented animals. Behind them was the backdrop of dark woods. A twisting brook threaded through it all. It was an almost too-perfect farm scene. The only problem was that I couldn't just lie there on the springy pasture for the rest of the afternoon.

I thought about how amazing it was that the farm existed at all. This was exactly the way farms had been before industrial food and feedlots and giant wet mills. Yet I had not traveled back in time. This farm was living and thriving today just 150 miles from Washington, D.C.

I'd come to Polyface Farm to find out if it was possible for a non-industrial food chain to survive in the twenty-first century. Was this farm just a lone holdout against industrial food? Or did it represent a new wave of local organic farms that could survive outside the industrial food chain? In short, I wanted to know if this kind of farming was the past or the future.

Looking at those green pastures that afternoon, I thought the only thing missing from the scene was a happy shepherd. But then I saw a tall fellow loping toward me, wearing broad blue suspenders and a floppy straw hat. It was Joel Salatin, owner of Polyface, returning from the barn. Most farmers wear a trucker's cap marked with the logo of an agribusiness giant. Salatin's hat had no logo and it was made of grass, not plastic. This was fitting because grass, not petroleum, is the foundation of his farm's success.

THE GRASS FARMER

Polyface Farm raises chicken, beef, turkeys, eggs, rabbits, and pigs, plus tomatoes, sweet corn, grapes, and berries. They do all this on 100 acres of pasture mixed in with another 450 acres of forest. But if you ask Joel Salatin what he does for a living he'll say, "I'm a grass farmer."

The first time I heard this I didn't get it at all. People can't eat grass, and he doesn't sell any of his hay to other farmers. How could he be in the grass business? But of course, Salatin was right. As I was to learn during my stay, the cows, pigs, chickens, turkeys, and rabbits at Polyface (as well as Salatin and his family) all depend on grass in one way or another.

(Grass, of course, is not a single plant. It is our name for the whole collection of plants that grow together in a pasture or meadow.)

Polyface Farm is the opposite of an industrial farm like George Naylor's or Earthbound. Those industrial farms grow giant monoculture fields. Their farms run like factories. They put in the seed and fertilizer (raw materials) and out comes corn or soybeans (product). It's a pretty straight line from start to finish.

Nothing at Polyface works in a straight line. The animals and crops seem to move in circles like some sort of compli-

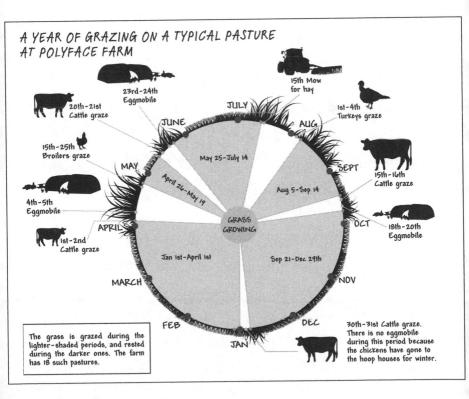

A YEAR OF GRAZING ON A TYPICAL PASTURE AT POLYFACE FARM

23rd–24th Eggmobile

20th–21st Cattle graze

15th Mow for hay

1st–4th Turkeys graze

JULY

JUNE

AUG

15th–25th Broilers graze

MAY

May 25–July 14

SEPT

15th–16th Cattle graze

4th–5th Eggmobile

April 26–May 19

Aug 5–Sep 14

GRASS GROWING

1st–2nd Cattle graze

APRIL

OCT

18th–20th Eggmobile

Jan 1st–April 1st

Sep 21–Dec 29th

MARCH

NOV

FEB

DEC

JAN

The grass is grazed during the lighter-shaded periods, and rested during the darker ones. The farm has 18 such pastures.

30th–31st Cattle graze. There is no eggmobile during this period because the chickens have gone to the hoop houses for winter.

cated dance. Each plant and animal plays its part and Joel Salatin is the choreographer. The pastures are the stage and the main action of the dance is to rotate the animals through the pastures.

PASTURES OF PLENTY

The pasture I was resting in was a good example. It was the third week of June and the field had already been occupied several times. It had been grazed twice by beef cattle. After the cattle it had been home to several hundred laying hens. Later, the grass had been cut to make hay that would feed the farm's animals through the winter.

I asked Salatin why the chickens had been let loose in the pasture instead of fed in a chicken coop. "Because that's how it works in nature," he explained. "Birds follow and clean up after herbivores."

Joel calls the hens his "sanitation crew." In the pasture, they pick tasty grubs and fly larvae out of the cowpats. (Larvae are one stage in the life cycle of insects. For example, caterpillars are butterfly larvae.) Eating the grubs and larvae cuts down on bugs and parasites—in this case, tiny organisms that live on or in the cow—that would bother the cattle. And while the chickens are nibbling on the grasses, they add a few thousand pounds of nitrogen to the pasture with their own droppings—and produce several thousand rich and tasty eggs. After a few weeks' rest, the pasture will regrow and feed the cows again.

By the end of the season Salatin's animals will have transformed his grasses into an astounding amount of food. Yet even more amazing is the fact that this pasture will be in better, not worse, shape. Its soil will be deeper, more fertile, and even springier underfoot (this thanks to the increased earthworm traffic). And the whole process is powered by the sun. No fossil fuels or added fertilizer or chemicals needed.

GRASS AND HUMANS—BFF?

When we looked at beef ranching, we learned how grasses and herbivores formed a partnership over millions of years of evolution. In the same way, human beings and grasses also have been partners. People in prehistoric times often hunted the big herbivores that dined on grass. Those hunters would regularly set fire to the prairie to keep it free of trees and nourish the soil. In a sense, they too were "grass farmers." They helped the grass, and the grass in turn fed the animals they hunted.

The bonds between humans and grass grew even stronger about 10,000 years ago. About that time people learned to plant and grow grasses like wheat, rice, and corn. These grasses were different because they produced big, rich seeds. Humans could harvest and eat those seeds. They didn't need herbivores to turn the grass into meat.

Grains like wheat and corn are grasses, but they're different from the grasses in Joel Salatin's meadow. Meadow grasses can reproduce even if they are eaten (or mowed) before they can make seeds. They do this by sending out shoots or runners that become new plants. They also have deep root systems that help them to recover quickly from grazing or prairie fire. These roots survive through the winter and then start growing new leaves in the spring. Plants that do this are called perennials because they come back year after year.

Wheat, rice, and corn are annuals. That means they don't put down a deep root system. Instead, they survive by making seeds, which have to be planted every year. Because these seeds are edible, human beings took these annuals and helped them spread across the globe. We cut down forests and plowed up the prairies to make room for the giant seed-bearing grasses. They are the backbone of our agriculture and our food supply.

INDUSTRIAL VS. ORGANIC

So if you think of corn as a big, annual grass, then George Naylor in Iowa is also a grass farmer. But Naylor's farm is one link in a chain that includes fossil fuels, artificial fertilizer, pesticides, heavy machinery, feedlots, antibiotics, and processing plants. The oil comes mostly from the Middle East, the corn comes from Iowa, the beef is slaughtered in Kansas, and then the meat has to be shipped by truck across the country to a Walmart or McDonald's near you.

You can think of the industrial food system as a great machine. It's a machine that stretches over thousands of miles. It runs on fossil fuel and creates tons of waste and pollution.

THE GRASS-ROOTS TRUTH

If the sixteen million acres now being used to grow corn to feed cattle in the United States became well-managed pasture, that would remove fourteen billion pounds of carbon from the atmosphere each year, the equivalent of taking four million cars off the road.

Polyface Farm stands about as far from industrial agri-business as you can get. Almost everything the farm uses is grown on the farm. Almost all of the energy used to make the food comes from the sun. There are no pesticides, no artificial fertilizer, no pollution, and no extra waste. Everything is recycled. Just compare the two farms:

NAYLOR FARM	POLYFACE FARM
Industrial	Ecological
Annual species	Perennial species
Monoculture	Diverse crop species
Fossil fuels	Solar energy
Global market	Local market
Imported fertility	Local fertility

ORGANIC VS. BEYOND ORGANIC

As I discovered in that first phone call, Polyface is so outside the industrial food chain that Salatin won't even sell his beef, chicken, or pork by mail. You can't order them on a website.

"We never called ourselves organic," he went on to explain. "We call ourselves 'beyond organic.'" He talked about the difference between one of his chickens and an organic chicken you can buy in a supermarket. The supermarket chicken is raised in "a ten-thousand-bird shed that stinks to high heaven." His chickens do eat non-organic grain, but they "see a new paddock of fresh green grass every day." Then he asked, "So which chicken shall we call 'organic'?"

13
Grass

MONDAY

We see grass all the time—on lawns, by the side of the highway, on baseball fields (if they aren't artificial turf). But have you ever really *looked* at grass?

During my week at Polyface, I learned to look at grass from lots of different angles. For example, I learned to look at a field of grass the way a cow does. You might think a field of grass is all the same. But to a cow, a fresh pasture is like a salad bar, with lots of different things to eat.

From the mix of green leaves and stems, a cow can easily pick out a tuft of emerald green clover next to a spray of bluish green fescue. These two plants are as different to her as vanilla ice cream is from cauliflower. The cow opens her meaty wet lips, curls her sandpaper tongue around the bunched clover like a fat rope, and rips the mouthful of tender leaves from its

MEET THE GRASSES

When I started working for Joel Salatin he insisted that even before I met any of his animals, I had to get down on my belly in a pasture to meet his grass. We took an ant's-eye view and he ticked off the types of grass found in a single square foot of pasture. There was orchard grass, foxtail, fescues, bluegrass, and timothy. Then he showed me the legumes: red clover and white, plus lupines. Finally he showed me examples of a group of plants called forbs, broad-leaved species like plantain, dandelion, and Queen Anne's lace.

And those were just the plants. Below and out of sight were earthworms, woodchucks, moles, and burrowing insects. They lived alongside creatures like bacteria, phages, nematodes, and miles upon miles of fungi.

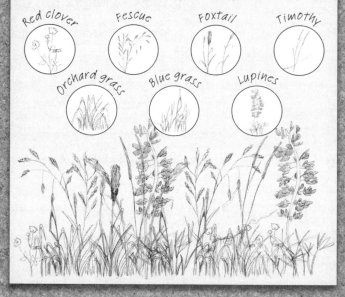

crown. She'll get to the fescue, but not before she's eaten all the clover ice cream she can find.

A cow also knows there are things in the pasture to avoid, plants that will make her sick. We might fail to notice the handful of Carolina nightshades or thistles among the other plants. But when the cows are done grazing tomorrow, those plants will still be standing, like forlorn pieces of broccoli left on a picky eater's plate.

THE LAW OF THE SECOND BITE

Joel Salatin calls himself a grass farmer. In the end everything he raises on his farm comes from grass. How do the grasses perform this miracle? They do it by capturing the energy of the sun and using it to make leaves cows can eat. So maybe he's really a sun farmer.

To Joel, sustainable organic farming means using this free solar energy instead of fossil fuel energy. "These grass blades are our photovoltaic panels," he says. He's built a complex farm system around this simple idea. To make it work, he needs to know an awful lot about grass. And the most important thing to know about grass, he told me, is when it likes to be eaten.

As I explained, grass has evolved to be in partnership with grass eaters. It survives very well if its leaves are chewed off. The secret, Joel told me, is not to let the cows take a second bite until the grass has had time to recover. That takes about fourteen days. He calls it the "law of the second bite."

If this were a real law, most of the world's ranchers and dairy farmers would be outlaws, because they let their cows stay in the same pasture without stop. Without a chance to recover, clover and other cow favorites soon disappear. The root system of the entire field weakens. Instead of a lush pasture, the farmer soon has a field full of brown bald spots and plants that cows won't touch.

Joel keeps his cows from getting that second bite by moving them every day. Near the end of my first day as a Polyface farmhand, when all I really wanted to do was lie down, there was still one more important chore to perform. We had to move the cows.

A MOVING EXPERIENCE

Throwing and stacking fifty-pound bales of hay all afternoon had left me bone tired, so I was mightily relieved when Joel proposed we drive his ATV to the upper pasture where the cows had spent their day. (It's a basic rule that the more weary you feel, the more kindly you look on fossil fuel.) We stopped by the toolshed for a freshly charged car battery we'd use to power the electrified fence. Then we sped up the rutted dirt road and soon bumped to a halt at the upper pasture. Eighty or so cattle were bunched together in a section of a much larger field. A portable electric fence kept them from roaming.

The cows had been in that spot for only one day. During that time they had eaten down just about everything within reach. Now it was time for them to move on, giving the grasses a chance to recover. Moving every day also keeps the cows healthier, because they can get away from their droppings, which can contain unhealthy parasites.

Joel disconnected the electric fence from its battery and held down the wire with his boot to let me into the paddock. Clearly Joel's cattle knew what was about to happen. The cows that had been lying around roused themselves, and the bolder ones slowly lumbered over in our direction. One of them stepped right up to nuzzle us like a big cat. "That's Budger," Joel told me. You wouldn't mistake Joel's cattle for show cattle. None of them are purebred. Instead they're a mix of Angus, Brahmin, and other breeds. Yet their coats were sleek, their tails were clean, and they had remarkably few flies on them.

It took the two of us no more than fifteen minutes to put up a new fence around an area next to the old one, drag the watering tub into it, and set up the water line. The grasses in the new paddock were thigh-high and lush, and the cattle plainly couldn't wait to get at them.

The moment arrived. Looking more like a restaurant maître d' than a cowboy, Joel opened the gate between the two paddocks. He removed his straw hat and swept it grandly in the direction of the fresh salad bar, and called his cows to their dinner. After a moment of hesitation, the cows began to move, first singly, then two by two, and then all eighty of them sauntered into the new pasture, brushing past us as they looked around for their favorite grasses. They lowered their great heads, and the evening air filled with the muffled sounds of smacking lips, tearing grass, and the low snuffling of contented cattle.

The last time I had stood watching a herd of cattle eat their supper I was standing up to my ankles in cow manure in Poky Feeders pen number 43. At Poky, the feed had to be harvested by machine, transported by train, processed in a mill, then trucked to the feedlots. Joel's cows were harvesting their own feed: grasses that had grown right there, powered by little more than sunlight. The food chain in this pasture could not be any shorter. And at the end of their meal there'd be nothing left to clean up, since the cattle would spread their waste exactly where it would do the most good.

UNDER THE GRASS

The food chain at Polyface is short and simple. But there's a lot more going on than meets the eye. For example, Joel moves his cattle in the evening because he knows that's when the grass is sweetest. The leaves spend the whole day using sunlight to make food—sugars. Mixed in with the sugars are important minerals the grasses have drawn up from the soil.

If you could look underground, you'd see even more. When cattle eat the leaves of a grass, the plant will kill off some of its roots, to balance itself out. Part of the root system dies and begins to decay. Then the bacteria, fungi, and earthworms will get to work breaking the old roots down into rich brown humus. (Humus is the part of soil that used to be living organic matter.) So by taking a bite of grass, a cow actually helps create new soil.

Because the cattle move on every day, they don't wipe out their favorite types of grass. As we've seen, this means that a pasture holds a dozen or more types of plants—a real example of biodiversity. A mixture of tall and short plants means that more of the solar energy that falls on the pasture is turned into growth. Biodiversity also means the pasture is green almost all year long. Some grasses grow more in the spring, others have their growing season in the summer. For this reason, an acre of mixed grasses can actually produce more carbohydrate and protein in a year

GRASS AND GLOBAL WARMING

Like a forest, Joel's pastures remove thousands of pounds of carbon from the atmosphere each year. Trees take in carbon too, but they store most of it in their trunks and branches. Grasslands, however, store most of their carbon in their roots. When those roots die off and become humus, the carbon becomes part of the soil. Because of this, grasslands are great at reducing carbon in the atmosphere and fighting global warming.

than an acre of field corn. And a field of mixed grasses with a deep root system is much more likely to survive dry spells and droughts.

These are just some of the incredible things that happen because Joel Salatin doesn't let his cows graze in the same spot too long. The amount of time it takes grass to recover is constantly changing too. It can vary depending on temperature, rainfall, sunlight, and the time of year. And of course, Joel has to figure in that different size cattle eat different amounts of grass.

This is another way "grass farming" is very different from the "ride and spray" farming on big industrial farms. It takes a lot of thought and planning to make sure the cows get to the right piece of pasture at the right time. It sometimes seems like grass farmers need to know personally every single blade of grass on their farms.

MONDAY SUPPER

Once the cattle were settled in their paddock for the night, we rolled down the hill to dinner. We ditched our boots by the back door and washed up in a basin in the mudroom. Then we sat down to a meal prepared by Joel's wife, Teresa, and Rachel, the Salatins' eighteen-year-old daughter. Joel began the meal by closing his eyes and saying his own version of grace. It included a fairly detailed list of what had been done on the farm that day. The farm's two young interns, Galen and Peter, joined us at the big pine table. They focused so intently on eating that they uttered not a word. The Salatins' son, Daniel, twenty-two, is a full partner in the farm, but most nights he has dinner with his wife and baby son in their house up the hill. Joel's mother, Lucille, lives in a trailer home next to the house. It was in Lucille's guest room that I was sleeping.

Everything we ate had been grown on the farm, with the exception of the cream of mushroom soup that was the sauce in the chicken and broccoli casserole. Rachel passed a big platter of delicious deviled eggs. Though it wasn't even the end of June, we tasted the first sweet corn of the season. It had

The Salatin family and farm crew. From left to right: Peter, Daniel, Lucille, Galen, Teresa, and Joel.

been grown in the hoop house where the laying hens spend the winter. There was plenty of everything, and there were a lot of jokes about the interns' giant appetites. To drink, there was a pitcher of ice water.

I told everyone that this was probably the most local meal I'd ever eaten. Teresa joked that if Joel and Daniel could just figure out how to make paper towels and toilet paper from the trees on the farm, she'd never have to go to the supermarket. It was true: We were eating almost completely off the grid. The farm and the family was a self-contained world, in the way I imagine all American farm life once was.

At dinner I got Joel and Teresa talking about the history of Polyface. "I'm actually a third-generation alternative farmer," Joel said. His grandfather Fred Salatin had farmed a half-acre lot in Anderson, Indiana. Joel's father, William Salatin, bought the land that would become Polyface in 1961. Back then, the 550 acres were in bad shape.

RESTORING THE LAND

"The farm had been abused by tenant farmers for 150 years," Joel said. The land is hilly and really too steep for row crops. Still, several generations of tenant farmers had grown corn and other grains there. As a result, most of the soil was either no longer fertile or had washed away. "We measured gullies fourteen feet deep," Joel explained. "This farm couldn't stand any more plowing. In many places there was no topsoil left whatsoever—just outcroppings of granite and clay. We've been working to heal this land ever since."

William Salatin worked in town as an accountant while he figured out how to build the farm. A lot of his accounting clients were farmers too. When he saw the trouble they were having staying in business, he decided to try a different approach. Instead of building silos and growing grain, he started growing grass. He stopped buying fertilizer and started composting. He also let the steeper, north-facing hillsides return to forest.

Gradually the farm began to recover. Grasses colonized the gullies, the thin soils deepened, and the rock outcrops disappeared under a fresh layer of sod.

"I still miss him every day," Joel said. "Dad was definitely a little odd, but in a good way. He lived out his beliefs. But you want to know when I miss him the most? When I see all the progress we've made since he left us. Oh, how proud he would be to see this place now!"

14
The Animals

TUESDAY

It's not often I wake up at six in the morning and find I've overslept, but it happened to me on my second morning at Polyface. By the time I hauled my six-foot self out of the five-foot bed in Lucille's guest room, everyone was already at work. In fact, morning chores were nearly done. Shockingly, chores at Polyface start as soon as the sun comes up. Even worse, they start before breakfast. Before coffee!

I stepped out of the trailer into the warm early morning. Through the mist I could make out the figures of the two interns, Galen and Peter. They were moving around on the hill to the east. That's where a group of portable chicken pens sat on the grass. One of the most important morning chores was feeding and watering the chickens and moving their pens. I was supposed to be helping, so I started up the path, hoping to get there before they finished.

As I stumbled up the hill, I was struck by how very beautiful the farm looked in the hazy early light. The thick June grass was coated with dew. The bright green pastures stood out against patches of black forest. It was hard to believe this hillside had ever been the gullied wreck Joel had described at dinner. One type of farming had destroyed the land. Now another type of farming was restoring it.

WHY DID THE CHICKEN CROSS THE PASTURE?

By the time I reached the pasture Galen and Peter had finished moving the pens. Luckily, they were either too kind or too timid to give me a hard time for oversleeping. I grabbed a pair of water buckets, filled them from the big tub in the center of the pasture, and lugged them to the nearest pen. Fifty of these pens were spread out across the damp grass. Each was ten feet by twelve feet wide and two feet high, with no floor. Inside each one were seventy broiler chickens. (Broilers are raised to be, well, broiled—or grilled or fried.) The pens are floorless to allow the birds to get at the grass.

Joel had explained that the pens were arranged very carefully. Each one would be moved ten feet a day. At the end of fifty-six days the pens would have covered every square foot of the meadow. Fifty-six days is the amount of time it would take the chickens to grow big enough to be slaughtered.

Directly behind each pen was a rectangular patch of closely cropped grass. That was where the pen had been the day before. The ground there looked like a really awful piece of modern art, thickly spattered with white, brown, and green chicken poop. It was amazing what a mess seventy chickens could make in just one day. But that was the idea: Give them twenty-four hours to eat the grass and fertilize it with their droppings, and then move them onto fresh ground.

Joel moves the chickens every day for the same reason he moves the cows every night. The chicken manure fertilizes the grass, supplying all the nitrogen it needs. But left in one place, the chickens would eventually destroy the soil. They'd peck the grass down to its roots and poison the soil with their "hot," or nitrogen-rich, manure. This is why the typical chicken yard quickly winds up bare and hard as brick.

Joel says the chickens get about 20 percent of their diet from the fresh grass, worms, grasshoppers, and crickets they find. He also feeds them a mixture of corn, toasted soybeans, and kelp, which we scooped into long troughs in their pens. The chicken feed is one of the only raw materials he buys for the whole farm.

THE INCREDIBLE EGGMOBILE

After we had finished watering and feeding the broilers, I headed up to the next pasture, where Joel was moving the

The Eggmobile is home to four hundred laying hens.

Eggmobile. The Eggmobile is one of Joel's proudest innovations. It looks like a cross between a henhouse and a covered wagon from the old west. The Eggmobile is home to four hundred laying hens. On each side of the wagon are rows of nesting boxes. The boxes open from the outside so someone can get at the eggs. Every night the hens climb the little ramp into the safety of the coop and Joel latches the door behind

Every morning the broiler pens are moved to fresh pasture, following the cattle around the farm. Each pen is home to seventy chickens.

them. In the morning he moves them to a fresh pasture.

When I got there, Joel was bolting the Eggmobile to the hitch of his tractor. It wasn't quite seven a.m. yet, but he seemed delighted to have someone to talk to. Talking about farming is one of his greatest pleasures.

"In nature you'll always find birds following herbivores," Joel had explained. In the wild, turkeys and pheasants follow bison herds. In Africa, you'll see birds like egrets perched on the nose of a rhinoceros. In each case the birds dine on the insects that would otherwise bother the herbivore. They also pick insect larvae and parasites out of the animal's droppings.

Joel climbed onto the tractor, threw it into gear, and slowly towed the rickety henhouse fifty yards or so. He placed it in the middle of a paddock where his cattle had been three days earlier. It seems the chickens don't like fresh manure, so he waits three or four days before bringing them in—but not a day longer. "Three days is ideal," he explained. "That gives the larvae a chance to fatten up nicely, the way the hens like them, but not quite long enough to hatch into flies." Fly larvae may not seem appetizing to you and me, but that protein-rich diet makes the chickens' eggs unusually rich and tasty.

THE SANITATION CREW

Once the Eggmobile was in position, Joel opened the trap-door, and an eager, noisy parade of Barred Rocks, Rhode

Island Reds, and New Hampshire Whites filed down the little ramp, fanning out across the pasture. The hens picked at the grasses but mainly they were all over the cowpats. They performed a crazy kind of dance with their claws to scratch apart the caked manure and expose the meaty grubs within.

"I'm convinced an Eggmobile would be worth it even if the chickens never laid a single egg," Joel told me. Because of the chickens, Joel doesn't have to treat his cattle with toxic chemicals to get rid of parasites. This is what Joel means when he says the animals do the real work on his farm. "I'm just the orchestra conductor, making sure everybody's in the right place at the right time."

Eggs bring in more money than anything else Joel sells. To take advantage of that, most farmers would buy more chickens to lay more eggs. But Joel knows if he added a lot more chickens to the farm it would throw the system off balance. Too much chicken manure could kill the grass. Suddenly the manure would become a waste product. Plus, where would the new chickens get larvae for their protein? Joel would have to buy more cows. But how could he grow enough grass to feed them?

"It's all connected," he told me. "This farm is more like an organism than a machine, and like any organism it has its proper scale. A mouse is the size of a mouse for a good reason, and a mouse that was the size of an elephant wouldn't do very well."

LETTING CHICKENS BE CHICKENS

Most industrial farmers don't worry about keeping things in balance. Their main concern is paying for inputs and getting the most possible outputs. If that means forcing cows to eat corn, even when it is unnatural for them, then that is what must be done.

At Polyface, the Salatins try to work with the natural instincts of their animals, not against them. When Joel lets his chickens loose in a pasture, he is using their natural instinct to clean up after herbivores. The chickens get to do, and eat, what they evolved to do and eat. Instead of treating chickens as egg-laying (or meat-growing) machines, Polyface honors their inborn "chickenness." It is the same for all the animals on the farm.

The Salatins also raise rabbits. Like the hens, the rabbits spend part of their time in portable rabbit hutches in the pastures. The rest of the time, they live in cages suspended over a deep bedding of woodchips. The woodchips are home to earthworms, and of course, there are hens loose in the woodchips, eating the worms. The scratching of the hens turns the chips and the rabbits' nitrogen-rich urine into valuable compost.

The Polyface turkeys also spend time in the pastures. They are moved every three days. Joel has built them a moveable shademobile, which he calls the Gobbledy-Go. The turkeys

© Micxael Pollxx

Polyface turkeys emerging from their moveable shademobile, called the Gobbledy-Go.

rest under the Gobbledy-Go by day and roost on top of it at night. Joel likes to put his turkeys in the orchard, where they eat the bugs, mow the grass, and fertilize the trees and vines. Putting turkeys and grape vines together means getting two crops off of the same piece of land.

During the winter, the cows and other animals come off the pastures and into the barns. But Polyface's "beyond organic" methods don't stop, they just move indoors. The cow barn is a simple open-sided structure where the cattle eat twenty-five pounds of hay and produce fifty pounds of manure each day. (Water makes up the difference.) Joel just leaves the manure where it falls. Every few days he covers it with a layer of woodchips or straw. This layer cake of manure, woodchips, and straw gradually rises beneath the cattle. By winter's end the bedding, and the cattle, can be as much as three feet off the ground. As the manure/woodchip mix decays it heats up, warming the barn. Joel calls it his cattle's electric blanket.

HAPPY PIGS

There's one more secret ingredient Joel adds to each layer of this cake: a few bucketfuls of corn. Over the winter, the corn ferments. That means fungi in the manure turn some of the corn into alcohol. (This is the same fermenting process used to make wine or beer.) Why does Joel want fermented corn in his manure pile? Because there's nothing a pig enjoys more than getting tipsy on corn, and there's nothing a pig is better equipped to do than root it out with his powerful snout and exquisite sense of smell. "I call them my pigaerators," Joel told me proudly.

As soon as the cows head out to pasture in the spring, several dozen pigs come in and hunt for the corn in the manure pile. As they dig, they turn the compost over and air it out. This kills any harmful bacteria and after a few weeks the rich, cakey compost is ready to be spread on the fields.

"This is the sort of farm machinery I like," Joel told me one afternoon as we watched his pigs do their work. "It never needs its oil changed, grows over time, and when you're done with it you eat it." Buried clear to their butts in composting cow manure, the pigaerators were a bobbing sea of wriggling hams and corkscrew tails. If pigs can be happy, these were the happiest pigs I'd ever seen.

Salatin reached down deep where his pigs were happily rooting and brought a handful of fresh compost right up to my nose. What had been cow manure and woodchips just a few weeks before now smelled as sweet and warm as the forest floor in summertime. Joel will spread the compost on his pastures. There it will feed the grasses, so the grasses might again feed the cows, the cows the chickens, and so on until the snow falls. That handful of compost was proof that when grass can eat sunlight and food animals can eat grass, there is indeed a free lunch.

The type of farming the Salatins do isn't easy. George Naylor works his fields maybe fifty days a year; Joel and Daniel and two interns are out there sunrise to sunset almost every day.

Yet Joel and Daniel plainly enjoy their work. One reason is that their type of farming takes a lot of thought and problem-solving. They like the challenge of getting all the pieces of their farm working together. They also get great satisfaction from the care they give to their land and their animals. Over and over again, I was struck by how healthy their animals were—all without a single ounce of antibiotics or chemicals. Because they are not raising identical chickens or cows in giant, crowded sheds, a single illness doesn't represent a threat to them. Instead, when an animal gets sick, the Salatins try to figure out what is going wrong in their system. As Joel puts it, "Most of the time pests and disease are just nature's way of telling the farmer he's doing something wrong."

TREES GROW GRASS

All of this produces some pretty impressive results. I asked Joel how much food Polyface produces in a season, and he rattled off the following figures:

30,000 dozen eggs

10,000 broilers

800 stewing hens

50 beef cattle (25,000 lbs of beef)

250 hogs (25,000 lbs of pork)

1,000 turkeys

500 rabbits

It was hard to believe they got that much food from one hundred acres of grass. Then Joel corrected me. He said that the 450 acres of forest were also an important part of the farm operation. I didn't get that at all. What in the world did the forest have to do with producing food?

Joel counted off the ways. First, the forest held the farm's water supply. Many of the farm's streams and ponds would simply dry up if not for the cover of trees. Second, the trees keep the farm cooler in the summer. That reduces the stress on the animals from too much heat. The trees also act as a windbreak—when the grass is sheltered from the wind it can grow higher. It doesn't stop there. More trees mean more wild birds. More birds on a farm mean fewer insects. Forests mean that coyotes and weasels have plenty of chipmunks and voles to eat, so they don't hunt chickens. And some of the trees are made into woodchips that go into the farm compost.

I had thought of the farm as just the hundred acres of pasture. For Joel, it was all one biological system, the trees and the grasses and the animals, the wild and the domestic. On an industrial farm, the trees would have been thought of as a waste of valuable crop land. But at Polyface, it was understood that the trees helped the grass to grow and the forest fed the farm.

15

The Slaughterhouse

WEDNESDAY MORNING

I woke up Wednesday and wished for a moment I had over-slept again. It wasn't because I was tired, although I was. It was because I knew this was the day we were going to "pro-cess" the broilers. To put it plainly, we were going to spend the morning killing chickens.

So far, I'd enjoyed the beauty of this organic food chain. I'd watched as the sun fed the grass, the grass fed the cattle, and the cattle fed the chickens. There was one more link in that food chain, however. That last link was when the chickens fed us. An important part of that last step took place right here on the farm, in an open-air shed out behind the Salatins' house. That's where, six times a month, several hundred chickens are killed, scalded, plucked, and gutted.

I had been trying not to think about this last link, and of

course that's what most of us do. We avoid thinking about, or having anything to do with, the slaughter of the animals we eat. Even most farmers have nothing to do with it.

Not here. Joel insists on slaughtering chickens on the farm. He'd slaughter his cattle and hogs here too if only the government would let him. Joel has many reasons for wanting to do the killing himself. Some are economic, some ecological, some are political, and some are spiritual. "The way I produce a chicken is an extension of my worldview," he'd told me the first time we'd talked. To him that means every step of a chicken's life must be managed correctly, including its end.

THE CHICKEN ROUNDUP

So that morning I managed to get up right on time—5:30 a.m., to be exact. I made my way to the broilers' pasture. We had to catch and crate three hundred chickens. While we waited for Daniel to show up with the chicken crates, I helped Peter move the pens to a new spot of grass.

After a while Daniel drove up on the tractor, towing a wagon piled high with plastic chicken crates. We stacked four of them in front of the pens and then he and I got to work catching chickens. After lifting the top off the pen, Daniel used a big plywood paddle to crowd the birds into one corner. Then he reached in and grabbed a flapping bird by one leg and flipped it upside down. That seemed to settle

Daniel Salatin gathering up the chickens for slaughter.

the bird. Then he easily switched the dangling bird from his right hand to his left, freeing his right hand to grab another. I could see he'd done this many times. When he had five birds in one hand, I held open the door to the chicken crate and he stuffed them in. He could fill a crate with ten birds in less than a minute.

"Your turn," Daniel said. He nodded toward the cornered mass of chickens remaining in the pen. To me, the way he'd grabbed and flipped the birds seemed pretty rough. Their pencil-thin legs looked so fragile. Yet when I tried to be gentle with the birds as I grabbed them, they flapped around even more violently, until I was forced to let go. This clearly wasn't going to work. So finally I just reached into and blindly clutched at a leg with one hand and flipped it over. When I saw the chicken was none the worse for it, I switched it to my right hand (I'm a lefty). I went for a second and a third, until I had five chicken legs and a giant white pom-pom of feathers in my right hand. Daniel flipped open the lid on a crate and I pushed the pom-pom in.

SALATIN VS. THE USDA

After we had crated three hundred birds we went to breakfast (scrambled Polyface eggs and Polyface bacon). While we ate, Joel talked a little about the importance of on-farm processing. To hear him describe it, what we were about to do—kill a bunch of chickens in the backyard—was nothing less than a political act.

"When the USDA sees what we're doing here they get weak in the knees," Joel said with a chuckle. "The inspectors take one look at our processing shed, and they don't know what to do with us."

For example, government rules say the walls of a processing plant must be white. But Joel's shed doesn't have any walls. He believes fresh air keeps the shed cleaner than washing down walls with disinfectant.

Incredibly, the USDA rules don't set a limit for the amount of bacteria allowed in our meat. In fact, the rules assume that there will be bacteria in the meat, because in a giant slaughterhouse, there's no way to avoid it. In most big plants expensive machinery is used to remove or kill the bacteria on the meat. Those machines, like a lot of things required by the USDA, are way too expensive for a small, local meat processor.

More to the point, Joel says he doesn't need this machinery because his meat is already clean. To prove it, he's had his chickens tested by an independent lab. The tests showed that Polyface hens have a much lower bacteria count than supermarket chickens. Salatin is confident he could meet any health standard the government would set.

THE SHED

By the time we finished breakfast, a couple of cars had pulled into the driveway. There were two women who were raising their own chickens and wanted to learn how to process them. There were also a couple of neighbors Joel sometimes hires when he needs extra hands on processing day.

After a few minutes of neighborly chitchat, we all drifted toward our stations in the processing shed. The shed resembles a sort of outdoor kitchen on a concrete slab. There are no walls, just a sheet-metal roof perched on wooden posts. Arranged in a horseshoe along the edge are stainless steel sinks and counters, a scalding tank, and a feather-plucking machine. There's also a line of metal cones to hold the birds upside down while they're being killed and bled out.

I volunteered to join Daniel at the metal cones, the first sta-

The Polyface processing shed, where chickens are killed, scalded, plucked, and gutted.

tion on the line. Why? Because I'd been dreading this event all week and wanted to get it over with. Nobody was insisting I personally slaughter a chicken, but I was curious to learn how it was done and to see if I could bring myself to do it. I guess I felt that if I was going to be a meat eater, then at least once in my life I should take part in the killing of my food.

I stacked several chicken crates in the corner by the killing cones. Then, while Daniel sharpened his knives, I began lifting chickens from the crates. I placed each bird upside down into a cone. Each cone has an opening at the bottom for the chicken's head. Taking the squawking birds out of the crate was the hard part. As soon as they were snug in the cones, the chickens fell silent.

Once all eight cones were loaded, Daniel reached underneath and took one chicken's head between his first finger and thumb. Gently, he gave the head a quarter turn and then quickly drew his knife across the artery running alongside the bird's windpipe. A stream of blood shot from the cut and poured down into a metal gutter that funneled it into a bucket. Daniel explained that you wanted to cut only the artery, not the whole neck. That way the heart would continue to beat and pump out the blood. The bird shuddered in its cone and its yellow feet jerked around.

It was hard to watch the chicken die. I told myself that its suffering, once its throat was slit, was brief. I told myself that the birds waiting their turn appeared to have no idea what was going on. Honestly, there wasn't much time to reflect. We were working on an assembly line (or, really, a disassembly line). The work soon took over and I had no time to think. Within minutes the first eight chickens had bled out. Then they had to be lifted from the cones and moved to the scalding tank. Daniel was calling for eight more, and I had to hustle so as not to fall behind.

MY MEAT EATER'S DUTY

After he had slaughtered several batches, Daniel offered me his knife. He showed me the steps I was to follow: First you hold the chicken's little head in a V between your thumb and forefinger. Then you turn the head to expose the artery but avoid the windpipe. Then you slice down toward at a spot just beneath the skull. Since I am left-handed, I had to learn every step from the opposite direction. Then it was my turn.

I looked into the black eye of the chicken and, thankfully, saw nothing, not a flicker of fear. Holding its head in my right hand, I drew the knife down the left side of the chicken's neck. I worried about not cutting hard enough, but the blade was sharp and sliced easily through the white feathers covering the bird's neck. Before I could let go of the suddenly limp head, my hand was painted in a gush of warm blood. Somehow, a single droplet spattered the lens of my glasses. There would be a tiny red blot in my field of vision for the rest of the morning.

Daniel gave his approval of my technique and, noticing the drop of blood on my glasses, offered one last bit of advice: "The first rule of chicken killing is that if you ever feel anything on your lip, you don't want to lick it off." Daniel smiled. He's been killing chickens since he was ten years old and doesn't seem to mind it.

Daniel gestured toward the next cone; I guessed I wasn't done. In the end I personally killed a dozen or so chickens before moving on to try another station. I got fairly good at it, though once or twice I sliced too deeply, nearly cutting off a whole head. After a while the rhythm of the work took over and I could kill without worrying about it. That almost bothered me more than anything else. I saw how quickly you can get used to anything, especially when the people around you think nothing of it. In a way, the most morally troubling thing about killing chickens is that after a while it is no longer morally troubling.

When I stepped away from the killing area for a break, Joel clapped me on the back for having taken my turn at the killing cones. I told him killing chickens wasn't something I would want to do every day.

"Nobody should," Joel said. "Slaughter is dehumanizing work if you have to do it every day. Processing but a few days a month means we can actually think about what we're doing," he continued, "and be as careful and humane as possible."

FROM BIRD TO FOOD

After my break I moved down the line. Once the birds were bled out and dead, Daniel handed them, by their feet, to Galen. He dropped them into the scalding tank. There the birds were plunged up and down in the hot water to loosen their feathers. They came out of the scalder looking like floppy wet rags with beaks and feet. Next they went into the plucker. That's a stainless steel cylinder that resembles a top-loading washing machine with dozens of black rubber fingers projecting from the sides. As the chickens spin at high speed, they rub against the stiff fingers, which pull their feathers off.

After a few minutes they emerge as naked as supermarket broilers. This is the moment the chickens passed over from looking like dead animals to looking like food.

Peter pulled the birds from the plucker, yanked off the heads, and cut off the feet. Then he passed the birds to Galen for gutting. I joined him at his station, and he showed me what to do—where to make the cut with your knife, how to reach your hand into the bird without tearing too much skin. You have to reach in and pull out the bird's guts while trying to keep the digestive tract in one piece. As the innards spilled out onto the stainless steel counter, he named the parts: gullet, gizzard, gallbladder (which you must be careful not to pierce), liver, heart, lungs, and intestines (have to be careful here again). Some organs were to be sold, others were dropped in the gutbucket at our feet.

© Michael Pollan

Three hundred or so freshly slaughtered chickens floating in a steel tank of ice water.

I didn't get very good at gutting. My clumsy hands tore large openings in the skin. I accidentally broke a gallbladder, spilling a thin yellow bile that I then had to carefully rinse off the carcass. "After you gut a few thousand chickens," Galen said dryly, "you'll either get really good at it, or you'll stop gutting chickens."

GRASS FROM CHICKEN GUTS

We hadn't been at it much more than three hours when we were done. There were three hundred or so chickens floating in the big steel tank of ice water. Each of them had gone from clucking animal to oven-ready roaster in ten minutes, give or take.

We cleaned up, scrubbing the blood off the tables and hosing down the floor. Meanwhile customers began arriving to pick up their chickens. This was another reason Joel has a slaughterhouse with no walls. Polyface's customers know to come after noon on a chicken day, but there's nothing to prevent them from showing up earlier and watching their dinner being killed. They don't need USDA rules to ensure that the meat they're buying has been humanely and cleanly processed. They can see for themselves.

The customers pick their chicken out of the tank and bag it themselves. Then they put it on the scale in the shop next door to the processing shed. Teresa chatted with customers as she checked them out. Meanwhile Galen and I helped Joel compost chicken waste. This just may be the grossest job on the farm—or anywhere else for that matter. Yet as Joel would say, even the way Polyface handles its chicken guts is an extension of his worldview.

Joel went off on the tractor to get a load of woodchips from the big pile he keeps across the road. Meanwhile Galen and I hauled five-gallon buckets of blood and guts and feathers from the processing shed to the compost pile. The pile, only a stone's throw from the house, had a truly evil stink. It smelled like exactly what it was: rotting flesh.

Beside the old pile Joel dumped a few yards of fresh wood-chips. Galen and I raked this into a broad rectangular mound about the size of a double bed. We left a slight hole in the middle and that's where we spilled the buckets of guts. It was a glistening, multicolored stew. On top of this we added piles

Five-gallon buckets of blood, guts, and feathers, plus hun-dreds of chicken feet and innards waiting to be mixed with woodchips and made into compost.

of feathers, and finally the blood, which now was as thick as house paint. Then Joel came back with another load of chips, which he dumped onto the top of the pile. Galen climbed up onto the mass of woodchips with his rake, and I followed him with mine. The top layer of woodchips was dry, but you could feel the guts sliding around underfoot. It felt like walking on a mattress filled with Jell-O. We raked the pile level and got out of there.

At a slaughterhouse, the guts would end up being turned into "protein meal." Then it would be fed to factory-farmed pigs and cattle and even other chickens. But like every other bit of "waste" on this farm, Joel regards chicken guts as a form of biological wealth. It contains nitrogen he can return to the land along with carbon he's harvested from the woodlot. He knows that by spring, this mass of blood and guts and feathers will become a rich, black, sweet-smelling compost ready for him to spread onto the pastures and turn back into grass. He sees the beauty in the compost pile, and who knows? Maybe to him it doesn't even smell that bad.

16
The Market

"GREETINGS FROM THE NON—BAR CODE PEOPLE"

In the industrial food chain, the typical item of food travels 1,500 miles before it is eaten. Compared to that, the Polyface "beyond organic" food chain is incredibly short. Almost all of the three hundred chickens we'd processed Wednesday morning would be eaten within a few dozen miles of the farm.

Remember, Joel doesn't ship his products. That's what brought me to Polyface in the first place—Joel refused to ship me a steak. I was learning that even where and how he sold his products was an extension of his worldview.

Originally I thought Joel sold locally just to keep from burning fossil fuels. While that's certainly part of his thinking, it's only part. He sees his farm as part of a local food economy. He wants the sale of his eggs and meat to help other local businesses, like small shops and restaurants. He feels

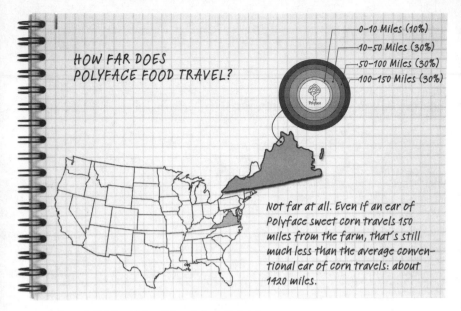

HOW FAR DOES
POLYFACE FOOD TRAVEL?

0–10 Miles (10%)
10–50 Miles (30%)
50–100 Miles (30%)
100–150 Miles (30%)

Polyface

Not far at all. Even if an ear of
Polyface sweet corn travels 150
miles from the farm, that's still
much less than the average conventional ear of corn travels: about
1420 miles.

Sources: Joel Salatin and the Leopold Center for Sustainable Agriculture.

selling his eggs or chickens in a chain supermarket supports
the industrial food industry, the very thing he is trying to get
away from.

The Salatins believe having a direct relationship with their
customers is very important. "Don't you find it odd that people will put more work into choosing their mechanic or house
contractor than they will into choosing the person who grows
their food?" he asked me. Once a year he sends out a news-
letter to his regular customers. A recent one began with this
greeting: "Greetings from the non–bar code people." That
kind of sums up the way he looks at himself, his farm, and his
customers. They are dropouts from the industrial agribusiness food chain, trying to build a new one.

SOLVING THE OMNIVORE'S DILEMMA

I met several of those customers on Wednesday afternoon as they came to collect the fresh chickens they'd reserved. These people were paying a higher price for Polyface food, and in many cases driving more than an hour to come get it. But they were not wealthy, upper-middle-class people. They were a real cross section of types, including a schoolteacher, several retirees, a young mom with her towheaded twins, a mechanic, an opera singer, a furniture maker, a woman who worked in a metal plant.

What brought them all together at Polyface Farm? Here are some of the comments I jotted down:

"This is the chicken I remember from my childhood. It actually tastes like chicken."

"I just don't trust the meat in the supermarket anymore."

"You're not going to find fresher chickens anywhere."

"All this meat comes from happy animals—I know because I've seen them."

"I drive 150 miles one way in order to get clean meat for my family."

"It's very simple: I trust the Salatins more than I trust the Walmart. And I like the idea of keeping my money right here in town."

What I was hearing, in other words, was the same omnivore's dilemma that had spurred me to write this book.

Somehow, getting meat and eggs from the Salatins helped these folks solve their dilemma, at least a little. Getting their food from Polyface lets them feel connected to their food—these customers know exactly where their food comes from. Plus, they think it tastes better. And of course, they might just enjoy spending a little time on a farm, chatting on the porch with the Salatins, and taking a beautiful drive in the country to get here.

YOU GET WHAT YOU PAY FOR

I asked Joel what he said to people who said his prices were too high.

"Whenever I hear people say clean food is expensive, I tell them it's actually the cheapest food you can buy. That always gets their attention. Then I explain that with our food, all of the costs are figured into the price. Society is not bearing the cost of water pollution, of antibiotic resistance, of food-borne illnesses, of crop subsidies, of subsidized oil and water—all the hidden costs to the environment and the taxpayer that make cheap food seem cheap."

He also reminded me that his meat would be considerably cheaper than it is if not for government regulations that forced him to send his cattle and hogs away to be processed.

Still, whatever the reason, organic and beyond organic food does cost more at the cash register. That is going to make it hard for some people to afford it. Yet for the great majority of Americans, the reason is not quite so simple. After all, most people would agree that food is more important than a new cell phone or cable TV or name-brand sneakers. Why is it that we pay for those things without blinking but won't pay an extra dollar for a dozen organic eggs? Nowadays many Americans are even willing to pay for water— something we can get for free from any tap. So why are we unwilling to pay more for better food?

Joel pointed out that people generally understand that quality costs more, except when it comes to food. "When someone drives up to the

FOOD FROM AFAR

Not only does the U.S. import crops from other countries that we grow ourselves, but we have been known to export food only to turn around and import the same kinds of food. And we're not the only country with such a crazy system. Here are some bizarre examples of truly global, and truly wasteful, food travels:

• Seattle-caught Dungeness crab is sent to China, where the meat is removed from the shells, and then returned to American tables.

• Half of Europe's peas are grown and packaged in Kenya.

• Norway ships cod to China to be turned into filets and then sent back to Norwegian supermarkets.

• Despite Spain's thriving citrus orchards, it still imports Argentine lemons while it's own fruit rots.

• Britain imports about 14,000 tons of chocolate-covered waffles a year, then exports 15,000 tons of the same kind of waffles.

• Scottish shrimp are often flown to China to be shelled and then brought right back to Europe.

RAISING THE BAR ON BAR CODES

Bar codes in the U.S. don't tell consumers anything. They hold information about the name, size, and price of items. Scanners at checkout counters read the bar codes and add up your bill. Stores also use the codes to keep track of what they have in stock. But there is no reason bar codes couldn't give us more information.

Supermarkets in Denmark have experimented with adding a second bar code to packages of meat. Shoppers can pass those labels under a special scanner in the middle of the store. When they do, information about the food appears on a monitor. The information includes details about the exact type of cow or pig, what kind of feed it was given, what drugs, if any, when it was slaughtered, and more. There's even a photo of the farm on which the animal was raised.

farm in a BMW and asks me why our eggs cost more . . . well, first I try not to get mad. Instead, I take him outside and point at his car. 'Sir, you clearly understand quality and are willing to pay for it. Well, food is no different: You get what you pay for.'"

Agribusiness has bombarded us with the message that all pork is pork, all chicken is chicken. They tell us one egg is exactly like any other, but that's just not the case. If that's what you think, then you won't pay a dollar extra for the same old carton of eggs. But when you know that some eggs are not only tastier, but also healthier to eat, then a dollar extra for a dozen seems like a bargain. When people know about their food, they start considering quality and not just price.

FARMERS' MARKETS AND BUYING CLUBS

A short food chain helps the consumer know what he or she is buying. It also helps the farmer in another important way. As we saw earlier, farmers in the industrial food chain are often on the edge of going bankrupt. One reason is they make less money than supermarkets, wholesalers, and food processors. In fact, out of every dollar spent on food in this country, ninety-two cents goes to these non-farmers. By selling directly to consumers Joel gets to keep more of that money.

That's why Joel makes more money from his chickens than his beef and pork. He processes the chickens himself, and doesn't have to pay someone else. So avoiding the industrial food chain isn't just a matter of principle. It's also good business.

Besides the farm store, Joel sells Polyface meat and eggs at farmers' markets in the Washington, D.C., area. The number of these farmers' markets in the U.S. has almost doubled in recent years, from 1,755 in 1996 to more than 4,000 in 2008. Polyface also sells to buying clubs. These are groups of families, usually in cities or suburbs, who put together a big order once or twice a month. One person in the club collects the orders and takes delivery of the food. The size of the order makes it worth the farmer's while to deliver, in Joel's case sometimes as far as Virginia Beach or Bethesda—half a day's drive.

THURSDAY MORNING

And then there is Joel's brother, Art, who makes deliveries to area restaurants once a week. On Thursday I woke to the sound of Art's panel truck noisily backing up to the salesroom door. The clock said 5:45 a.m. I threw on some clothes and dashed out to meet him.

Art is five years older than Joel and, on first impression, a very different sort of character. He's not nearly so sunny, or talkative: he's even a little cranky sometimes. He's more grounded in the world, more businesslike. But then, maybe he has to be. After all, Art spends a lot more time dealing with city traffic and parking and chefs who can sometimes be pretty picky.

Every Thursday Art mounts a carefully planned military-style operation. His mission is to supply restaurants in Charlottesville, Virginia, with meat and eggs from Polyface. He also sells produce, dairy products, and mushrooms from a half dozen other small producers in the Shenandoah Valley. He gets the orders from customers, tells the farmers what he needs, and they arrive with their trucks at Polyface at dawn on Thursday.

I spent the better part of Thursday riding shotgun in Art's panel truck. It's an old orange Dodge Caravan with a sign on the side that says: "On Delivery From Polyface Inc. Follow me to the Best Restaurants in Town." Which seemed to be more or less the case. Many of Charlottesville's best chefs buy from Polyface.

We made most of our deliveries after lunch, when the kitchens were relatively quiet. I helped Art haul in plastic totes the size of laundry baskets laden with meat and produce. The chefs had high praise for the quality of Polyface products, and clearly felt good about supporting a local farm.

Between stops, Art told me that it was the eggs that got him his new customers. I saw how this worked at a newly opened restaurant called the Filling Station. Art introduced himself and presented the chef with a dozen eggs. The chef cracked one into a saucepan. Instead of spreading out, the egg stood up nice and tall in the pan. The chef called his staff over to admire the bright orange color of the yolk. Art explained that it was the grass diet that gave the eggs their color. I don't think I'd ever seen people so interested in an egg yolk—they were clearly impressed.

SEASONAL FOOD

Unlike supermarket eggs, Polyface eggs are different at different times of the year. They turn paler in the winter, when the hens are not in the pasture. Art told me this was one of his biggest challenges. Many customers were not used to the idea of seasonal food.

We have forgotten that meats used to be as seasonal as fruits and vegetables. For example, lambs are born in the spring. They're not ready to be eaten for eight to ten months—in the next winter. Yet supermarkets sell "spring lamb," which is meat shipped in from New Zealand. The natural seasons for red meat are fall and winter. The natural seasons for chicken are the spring and summer. If local food chains are going to succeed, customers will have to get used to eating that way again. Will consumers be ready to give up the "convenience" of any food any time? Perhaps they will, if they see what they are getting in return.

Chefs around the country, like the ones who buy from Polyface in Virginia, are trying to teach consumers that food actually tastes better when it is fresh, in season, and grown without chemicals. These chefs, along with the buying clubs and the farmers' markets, are all part of a worldwide movement. It is a movement away from the industrial food chain and toward a more local, organic food system.

EAT YOUR VIEW

In Europe, there's a bumper sticker that says: "Eat Your View!" That's what the Polyface customers are doing—preserving the landscape by supporting the local farmers. They are part of an international movement to change the global food system. The movement includes farmers in Europe who try to preserve local food products and eating habits. Then there are farmers in India who have protested the sale of patented seeds by agribusiness. There are farmworkers in South America who protest the use of dangerous pesticides. And there are people in many countries who are trying to stop the spread of genetically modified food.

It's not surprising that food has become the focus of an international movement. Food is, after all, the center of our lives in many ways, even if we no longer pay very much attention to it. And it is one part of our lives we can still control. We can still decide, every day, what we're going to put into our bodies, what sort of food chain we want to be part of. We can vote with our forks.

Consumers in the U.S. have already made big changes in the food system. Our desire to have cleaner, healthier food has created a $20-billion market for industrial organics. Farmers like Joel Salatin, his customers, and all the people who buy from farmers' markets and food clubs are trying to make

SLOW FOOD

Slow food is an international movement founded in 1989 that now has chapters in 132 countries. The aim of the movement is to protect local food cultures and promote sustainable, organic, local farming. Members call their philosophy eco-gastronomy. This is how they describe it:

"Slow food is good, clean and fair food. We believe that the food we eat should taste good; that it should be produced in a clean way that does not harm the environment, animal welfare or our health; and that food producers should receive fair compensation for their work."

another change. They are making the word *local* just as powerful as the word *organic*.

Changing to a truly local food economy won't be easy. It might not even be completely possible. But the advantages of moving in this direction are very clear. When consumers know once again how their food is produced, they are naturally going to want it produced in the cleanest, most humane and environmentally healthy ways. Eating locally is also an act of conservation. Keeping local farms in business keeps the countryside from being overrun by cities and suburbs.

"Eat Your View!" takes work. It means not being able to buy a tomato in December. It means giving up many processed foods. And once you give up processed foods, you have to learn to cook, a skill that is disappearing from many American homes. Are we prepared to go that far?

IF YOU BUILD IT, THEY WILL EAT

On my last day on the farm, a soft June Friday afternoon, Joel and I sat talking at a picnic table behind the house. A steady stream of customers dropped by to pick up their chickens. I asked Joel if he believed the industrial food chain would ever be replaced by a local food system.

"We don't have to beat them," Joel patiently explained. "I'm not even sure we should try." I guess I would sum up his view as: "If you build it, they will come." He believes that more and more consumers will make the choice to buy local, "beyond organic" food. The rest will take care of itself.

I think he has a point. We may need a great many food chains that combine organic food and slow food and local foods in different ways. There may be other food chains we haven't even thought of yet. Nature produces diversity. Polyface Farm is home to diversity. Maybe the food system should be diverse too.

Sitting on the porch with Joel, watching his customers buzzing about, I could see part of that new food system taking shape. It certainly seemed like a good start.

17
My Grass-Fed Meal

A WEEK'S PAY

Before I left the farm Friday, I gathered together the makings for that evening's dinner. I had originally thought about filling a cooler with Polyface meat and bringing it home with me to California to cook there. But after all of Joel's talks about eating locally and short food chains, that didn't seem right. So I decided to cook dinner for a few old friends who lived close by in Charlottesville. We would eat the food within a short drive of the farm where it had been grown.

From the farm's walk-in cooler I picked out two of the chickens we had slaughtered on Wednesday. I also took a dozen of the eggs I'd helped gather Thursday evening. Then I stopped by the hoop house and harvested a dozen ears of sweet corn. Joel refused to accept payment for the food, calling it my pay for the week's work.

On the way into Charlottesville, I stopped to pick up a few other items. I tried as best as I could to look for local produce. As much as possible I wanted this meal to be bar code–free. For my salad, I found some nice-looking locally grown arugula. At the wine shop I found a short shelf of Virginia wines, but here I hesitated.

EATING LOCALLY

Virginia is known for many things, but wine isn't one of them. Did buying local have to include the wine too? I hadn't had a sip of wine all week and was really looking forward to it. Then I spotted a wine for twenty-five bucks, an awful lot for a bottle from an area not generally known for its wines. I decided the wine makers must have been confident it was good, so I added the bottle to my cart.

I also needed some chocolate for the dessert I had in mind. The state of Virginia produces no chocolate to speak of. Since there was no local product, I was free to go for the good Belgian stuff. I did it without guilt, since even the most extreme eat-local types say it's okay to buy goods that can't be produced locally. That meant coffee, tea, sugar, and chocolate were safe. (Whew . . .)

During the week I'd given some thought to what I should make. Working backward, I knew I wanted to make a dessert that would feature Polyface eggs. All those chefs had said the eggs were magical. So I decided to try something that calls for a bit of magic—a chocolate soufflé. For a side dish, sweet corn was a no-brainer. No one had tasted corn yet this year. But what meat to serve?

Because it was only June, Polyface had no fresh beef or pork or turkey. Joel wouldn't begin slaughtering cattle and turkeys till later in the summer. He wouldn't get to the hogs until the fall. There was frozen beef and pork, but it was last season's. I wanted to make something fresh. Rabbit seemed risky. I had no idea whether my friends Mark and Liz liked it, or if their boys would want to eat bunny. So that left chicken. Which, truth to tell, left me feeling a little queasy. Was I going to be able to enjoy chicken so soon after working in the processing shed and gut-composting pile? I was about to find out.

POLYFACE CHICKEN A LA POLLAN

When I got to Mark and Liz's house, there were still several hours before dinner. I had decided to brine the chicken—a soak in saltwater brine causes meat to absorb moisture and breaks down the proteins that can toughen it on the grill. My plan was to slow roast the chicken pieces on a wood fire, and this would keep the chicken from drying out. So I cut each of the two birds into eight pieces and put them in a bath of water, kosher salt, sugar, a bay leaf, a splash of soy sauce, a garlic clove, and a small handful of peppercorns and coriander seeds.

To be honest, there was another reason I chose the brining and grilling method. Once the chickens were cut into pieces, they wouldn't look quite so much like the birds I had helped kill and gut on the farm. Soaking them in brine would change their taste and aroma. That would help cancel out the scents I remembered from the processing shed. Cooking changes the animals we eat and gives us some distance from the reality of the slaughterhouse. In the same way, when we buy a package of hamburger at a supermarket, we rarely think of the living cow. (There are, of course, those who prefer their fish, poultry, or pork served with the heads still on.)

After soaking them in the brine for a few hours, I removed and rinsed the chicken pieces. Then I spread them out to dry for an hour or two. Drier skin would brown and get crispy on the grill.

Mark and Liz had a gas barbecue, but I wanted some smoke and flavor of a wood fire. I snipped a couple of twigs off their apple tree and stripped off the leaves. Then I placed the twigs on top of the grill, where the green wood would smolder rather than burn. I turned the gas down low and, after rubbing a little olive oil on the chicken pieces, arranged them on the grill among the apple branches.

POLYFACE EGG SOUFFLÉ

While the chicken roasted slowly outside, I got to work in the kitchen preparing the soufflé. I was assisted by Willie, Mark and Liz's twelve-year-old son. Willie melted the chocolate in a saucepan and I separated the egg whites from the yolks. The yolks were a gorgeous carroty shade of orange. They were so firm that separating them from the whites was easy. After adding a pinch of salt, I began beating the egg whites. Beating whites makes them turn white and stiff. That's when you begin adding sugar and turn the beater on high. The beater forms billions of microscopic air pockets and stiffens the egg proteins. A soufflé grows in the oven because the heat causes these air pockets to expand. At least, that's the way it's supposed to work.

The egg whites doubled in size, then doubled again. Once they formed into stiff, snowy peaks, they were ready. Willie had already blended the yolks into his melted chocolate. Now we gently folded my egg whites into the thick syrup, then poured the airy, toast-colored mixture into a soufflé dish and put it aside.

Willie and I brought the corn out on the deck to shuck. The ears were so fresh that the husks squealed as you peeled them back. I explained to Willie that the corn had grown in a deep bed of composted chicken manure. That was probably not the sort of detail you'd want to mention on a menu. (Polyface corn a la chicken crap?) But Willie agreed there was something pretty neat about it.

I also told him that the variety of corn we were eating was called Golden Bantam. It dates back over a hundred years, before all corn was just "corn." Today's hybrid corn is bred to keep its sweetness over long-distance transport. At the same time, that breeding has made it lose a lot of its earthy corn flavor. Our corn had been picked that morning, just a short drive away. Since it didn't have to stand up to the stress of a cross-country trip, we were able to enjoy this corn the way it was supposed to taste.

GRASS, NOT GRAIN

I had made pretty much this same meal several times before. The list of ingredients looked the same. Yet I knew this wasn't the same food at all. That was because the chickens had spent their lives outdoors on pastures rather than in a shed eating grain. When cattle, chickens, and other animals eat grass—and not just corn or other grains—they are actually healthier for us to eat. So is the milk or eggs that come from grass-fed animals. This is no accident. Humans evolved to eat meat from wild animals, animals that ate little or no grain. Animals raised outdoors on grass have a diet much more like that of the wild animals. It makes sense that their meat, milk, and eggs would be better for us.

Green grass has large quantities of beta-carotene, vitamin E, and folic acid. These natural chemicals are important for a healthy diet. Animals that eat grass have high levels of these and other important nutrients. (It's the beta-carotene

CORN-FED FISH?

Doctors often suggest eating fish like salmon to make sure we get enough omega-3 fatty acids. Wild salmon have a high level of omega-3 fatty acids because they eat other fish that have eaten algae and phytoplankton. (Think of algae and phytoplankton as the grasses of the sea.) Wild salmon wind up with the omega-3s found in those sea "grasses."

However, farm-raised salmon are being fed more like feedlot cattle, often on grain. The result is their omega-3 levels fall well below those of wild fish. So farm-raised (corn-fed) salmon might actually be less healthy for us than grass-fed beef, which has high levels of omega-3s.

that gives the Polyface egg yolks their carroty color.)

Animals raised in pastures have less fat than grain-fed animals. Part of this is because pasture-fed animals get exercise. Not only that, but the kind of fats in pastured animals are the ones that are healthier for us to eat. For example, they have higher levels of polyunsaturated fats instead of monounsaturated fats. They also contain more omega-3s. These are essential fatty acids and they are very important for human health. Among other things, omega-3s are important for the growth of brain cells and other neurons.

Omega-6 is another fatty acid essential to humans. Our bodies need both of these and they need them in the right balance. (Omega-3s are made in the leaves of plants. Omega-6s are made in the seeds.) There is a lot of evidence that a healthy diet has a pretty even balance of omega-3 and omega-6. And that's exactly the balance in the meat of wild animals. It makes a lot of sense when you think about it. Human beings evolved to survive and be healthy on a diet of wild meat and plants.

Now go one step further. The meat of grass-fed cows also has the same healthy balance of omega-3 and omega-6. Why? Because grass-fed cows are eating the same diet as their wild ancestors.

It turns out that corn-fed cows don't have the healthy balance of omegas. Their meat has a ratio of about 14 omega-6 to 1 omega-3. Some scientists think this imbalance might help explain the high levels of heart disease in our society. In other words, it's not eating meat so much as eating *corn-fed* meat that is bad for us.

The point is that all beef is not the same. All salmon is not the same. All eggs are not created equal. The type of animal you eat may matter less than what the animal you're eating has itself eaten.

Once shoppers know this, they begin to look at food costs differently. Polyface Farm's eggs at $2.20 a dozen might be a better deal than supermarket eggs at $0.79 a dozen. Polyface grass-fed chickens produce eggs with more omega-3s, beta-carotene, and vitamin E. And they do it in a way that's better for the environment. Doesn't that sound like a bargain?

THE MEAL

Okay, so a pastured chicken might be better for you, but how different does it actually taste? It certainly smelled wonderful when I raised the lid on the barbecue to put the corn on. The chicken was browning nicely, the skin beginning to crisp and take on the toasty tones of oiled wood. The corn, on which I'd rubbed some olive oil and sprinkled salt and pepper, would take only a few minutes. All it needed was to heat up and for a scattering of kernels to brown.

While the corn finished roasting, I removed the chicken from the grill and set it aside to rest. A few minutes later I called everyone to the table. Ordinarily I might have felt a little funny hosting a dinner in someone else's home. But Mark and Liz are such close friends, it seemed perfectly natural to be cooking for them. That's not to say I didn't feel the cook's usual worries about whether everything would come out right. Liz is a great cook too, so I was anxious to measure up.

I passed the platters of chicken and corn and proposed a toast. I offered thanks first to my hosts (who were also my guests) and then to Joel Salatin and his family for growing the food before us (and for giving it to us), and then finally to the chickens, who in one way or another had provided just about everything we were about to eat. This was my non-religious version of grace, I suppose.

We dug in and, as usually happens during a good meal, there was little talking at first, just a few murmurs of satisfaction. I don't mind saying the chicken was out of this world. The skin had turned the color of mahogany and the texture of parchment. The meat itself was moist, dense, and almost shockingly flavorful. I could taste the brine and apple wood, of course. But even more important, the chicken held its own against those strong flavors. This may not sound like much of a compliment, but to me the chicken smelled and tasted exactly like chicken. Liz agreed, saying it was a more "chickeny" chicken. What accounted for it? I know what Joel would have said: When chickens get to live like chickens, they'll taste like chickens too.

GRASS-FED MAGIC

Everyone was curious to hear about the farm, especially after tasting the food that had come off it. Liz and Mark's older son, Matthew, who is fifteen, asked a lot of questions about killing chickens. (He's currently a vegetarian and would only eat the corn.) I didn't think it was wise to go into detail at the dinner table. But I did talk about my week on the farm, about the Salatins and their animals. I explained the circle of chickens and cows and pigs and grass. I managed to avoid the details of manure and grubs and composted guts.

Slowly the conversation drifted off from my adventures as a farmhand. We talked about Willie's songwriting (he is, mark my words, the next Bob Dylan), Matthew's summer football camp, Mark's and Liz's writing, school, politics, the war in Iraq, and on and on. Being a Friday late in June, this was one of the longest evenings of the year, so no one felt in a rush to finish. Besides, I'd just put the soufflé in to bake when we sat down, so dessert was still a ways off.

While we talked and waited for the soufflé to complete its magic rise, the smell of baking chocolate seeped out of the kitchen and filled the house. Though I had avoided talking about it, my mind went to the long chain from manure to grass to cow to grubs to chicken to eggs. The chain didn't stop there, for I had turned the eggs into something else—at least I hoped I had. When at last I told Willie the time had come to open the oven and cross your fingers, I saw his smile blossom first, then the great crown of soufflé puffing out from the cinched white waist of its dish. Triumph!

There's something amazing about any soufflé, how a half dozen eggs flavored by nothing more than sugar and chocolate can turn into something so air-like. (*Soufflé*, "to blow," comes from the Latin word for breath. When done right, it's more like a breath of food, rather than something solid.) This particular soufflé was good, not great. Its texture was slightly grainier than it should have been, which makes me think I may have beaten the whites a little too long. But it tasted wonderful, everyone agreed, and as I rolled the rich yet weightless confection on my tongue, I closed my eyes and suddenly there they were: Joel's hens, marching down the gangplank from out of their Eggmobile, fanning out across the early-morning pasture, there in the grass where this magical bite began.

THE MEAL:

Source: Wild Northern California

Eaten: At home in Berkeley, CA

MENU:

Appetizer: Fava bean toasts and sonoma boar pâté

Mains: Egg fettuccine with power fire morels, braised leg and grilled loin of wild sonoma pig

Sides: Wild East Bay yeast levain, very local garden salad

Dessert: Fulton Street bing cherry tart

Claremont Canyon chamomile tea, 2003 Angelo Garro Petite Syrah

© Alisha Niehaus

PART FOUR

The Do-It-Yourself Meal:

Hunted, Gathered, and Gardened Food

18
The Forest

SURVIVOR: FOOD

There was one more meal I wanted to make. It was the meal at the end of the shortest food chain of all. What I had in mind was a dinner made entirely from foods I had hunted, gathered, and grown myself. Now, there are some people in the world (not many anymore) who make that sort of meal three times a day. I am not one of them.

The growing part was the only part I knew I could handle. I've been a gardener most of my life, and have made countless meals from my garden. That left hunting and gathering.

I had never hunted in my life. Indeed, I had never fired a gun. (Unless you count cap pistols.) I've always thought of myself as pretty clumsy. Walking around with a loaded gun never seemed like a good idea.

Thanks to my mother, I did have some childhood experience as a gatherer. During the summer she would take us to the beach at low tide to dig for clams. We'd walk along the sand, looking for the airholes the clams made. Then we'd dig them up, until they squirted us in self-defense. At the end of summer we would pick beach plums that she would make into a delicious jelly the color of rubies. All winter long her beach plum jelly brought back memories of summer vacation: August on toast.

What I most remember from these early foraging (food-gathering) trips were the scary warnings from my mother. Some mushrooms and berries have poisons in them, and she made sure I knew exactly how terrible it would be to eat one of them. When she was done I thought eating wild mushrooms was as dangerous as touching a downed power line. As a result I only gathered fruits I absolutely knew, like blueberries. And I never, ever touched a wild mushroom.

WARNING: POISONOUS

Only around 100 of the nearly 10,000 different kinds of mushrooms—just 1 percent!—are safe to eat.

This Amanita muscaria, with its distinctive red color and white speckles, is one of the most poisonous species.

But I was determined to have wild mushrooms on the menu of my do-it-yourself meal. I think that's because mushroom hunting seems to be a perfect example of the omnivore's dilemma. Is that mushroom good food or is it poison? I'd have to learn to tell the difference.

THE FIRST FOOD CHAIN

Why go to all this trouble? It's not as though we can bring back hunting and gathering as a way of life for most people. There's just not enough wild game and fruit to feed everyone. Of course, if we *did* go back to that way of life, some of us might really enjoy it. Ancient hunter-gatherers worked much less than modern-day humans. It took them about seventeen hours a week to hunt and gather enough food for them and their families. Compare that to the forty-hour (or more) workweek we have today. And you'll be surprised to learn that hunter-gatherers ate better, grew taller, lived longer, and were healthier than "civilized" people. It's only in the last century that modern society has been able to match the health of its hunter-gatherer ancestors.

But whether we'd like it or not, we are clearly not returning to those days. So why did I want to make this last meal? Because it was as close as I could get to the original food chain, the way people fed themselves for the tens of thousands of years before agriculture. It is the food chain we evolved to be part of. I thought this meal might take me back to a time when the omnivore's dilemma wasn't as complicated, when we had a more direct connection with our food. It would give me a chance to look at the omnivore's dilemma in a new (or rather old) light.

It has often struck me that even though modern Americans don't ever need to grow, hunt, or gather our own food, a lot of us still do. We garden, we hunt, we pick wild mushrooms or berries. Even if all you can do is grow a few tomatoes in your backyard (and even if those tomatoes end up costing twice as much as the ones you can buy in the supermarket), you do it anyway. Why? I think it's an effort to be connected once again to our food. We don't want to be passive consumers, sitting at the end of a food chain and eating what we are served. My meal would be an extreme experiment in being an active and conscious eater.

I had been part of three different food systems—industrial, industrial organic, and beyond organic. Now I was going to *be* the food system. There would be nothing between me and my food, from start to finish.

POLLAN THE HUNTER

I have to confess that there was more behind my desire to go hunting. Hunting is one of those skills that the all-American boy is supposed to have. (At least in some parts of the country.) Even the writer and philosopher Henry David Thoreau said so. "We cannot but pity the boy who has never fired a gun," he wrote in his famous book *Walden*. This idea had always annoyed me. Was I less of a boy (or man) because I had never been hunting?

Now I was finally going to hunt. Yet deciding to hunt was one thing; doing it was another. How was I going to learn to fire a gun, let alone hunt? Did I need a license? What if I actually managed to kill something—*then* what? How do you "dress" an animal you've killed? (*Dress* is the word used to skin and gut an animal. A pretty weird choice of words when you think about it.) And what about those killer wild mushrooms? Would I be able to learn enough to overcome my fear of eating them?

What I badly needed, I realized, was a kind of hunter-gatherer tutor. I needed someone skilled in the arts of hunting and gathering who also knew a lot about the animals, plants, and fungi of northern California. Oh, yes, I forgot to mention that. On the eve of this experiment I had just moved to northern California, far away from

A FUNGUS AMONG US

Mushrooms are fungi (that's the plural of fungus). Fungi aren't plants and they aren't animals. In scientific classification, they belong to their own kingdom. The kingdom of fungi also includes yeast, mildew, and mold. (Not very tasty, I know, but there it is.)

A mushroom is actually just part of a fungus. Most of the fungus is underground. What we call a mushroom is the fruiting body or reproductive part of the fungus. It only appears when the fungus is ready to produce spores (which are kind of like seeds). You can think of a mushroom as something like the flower of a fungus.

the New England woods and fields I knew. I was going to have to learn to hunt and gather and garden on what amounted to a different planet, full of animals and plants I didn't know. What did people hunt here, anyway, and when did they hunt it? What time of year do the mushrooms mushroom around here, and where? I had a lot to learn.

MY FORAGING GUIDE

As luck would have it, a perfect tutor appeared in my life at exactly the right moment. Angelo Garro is a stout, burly Italian with a five-day beard, sleepy brown eyes, and a passion about getting and preparing food. Shortly after we moved to California, I started running into Angelo.

We'd be invited to a dinner party and there would be Angelo among the guests. Only unlike the other guests, Angelo always had some story to tell about the meal. Maybe he'd gotten the halibut from a fishing boat that morning. Or he'd picked the fennel along the highway on the drive over. Or he'd made the wine or the ham himself. And unlike the other guests, Angelo always wound up in the

Angelo Garro with a chanterelle.

© Michael Pollan

kitchen cooking the dinner or passing platters of his famous fennel cakes. Meanwhile he would explain the proper way to make pasta or salami or balsamic vinegar. (Hint: For the last one, you need at least ten or twelve years and the right kind of barrels.) The guy was a one-man traveling Food Network.

After a few of these dinners, I began to piece together Angelo's story. He's a fifty-eight-year-old Sicilian who left home at eighteen, following a girl to Canada. Twenty years later he followed a different girl to San Francisco, where he has lived ever since. He makes his living forging wrought iron items like garden gates and fences, railings, stairs, and fireplace tools. He lives in a forge that has been a blacksmith shop since the time of the California Gold Rush in 1849. Yet his consuming passion is food. He seems driven to recapture the flavors of his childhood back in Sicily. A successful dish, he will say, is one that "tastes like my mother."

Several months after I met Angelo he appeared again, this time, strangely enough, on my car radio. He was being interviewed on public radio for a story about foraging. The reporter followed Angelo on a porcini mushroom hunt and then into a duck blind at dawn. While he waited for the sun and the ducks to rise, Angelo spoke in a whisper about his past and his passions. "In Sicily I could tell by the smell what time of the year it was," he said. "Orange season, oranges, persimmons, olives, and olive oil.

"I have the passions of foraging, passion of hunting, opera, my work," he told the reporter. "I have the passion of cooking, pickling, curing salamis, sausage, making wine in the fall. This is my life. I do this with my friends. It's to my heart."

Even before the radio segment ended I knew I had found my guide. The next time I bumped into Angelo I asked him if I could tag along on his next foraging trip. "Sure, okay, we go hunt chanterelle in Sonoma. I call you when it's time." Feeling bolder, I asked about going hunting too. "Okay, we could hunt one day, maybe some duck, maybe the pig, but first you need license and learn to shoot."

The pig? Clearly there was even more to learn than I had thought.

HUNTING FOR DUMMIES

It took me a couple of months to sort out the rules for getting a hunter's license. They involved taking a hunter education course and taking a test. It seems they'll sell a high-powered rifle to just about anybody in California, but it's against the law to aim the thing at an animal without a fourteen-hour class and a multiple-choice exam. The next class was on a Saturday two months off.

Once I knew I would be going hunting and gathering, something strange happened. I started looking for food everywhere I went. Suddenly a walk in the woods wasn't just a walk. It was now a search for supper. Woody Allen once said as a joke that "nature is an enormous restaurant." Maybe he was right.

I started dividing everything I saw into two groups. Some things were probably good to eat. Others were not. Of course, in most cases I had no real idea which was which. Still, I began to notice things. I noticed the soft yellow globes of chamomile flowers on the path I hiked most afternoons. They're used to make chamomile tea. I spotted clumps of miner's lettuce off in the shade. That's a tasty green I had once grown in my Connecticut garden. And there was wild mustard, another green, growing out in the sun. There were blackberries in flower. I even saw some wild birds that were good to eat: a few quail, a pair of doves. I began looking at field guides to help me identify all the different unfamiliar species.

Okay, maybe I went a little overboard. You don't really want to turn nature into a big restaurant. But looking for food did change the way I looked at nature. It made me look more closely at everything. It made me pay attention in a way I hadn't in years.

THE OMNIVORE'S DILEMMA, PART II

Hiking in the Berkeley hills one afternoon in January I followed the path into a grove of big oaks. I was looking for chanterelle mushrooms. I knew that they grew around old live oak trees. The problem was that up until now, I'd only seen a chanterelle over pasta or in the market. Would I be able to recognize a wild one?

I knew I was looking for a yellowish-orange, thick trumpet shape. I carefully scanned the fallen leaves around a couple of oaks, hoping to spot one. Nothing. After a while I decided to give up. Then I noticed something bright and yellow pushing up through the carpet of leaves. It was not two feet from where I'd just stepped. I brushed away the leaves and there it was, this big, fleshy, vase-shaped mushroom that I was dead certain had to be a chanterelle.

Or was it?

Was I really *dead* certain?

I took the mushroom home, brushed off the soil, and put it on a plate. Then I pulled out my field guides. Inside one I found a picture and a description. Everything matched the mushroom on my plate. The color was right. So were the shape, the smell, and the markings on the underside. I felt fairly confident this was a chanterelle. But confident enough to eat it? Not quite. The field guide said there was something called a "false chanterelle." It looked roughly the same as the real one. Uh-oh.

My mother's mushroom warnings rang in my ears. I couldn't trust my eyes. I couldn't quite trust the field guide. So whom could I trust? Angelo! But that meant driving my lone mushroom across the bridge to San Francisco. That seemed a little nuts. I realized if I was that worried, I'd never

Chanterelles: the real thing.

Clitocybe illudens: the imposter.

be able to enjoy it. So I threw it out.

That chanterelle (or was it a false chanterelle?) reminded me of the basic problem that had started me on my food chain journey—the omnivore's dilemma. My first found mushroom had become a victim of this very dilemma. Not a very promising way to start. Of course, choosing between two boxes of breakfast cereal is a little different from deciding if a mushroom will poison you. But at its heart, the problem is the same—we have to figure out what is safe and good to eat.

By going back to a hunter-gatherer meal, I would have to solve the problem of what to eat the old-fashioned way. There would be no industrial food chain between me and my food. I'd have to gain direct knowledge of the plants, animals, and fungi I was going to eat. I'd see them in their natural state. I would have the help of some friends, but when it came down to it, I would have to solve the omnivore's dilemma myself.

And speaking of dilemmas, I was about to face another one. In my travels I had learned a lot about where our meat comes from. I had seen the factory farms and feedlots. I had even slaughtered some chickens at Polyface Farm. That experience had left me unsettled. I was beginning to have conflicts about eating animals. How did I feel about it? Was it right? I thought that hunting would bring me face-to-face with those conflicts. I'd either work them out or I'd have to stop eating meat.

19
Eating Animals

THE MEAT EATER'S DILEMMA

Here's a dilemma for you. I was sitting in the Palm, a famous steakhouse, trying to enjoy a rib-eye steak cooked medium rare. On the table in front of me, open to the first page, was a copy of a book about animal rights called *Animal Liberation*. If that sounds like a recipe for indigestion, well, that was sort of the idea. I was a meat eater who was wrestling with the idea of eating meat. I wanted to tackle the problem head-on and so there I was, with a delicious steak and a book that said it was wrong to eat that steak.

It had been a long time since I had felt any dilemma about eating meat, but some things had changed. I had owned (and visited) my own steer. I had worked the killing cones in Joel Salatin's processing shed. Now I was getting ready to hunt and kill a wild animal. I had a lot to think about.

I was especially thinking about my steer, number 534. I knew that on the next day, he was going to be sent to the slaughterhouse. I had followed his life so far, from when he was a calf on the prairie to his days in the feedlot, but his death was the one event I was not allowed to witness.

This didn't surprise me. The meat industry does not want Americans to know what happens in a slaughterhouse. Then again, most of us don't want to know. We don't want to think about the living animals that become our food. But I had resolved to think about it. Maybe it was a little late, but I wanted to see if I could defend what I had already done and what I was about to do.

TO MEAT OR NOT TO MEAT?

Animal Liberation is one of those rare books that demands you either defend the way you live or change it. It is by Peter Singer, a leader of the animal rights movement. The book has converted countless thousands to vegetarianism. It didn't take me long to see why: Within a few pages he had thrown me and my meat eating on the defensive.

Singer's argument is simple. He does not argue that animals are as intelligent as human beings. He doesn't argue that they should be treated the same as human beings. He merely points out that animals can suffer just as we do.

A cow is different from us in many ways. But Singer says

that a cow is not different at all in this one very important way: It feels pain and suffers just as we do. If we think suffering is wrong, how can we allow suffering of animals to go on?

Singer had planted a troubling notion, one that stuck in my mind. In the days that followed, I read other animal rights thinkers: writers like Tom Regan, James Rachels, Joy Williams, and Matthew Scully. These writers all ask: Is it all right to allow animals to suffer just because they are animals? Isn't that a kind of discrimination? I began to think they might be right. Not too long ago, racism and discrimination against women was accepted by a lot of people. Now those ideas are rejected by most Americans. Maybe some time in the future people will look back at our treatment of animals in the same way.

Singer says we have a simple choice to make. We have to choose between our desire to eat meat and allowing the suffering of animals to continue. Put it that way and it seems you have no choice. You have to stop eating animals.

So that is what I did, at least temporarily. I felt that until I had worked out exactly how I felt about these issues, I had better give up eating meat. So on a September Sunday, after dining on a delicious barbecued tenderloin of pork, I became a reluctant—and, I hoped, temporary—vegetarian.

THE VEGETARIAN'S DILEMMA

Becoming a vegetarian wasn't as simple as you might think. Like all vegetarians, I had to decide on my rules and exceptions. For one thing, I did not become a vegan (I still ate eggs and dairy). I decided that eggs and milk can be gotten from animals without hurting or killing them—or so, at least, I thought. I was also willing to eat animals without faces, such as clams and oysters. I believe these animals do not have enough of a nervous system to suffer pain. No one knows for certain if this is true, but many scientists and animal rights supporters (Peter Singer included) accept the argument.

Rules in place, I settled into my new vegetarian lifestyle. It was harder than I thought it would be. Cooking a good vegetarian dinner takes a lot more thought and work. (All that chopping of vegetables!) Cooking a steak or a chicken is a lot easier.

I also found that being a vegetarian makes it harder to eat with other people. My friends now had to change their eating plans for me, and this made me uncomfortable. As a guest, if I forget to tell my hosts in advance that I don't eat meat, they feel bad. But if I do tell them, they'll make something special for me, and I'll feel bad. If we go out to a restaurant, it has to be someplace where I can get something to eat. Steakhouses are definitely out.

Being a vegetarian also meant giving up traditions I value:

the Thanksgiving turkey, my mother's beef brisket at Passover, or even franks at the ballpark. Such foods connect us to our family, religion, nation, and history. Meat eating has been a part of human culture for tens of thousands of years. It's part of our biology too. Our bodies, from our teeth to our brains, evolved to help us hunt, cook, and eat meat. The desire to eat meat may be an instinct, something that is in our genes. Of course, as humans we can and sometimes should learn to rise above our instincts. I'm just saying that giving up meat is not something that comes easily, at least for me.

THE VEGETARIAN'S DILEMMA

Even a vegetarian can't avoid a dilemma—there are a variety of different styles.

Vegetarian
Generally, a vegetarian is a "lacto-ovo" vegetarian, which means she doesn't eat meat or fish, but does eat dairy (lacto) and eggs (ovo). Lacto vegetarians eat dairy but not eggs, and ovo vegetarians eat eggs but not dairy.

Pescatarian
A pescatarian doesn't eat meat, but does eat fish.

Vegan
Vegans don't eat meat, dairy, eggs, or any product containing ingredients that come from animals. Some vegans also extend this policy throughout their lifestyle, and do not buy leather, wool, silk, or certain cosmetics.

Raw foodist
Raw foodists do not eat any food that has been heated above a certain temperature, in the belief that heat damages certain healthy enzymes in food.

Flexitarian
This term for a person who does eat some meat—but only seldomly—is becoming more common.

ANIMAL SUFFERING

But even with all the conflicts I had about being vegetarian, none of the things that bothered me seemed more important than stopping animal suffering. The question that I needed to answer was this: Is there a way to raise farm animals and kill them for food without causing suffering?

Scientists agree that higher animals—mammals like cows or pigs or apes—feel pain pretty much as we do. But suffering is more than pain. A lot of human suffering comes from our emotions—fear, shame, worry, or regret. Animals don't seem to suffer from emotions the way humans do. Animals can't feel the same fear of death as a human, because they can't

Laying hens crammed into cages at a factory egg farm.

photo courtesy of PETA

imagine the future. I've watched cows walk up a ramp into a slaughterhouse. They seem to be feeling no fear or panic. They don't seem to be suffering at all.

So can animals suffer if they can't think like human beings? After wrestling with the question for some time, I decided that animal suffering is real but different from human suffering. Still, I want to make one thing very clear. Even if animals can't suffer like human beings, there is no excuse for the cruelty that goes on in our factory farms and feedlots. Believe me, the people who run those places don't waste any time thinking about animal suffering. If they did, they'd have to go out of business.

So far I've told you about how chickens and cows are raised on factory farms. It turns out that conditions are even worse for the chickens in egg farms. I haven't managed to actually get into one of these places. I tried—journalists are not welcome. But you can read about what happens right in the industry trade magazines. What they tell us is horrifying.

At a factory egg farm, the laying hen spends her brief life jammed into a wire cage with six other hens. The cage is so small that a single page of a newspaper could cover the floor. Being trapped in a tiny cage with six other birds goes against every natural instinct of a chicken. As a result the hens do things no normal chicken would do. They attack and try to eat each other. They rub their breasts against the wire of the cage until they are bald and bleeding. This is the chief reason broilers don't get put in cages. To scar so much high-value breast meat would be bad business.

Pain? Suffering? Madness? Whatever you want to call it, some of the hens simply can't take it. Ten percent just die in their cages. The companies that run the farms expect this death rate and figure it into the cost of production.

The fate of the survivors might be worse. When their egg production begins to drop, the hens will be "force-molted"—starved of food, water, and light for several days in order to stimulate a final spurt of egg laying before their life's work is done.

BLIND BUSINESS

When you refuse to look away from the industrial food system, this is what you see. You see the cruelty required to produce eggs that can be sold for seventy-nine cents a dozen. We don't look, or we are kept from looking by agribusiness companies. Why don't they see the cruelty they are causing?

Big business is often blind, except to profit. Morality just doesn't enter into a spreadsheet. Customs, culture, ideas about right and wrong all fall away under the pressure to increase production and get a higher return on investment. Mercy toward animals is just one of the principles that gets thrown out the window. Mercy to human beings often follows. It is no accident that the non-union workers in these factories receive little more consideration than the animals.

The food industry won't even use the word *suffering*. Instead they talk about "stress." Solutions to stress must be found, because it hurts production and therefore profits. But the solutions often involve more cruelty. If chickens are pecking at each other in cages, the industry doesn't let them out of their cages. Instead factory farms clip the beaks off their laying hens. When hogs bite each other's tails because of stress, the industry cuts off their tails. But not the whole tail. They leave a stub so the bite is more painful. That "teaches" the pigs to avoid being bitten.

It's painful just to write these things and I'm sure it's painful to read them. It all sounds like a nightmare. But it's real life for the billions of animals unlucky enough to have been born into the industrial food chain. In response to the horrors of the factory farm, becoming a vegetarian seems pretty reasonable.

ANIMAL HAPPINESS

Yet are those our only choices? Must we either take part in the crime of factory farms or give up meat? I have seen other types of farms and other ways to treat farm animals. I'm thinking of the hens I saw at Polyface Farm, fanning out over the cow pasture on a June morning, pecking at the cowpats and the grass. Those chickens were doing everything a chicken naturally wants and needs to do. If there is such a thing as animal happiness, then those animals were happy.

It is true that farms like Polyface are but a tiny speck compared to the industrial food chain. But they do exist. And they show that there is another way to raise and slaughter animals. Of course, many people in the animal rights movement think even a farm like Polyface is a "death camp." They think any use of animals for food is morally wrong, not just killing them for meat, but using their milk or eggs. But comparing a farm like Polyface to a concentration camp is to ignore reality—the reality of domesticated animals.

Chickens and cows are domestic animals. They have evolved to live with human beings. A good life for a chicken or a cow means doing all those things its nature tells it to do. That means chickens need to scratch in the dirt. Cows need to eat grass. And cows and chickens need humans to help them do those things. Animal rights people say we should free domestic animals, but domestic animals cannot survive in the wild. They cannot lead a good life apart from human beings. (Pigs can sometimes survive in the wild, as we will see.)

Animal rights supporters say that raising farm animals is a form of slavery. This is based on the false idea that humans went out and forced animals to be domesticated. But the history of domestication is much more complicated. Zoologists will tell you that certain animals more or less "chose" domestication. Individual wild animals discovered that they could better survive by hanging around human beings, eating their crops or leftovers. A deal was made. It was never written down or spoken, but it was a deal nonetheless. Humans began providing the animals with food and protection. In exchange the animals provided the humans their milk, eggs, and—yes—their flesh. The animals grew tame and lost their ability to fend for themselves in the wild. Humans helped this along by breeding the individuals that were tamer.

From the animals' point of view the bargain with humanity turned out to be a tremendous success, at least until our own time. Cows, pigs, dogs, cats, and chickens have thrived, while their wild ancestors have almost disappeared. (There are ten thousand wolves left in North America and fifty million dogs.) For many animals, domestication has been a winning strategy. Some people speak of animal liberation, but what would liberation mean to the millions of cows and chickens on our farms? It would mean a swift and unpleasant death, starvation, or attack by predators. And eventually it would mean the end of chickens, cattle, and many of the other domesticated species that at this point depend on us for their continued existence—depend, that is, on us eating them.

In nature there are always predators and prey. Have chickens, cows, and pigs traded one set of predators for another? Yes. They traded a life of being hunted in the wild for a life of being raised, bred, and eaten by humans. They have no other option now.

A VEGAN WORLD?

There was one other problem I had with being a vegetarian. I just didn't see how we could have a world in which people ate only plants. It would pose serious problems.

A vegan world could not be fed with local food chains. The globe is full of places where it is much easier to raise animals than crops. The rocky, hilly land of New England is a good example. To put New England on a vegan diet would mean most of its food would have to be imported from elsewhere.

Without animals to supply fertility (through their manure) you can't have small sustainable farms. You'd have to rely on chemical fertilizer from the industrial food chain.

You have to ask yourself which is better, tofu from an industrial food chain farm, shipped thousands of miles across the country, or an organic chicken raised on a small farm a few miles from my house? I would choose the chicken over the tofu.

As you can probably tell, after a lot of soul-searching I decided to give up my short experiment with being a vegetarian. I was glad I had done it, because it forced me to think hard about these questions. But in the end I decided that killing animals is not wrong in principle. What matters is the way we treat them when they are alive and the way we slaughter them when it's time for them to be eaten. Perhaps vegetarians and concerned meat eaters can at least agree on this: We have to work much harder to make sure that animals on farms are treated with respect. They have to be allowed to live lives that fit their natures. Then when it is time for the slaughterhouse, their deaths should be swift and painless.

MY STEER BECOMES A STEAK

The day after my steak-and-Singer dinner at the Palm I found myself on a plane flying from Atlanta to Denver. A couple of hours into the flight the pilot came on the public address system to announce that we were passing over Liberal, Kansas. This was very weird. The pilot hadn't said one word until then. This was the first, last, and only landmark that he pointed out. Why had he chosen that town?

It wasn't just weird, it was spooky. For Liberal, Kansas, happened to be the town where my steer, possibly that very day, was being slaughtered. I'm not a superstitious person, but this gave me the creeps. I could only wonder what was going on just then, thirty thousand feet below me, on the kill floor of the National Beef Plant. Was steer number 534 about to meet his fate?

I could only wonder because the company had refused to let me see. When I'd visited the plant earlier that spring I watched steers being unloaded from trailers into corrals. I watched them being led up a ramp and through a blue door. I was not allowed to see what happened inside, on what is called the kill floor. But as it turned out, I was able to ask an expert, the person who had actually designed that very ramp and the killing machinery behind the blue door.

A CLEAN KILL

Temple Grandin is an animal handling expert who has consulted for McDonald's. Her job is to make sure the killing of cows at National Beef is as quick and painless as possible. Before she began her work, there were many stories coming from the plant about cows that were still alive when they were being skinned and butchered. McDonald's hired Grandin to make sure that sort of thing never happened.

Here's how Grandin described what happened to steer 534 after he passed through the blue door:

"The animal goes into the chute single file. The sides are high enough so all he sees is the butt of the animal in front of him. As he walks through the chute, he passes over a metal bar, with his feet on either side. While he's straddling the bar, the ramp begins to decline at a twenty-degree angle, and before he knows it, his feet are off the ground, and he's being carried along on a conveyor belt. We put in a false floor so he can't look down and see he's off the ground. That would panic him."

I had been wondering what 534 would be feeling as he neared his end. Would he have any hint—a scent of blood, a

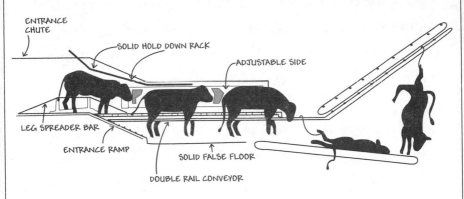

THE DOUBLE-RAIL CATTLE SLAUGHTER SYSTEM

ENTRANCE CHUTE

SOLID HOLD DOWN RACK

ADJUSTABLE SIDE

LEG SPREADER BAR

ENTRANCE RAMP

SOLID FALSE FLOOR

DOUBLE RAIL CONVEYOR

Cattle walk up a ramp and straddle a bar that positions their legs astride the moving double rail. Then they are stunned and a shackle is attached to one rear leg. The animals are discharged onto conveyors which transport them to the bleed area. The double rail system is now being used in fourteen large beef plants, which slaughter approximately one-third of North American cattle.

Information and diagram courtesy of Dr. Temple Grandin, Professor, Department of Animal Sciences, Colorado State University.

sound of terror from up the line—that this was no ordinary day? Would he, in other words, suffer? Grandin answered me before I had time to ask.

"Does the animal know it's going to get slaughtered? I used to wonder that. So I watched them going into the squeeze chutes on the feedlot, getting their shots, and going up the ramp at a slaughter plant. No difference. If they knew they were going to die you'd see much more agitated behavior.

"Anyway, the conveyor is moving along at roughly the speed of a moving sidewalk. On a catwalk above stands the stunner. The stunner has a pneumatic-powered 'gun' that fires a steel bolt about seven inches long and the diameter of a fat pencil. He leans over and puts it smack in the middle of the forehead. When it's done correctly it will kill the animal on the first shot.

"After the animal is shot, while he's riding along a worker wraps one of his feet and hooks it to an overhead trolley. Hanging upside down by one leg, he's carried by the trolley into the bleeding area, where the bleeder cuts his throat. Animal rights people say they're cutting live animals, but that's because there's a lot of reflex kicking. What I look for is, is the head dead? It should be flopping like a rag, with the tongue hanging out. He'd better not be trying to hold it up—then you've got a live one on the rail. Just in case, they have another stunner in the bleed area."

DON'T LOOK AWAY

Temple Grandin's account answered some of my questions but raised others. After all, she designed the system, so of course she would describe it in the best possible light. I couldn't help thinking about all those times "you've got a live one on the rail." At National Beef they slaughter four hundred head of cattle every hour. McDonald's says it's okay if they have a 5 percent "error rate." That could mean twenty cows an hour suffer a painful death. Is that okay? Is it moral to eat meat from a slaughterhouse like National Beef? In the end we all have to decide for ourselves.

I believe the best solution is really Joel Salatin's. The killing at his farm is done out in the open, where anyone can see. After watching (and taking part) I decided I was all right with what had happened. No doubt some of us will decide we can't accept any killing of animals, no matter how it is done. But we can only decide if we know the truth—if we *look*.

I remember a story Joel told me about a man who showed up at the farm one morning. When Joel noticed a People for the Ethical Treatment of Animals (PETA) bumper sticker on the man's car, he figured he was in for an angry argument. But the man had a different reason to be there. He explained that he had been a vegetarian for sixteen years.

STEER 534?

A lot of people have asked me why I did not save steer 534. Believe me, I wrestled with the idea for a long time.

I had written an article about him and I heard from dozens of people urging me to rescue the animal. I had offers from Hollywood producers to buy him at any price I named. A vegetarian radio station in New Jersey wanted to do a telethon to save 534 and put him in a petting zoo. I rejected all the offers. Why?

First, 534 had been living in a feedlot, eating corn for months. He probably had liver damage and other health problems. He was not going to live to a ripe old age in a petting zoo.

Second, saving a single animal might have made the rescuers feel better, but it would do nothing to change life for the millions of other steers just like him. That's what is important for us to keep our eye on. If we want to do something for steers like 534, then we should demand reform of the industrial food system that raised him.

He was thinking about eating meat again but felt the only way he could do it was if he killed the animal himself. So Joel grabbed a chicken and took the man into the processing shed.

"He slit the bird's throat and watched it die," Joel recalled. "He saw that the animal did not look at him accusingly. He saw that the animal had been treated with respect while it was alive and that it could have a respectful death." The man realized that the animals on Salatin's farm were not being treated like unfeeling raw material, but like living creatures. I realized I'd seen this too, which explains why I was able to kill a chicken one day and eat it the next.

The brutality of the industrial food system in America is something that is pretty recent. No other country raises and slaughters its food animals quite as cruelly as we do. This crime of cruelty is only possible because we do not ask and we are not allowed to see what is going on in the meat industry. We need public information about what is happening every day to our farm animals. Imagine if there was a law that the walls of America's slaughterhouses had to be made of glass. If Americans could see what was happening behind those walls, they would not allow it to continue. Tail docking and beak clipping would disappear overnight. Slaughtering four hundred head of cattle an hour would promptly come to an end—for who could stand the sight?

20
Hunting

A WALK IN THE WOODS

Hunting is exciting. It embarrasses me to write that, but it's true. I discovered this the first time I went into a forest with a loaded rifle. Hunting makes everything sharper, more vivid. It made me pay attention like nothing else I have ever done.

As I walk out on my hunt, I notice how the breezes move the pine needles. Their shadows wave on the tree trunks and the forest floor. I notice the way the air feels. My eyes search deep into thickets, looking for the slightest hint of movement. I listen carefully to every little noise, the cracking of a branch or . . . wait: What was that? Just a bird.

Angelo, my hunting tutor, has taught me how to read the ground for signs of pig. Notice the freshly dug soil at the base of that oak tree? It's still wet—the sun hasn't dried it out yet. This means pigs have been rooting here overnight. See that smoothly scooped-out puddle of water? That's a wallow, but notice how the water is perfectly clear. Pigs haven't disturbed it yet today. We could wait here for them.

After hunting here for years, Angelo knows there are three groups of pigs sharing the oak forest in northern California where he took me hunting. Each group visits a slightly different set of good pig places. This grove of oaks is where they dig for acorns, roots, and grubs. In the afternoon heat they snooze in the dusty dirt beneath that tangle of manzanita trees. They cool off in those muddy wallows, leaving the marks of their hoofprints. Then they scrape the mud from their backs on that pine tree there, the one where the lower bark is rubbed smooth and tan.

THE WILD PIG

Part of me did not want to go hunting. The night before, I had nightmares. In one dream I was on a bobbing boat trying to shoot a destroyer that was firing its cannons at me. In another, the woods were crawling with Angelo's Sicilian relatives. In that dream I couldn't remember how my gun worked, if the safety was on or off.

I had tried out my rifle only once before taking it to the woods, at a firing range in the Oakland hills. By the end of the morning my paper target didn't show much damage. But my left shoulder ached for a week. I wasn't ready to buy a gun of

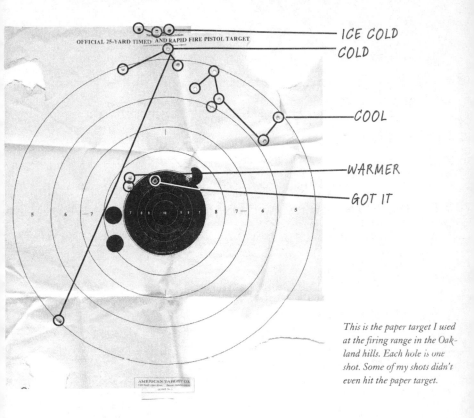

ICE COLD
COLD
COOL
WARMER
GOT IT

This is the paper target I used at the firing range in the Oakland hills. Each hole is one shot. Some of my shots didn't even hit the paper target.

my own, so Angelo had borrowed a fairly basic pump-action rifle, a .270 Winchester. I had been worried that I wouldn't have the nerve to fire at an animal. And after my session at the range, I began to worry that if I did fire, I would miss completely.

The plan was to hunt boar in the countryside north of San Francisco. A friend of Angelo's has a thousand-acre property up there and Angelo has permission to hunt on it. We could have hunted for deer or turkey or duck, but I felt more comfortable going for wild pig. The animal is not native, and is regarded as a pest in many parts of California. That made it easier for me. Wild pigs can be pretty nasty. One of their nicknames in California is "dog ripper." They destroy farmland and forest by ripping up the ground with their digging (or "rooting," as it is called).

So I had a good excuse for hunting pigs. But I also had another reason—I like pork, and since moving to California I'd often heard how tasty wild pigs are. When I asked Angelo why he hunted wild pig he didn't hesitate. He just kissed the tips of his fingers and said, "Because it is the most delicious meat. And there is nothing that tastes so good as boar prosciutto." (Prosciutto is a kind of ham.) "You'll see. You shoot a big one and we'll make some."

HAM HUNTING

In a sense, that's what Angelo was really hunting, not pigs so much as prosciutto. Maybe because he's been hunting his whole life, he doesn't talk about the thrill of it all. "For me it is all about the eating. Not the 'sport,'" he told

Jean-Pierre grew up hunting boar in northern France.

me. "I am not what you call a trophy hunter. I take what I need, enough to make a nice dinner for me and my friends, maybe some salami, a prosciutto, but then: That's it, I go home."

On my first hunt with Angelo we were joined by Richard, the owner of the property, and Angelo's friend Jean-Pierre. Jean-Pierre hadn't hunted in years, though he had grown up hunting boar with his relatives in northern France. He had on one of those green felt Alpine hats with the feather and a pair of tall black riding boots. Richard

INVADER PIGS

Wild pigs aren't strictly wild animals. They are really feral pigs. (Feral means domestic animals that are living in the wild.)

Pigs are not native to California or even America. Columbus brought them to the New World on his second voyage, in 1493. The Spanish brought them to California. They would release the animals into the woods, let them fatten on acorns and grasses, and then hunt them as needed. The wild pigs we were hunting were the descendants of these first Spanish pigs.

had on a full orange hunter's outfit and I was wearing my brightest orange sweater. (Hunters wear bright clothing so other hunters won't mistake them for a wild pig or a deer.)

We divided into pairs, me with Angelo. Our plan was to meet back at the cars for lunch around noon. Jean-Pierre and Richard walked off into the lower forest. Angelo and I rode up to the top of a grassy ridge on his four-wheel-drive ATV. The bike made a racket, but Angelo claimed it didn't bother the pigs and would allow us to cover a lot more ground than we could on foot.

"You are going to kill your first pig today," Angelo shouted over the roar of the engine. Given the nature of hunting, not to mention me, I understood this as less a prediction than a prayer.

After a while we parked the bike and set out on foot. Angelo told me to head for a wallow in a grassy opening at the bottom of a ravine. When I got close I was to find a tree with a good view of it and wait there, perfectly still, for twenty minutes until I heard him whistle. He would make his way toward the same spot from another direction, in the hopes of driving some pigs toward me.

HUNTER'S EYE

When I was alone, and could hear Angelo's footsteps no more, I fell into that state of extreme alertness I described earlier. It was as if I'd dialed up the volume on all my senses. I heard every little sound. I could see farther into the woods than I ever had before, picking out the tiniest movements. It was as if I had put on a new, strong pair of glasses for the first time. "Hunter's eye," Angelo called it when I told him about it later.

It was a completely different feeling than I get from just walking through the woods on a hike. It was the difference between being a spectator at a ball game and one of the players. It was the difference between being a tourist and belonging to a place. I felt part of the forest, instead of just a visitor.

We saw no pigs that morning, and around noon, we met back at the cars as planned. Jean-Pierre had shot a small boar and Angelo hung it from a nearby branch. Then we turned to eating. Being Europeans, Angelo and Jean-Pierre take lunch very seriously, even when out in the woods. "So I brought with me a few little things to nibble on," Jean-Pierre mumbled. "Me too," chimed Angelo. And out of their packs came course after course of the most astonishing picnic. They laid the feast on the hood of Angelo's SUV. There was:

GELLED LOBSTER AND HALIBUT

HOMEMADE SALAMI, PROSCIUTTO, AND MORTADELLA

HOMEMADE PÂTÉ OF BOAR

HOME-CURED OLIVES

CHICKEN SALAD

A GENEROUS SELECTION OF CHEESES AND BREADS

FRESH STRAWBERRIES

PASTRIES

And naturally, a bottle each of red and white wine.

It was a delicious lunch, but it took off some of my hunter's edge. After lunch Angelo stayed behind to dress the small pig and Jean-Pierre lay down in the grass for a nap. I was feeling pretty relaxed when Richard and I set off to look for another pig. Our rifles slung over our shoulders, we strolled down a shady trail and chatted as we walked. My attention floated away from the woods and the hunt.

READY. OR NOT.

Until I happened to glance up and saw directly in front of us, not thirty yards away, four large black shapes in the shadows. There they were, four pigs milling beneath an oak tree, eating acorns off the forest floor. They gave no sign that they'd spotted us or heard our yammering.

I grabbed Richard by the shoulder, put my finger to my lips, and pointed ahead. He stopped. "It's your shot," he whispered. "Go ahead. Take it." It's the custom when hunting that the first shot belongs to the person who spotted the animal. These pigs were mine.

One little problem. I had neglected to pump my rifle before we set out on the trail. There was no bullet in the chamber, and to cock my gun now would make a loud noise. The pigs would be on the run by the time I was ready to shoot. I explained all this in a whisper to Richard, who, unlike me, was ready. I gave him my shot.

Richard got down on one knee and slowly raised his rifle to his shoulder. I braced for the explosion, preparing to pump my gun the moment it came. Richard took his time, aiming carefully. The pigs had their heads down, eating acorns. Then the woods exploded. I saw a pig stagger and fall, then struggle drunkenly to its feet. I pumped my rifle, but it was already too late: The other pigs were gone. Richard fired again at the wounded pig and it fell. By the time we ran up to it, it was already dead. I felt a rush that made me light-headed and shaky.

The pig was a sow weighing perhaps a hundred pounds. She was too heavy to carry, so we took turns dragging her by her rear legs back toward the cars. Holding the pig by the ankle, I could still feel her warmth beneath the bristly skin.

When we got to the cars, Angelo trotted over to see the animal, excited and eager to hear our story. As we told him what had happened I could see the disappointment on his face. It had been my shot, my pig, but I hadn't taken it.

"You weren't ready," Angelo said in a level voice. "In hunting you always need to be ready. So, okay, you learned something today. Next time you will be ready and you will take your shot." He was trying hard not to sound like the disappointed father. I couldn't help feeling like the disappointing son.

I spent the rest of the afternoon hunting alone, walking the ridge, searching the shadows for signs of pig, looking and listening as hard as I could to will another animal out of the woods. When Angelo announced it was time to go home, I felt deflated.

A SECOND TRY

Well, I had gone hunting. Plus, Jean-Pierre offered me some cuts from his pig, so I had some meat for my meal. But I hadn't done what I'd set out to do—kill my own food. So I asked Angelo if I could go out with him again. He called me about a month later, said to meet him on a Monday morning, six o'clock sharp. We would be going back to Richard's property again and this time it would be just the two of us.

We spent the first part of the morning going to all of Angelo's pig spots. (Believe me, I made sure I had a round in my chamber.) It was hotter than last time, so Angelo felt the pigs would be keeping to the shadier parts of the property. We staked out a wallow deep in the woods, and then a clearing of ferns, but saw no signs of pig.

A little after nine in the morning we were walking together down a logging road cut into a steep hillside. Then we heard it. We were stopped in our tracks by a grunt so loud and deep that it seemed to be coming from the bowels of the earth. A very big pig was very close by. But where? What direction to look? We crouched down low, and I listened as hard as I've ever listened for anything before.

The next sound we heard was the sharp, clean crack of a branch coming from above us to our right. I looked up to the top of the thickly wooded hillside and that's when I saw it: a rounded black form, coming over the top of the hill. Then another shape, and another, a total of five or six, I couldn't be sure.

I touched Angelo on the shoulder and pointed toward the pigs. What should I do? Should I shoot? No, you wait, Angelo said. See—they're coming down the hill now. I followed the pigs with the barrel of my gun, trying to get one of them in my sight. I didn't have a clear shot—too many trees stood in the way. Take your time, Angelo whispered. They will come to us. And so they did, right down to the road directly in front of us.

MY PIG

I have no idea how long it took the pigs to pick their way down the steep hill, whether it was minutes or just seconds. At last the first animal, a big black one, stepped out into the clearing of the dirt road, followed by another that was just as big but much lighter in color. The second pig turned, giving me a shot at its flank. Now! Angelo whispered. This is your shot!

We were both down on one knee. I braced the rifle against my shoulder and lined up my sight. I felt calmer and clearer than I expected to as I took aim at the shoulder of the grayish pig. I held my breath, resisted a sudden urge to clamp my eyes shut, and gently squeezed.

The crystal stillness of the scene exploded. The pigs ran in panic, moving every which way at once, and then the blam!

of Angelo's shot directly behind made me jump. One pig was down; another seemed to stagger. I pumped my gun to fire again, but I was so excited that I pulled the trigger before I could lower my gun. The shot went wild, far over the heads of the rioting pigs. Angelo fired again and so did I. Then they were gone.

I DID IT—OR DID I?

We ran forward to the downed animal, a very large grayish sow sprawled on her side across the dirt road. A glossy bubble of blood grew directly beneath her ear. The pig thrashed briefly, attempting to lift her head, then gave it up. Death was quickly overtaking her. I was relieved she wouldn't need a second shot. We ran past her, looking for the others. Angelo said he thought he had grazed another one. I climbed down the embankment looking for it, but the hill was too steep and Angelo called me back up to the road.

He clapped me on the back. "Your first pig! Look at the size of it. And with a perfect shot, right in the head. You did it!"

Did I do it? Was that really my shot? I had my doubts. Yet Angelo insisted—he had fired at a different pig, a black one. "No, this is your pig, Michael, you killed it, there's no doubt in my mind. You got yourself a big one. That's some very nice prosciutto!"

I wasn't ready to see it as meat, though. What I saw was a dead wild animal, its head lying on the dirt in a widening circle of blood. I kneeled down and pressed the palm of my hand against the pig's belly above the nipples. Beneath the dusty, bristly skin I felt her warmth, but no heartbeat.

I was overcome with a strong mix of emotions. The first was a powerful feeling of pride: I had actually done what I'd set out to do. I had successfully shot a pig. I felt a flood of relief too, that the deed was done, thank God, and didn't need to be done again.

And then there was this wholly unexpected feeling of thankfulness. For my good fortune, I guess, and to Angelo, of course, but also to this animal, for stepping over the crest of that hill and into my sight, to become what Angelo kept calling her: your pig. I felt it wasn't my skill that had brought me this animal. It was a gift—from whom or what, I couldn't say—and thankfulness is what I felt.

There was one emotion I expected to feel but did not. I felt no sorrow or remorse. Those would come later. But at that moment, I'm slightly embarrassed to admit, I felt absolutely terrific—completely happy. Angelo wanted to take my picture, so he posed me behind my pig, one hand cradling the rifle across my chest, the other resting on the animal. I thought I should look serious for the picture, but I couldn't stop smiling.

FROM ANIMAL TO MEAT

Angelo posing with my pig after hanging it from the limb of an oak to be gutted and skinned.

Angelo made a cut across the pig's belly and pulled the skin loose. The inside-out skin looked like a sweater coming off.

The happy excitement didn't last. Less than an hour later I was hugging the pig's carcass as it hung from the limb of an oak. My job was to hold it steady while Angelo reached in and pulled out the guts. We had used a block and tackle and two hooks to raise the pig by its rear ankles. A scale attached to the rig gave the weight of the animal: 190 pounds. The pig weighed exactly as much as I did.

Dressing the pig meant getting much closer to it than I really wanted. Angelo made a shallow cut across the pig's belly and began to gently work the hide loose. I held down a narrow flap of skin while he cut into the fat behind it, leaving as much of the creamy white layer as possible. "This is really good fat," Angelo explained, "for the salami." The flap of skin grew larger as we worked our way down the body and then slowly pulled it down over the pig's shoulders. The inside-out skin looked like a sweater coming off. What hunters call dressing an animal is really an undressing.

As we drew the skin down over the rib cage it exposed the bullet, or what remained of the bullet. It had passed through the animal and torn a ragged slot in the last rib, where it came to rest just beneath the hide. "Here's a souvenir for you," Angelo said, pulling the bloody, mangled chunk of metal from the bone like a tooth and handing it to me.

Using a short knife, Angelo made another shallow cut the length of the animal's belly. He talked while he worked, mostly about the dishes he could make from the different parts of the pig. I could not believe Angelo was still talking about food. The pig was splayed open now. I could see all its organs: the bluish intestine and the spongy pink pair of lungs. I'd handled plenty of chicken guts on Joel's farm, but this was different and more disturbing. That was probably because the pig's internal organs looked exactly like human organs.

I held the cavity open while Angelo reached in to pull out the liver ("for a nice pâté"). He cut it free and dropped it into a Ziploc bag. Then he reached in and pulled, and the rest of the guts tumbled out onto the ground in a heap. There was a stench so awful it made me gag. It was a mix of pig manure and piss with an odor of death. I felt a wave of sickness begin to build in my gut. I still had my arms wrapped around the pig from behind, but I told Angelo I wanted to take a picture. What I really wanted was a breath of fresh air.

THE JOY OF HUNTING

The disgust I felt was so strong I wondered how I could ever eat this animal now. How could I serve it to my friends? Some of the disgust I felt made sense. After all, part of the stench was from the waste in the pig's intestines. But it was more than that. When we kill an animal, especially a big mammal like a pig, it can't help reminding us of our own death. The line between their bodies and ours, between their deaths and ours, is not very sharp.

I recovered from my disgust enough to help Angelo finish dress-

© Michael Pollan

Angelo's walk-in cooler packed full of foraged mushrooms and curing meat.

ing my pig. Yet the emotions did not go away. They really hit me late that evening. Back at home, I opened my e-mail and saw that Angelo had sent me some pictures under the subject heading Look the great hunter! I was eager to open them, excited to show my family my pig. (It was hanging in Angelo's walk-in cooler.)

The image that appeared on my computer screen hit me like an unexpected blow to the body. A hunter in an orange sweater is kneeling on the ground behind a pig. From the pig's head comes a narrow river of blood, spreading out toward the bottom of the frame. The hunter's rifle is angled just so across his chest. One hand rests on the dead animal's broad flank. The man is looking into the camera with a broad, happy grin.

I looked from the dead, bloody pig to the big, happy grin on the man's face—my face. Then I hurried my mouse to the corner of the image and clicked, closing it as quickly as I could.

What could I possibly have been thinking? What was the man in that picture feeling? What was I so damned proud of, anyway? Suddenly I felt ashamed.

I had set out to do something new and difficult for me. I had messed up the first time I tried it. Now I had succeeded and it made complete sense that I would feel relief and pride. I was okay with that. But was it okay to feel joy over another creature's death?

I was confronted with yet another dilemma. What exactly

is the joy of hunting? I know what made me feel good when I was out in the woods. I enjoyed feeling totally alive and a part of nature. I enjoyed discovering new abilities that I didn't know I had. I enjoyed succeeding in my difficult task.

However, I also knew what made me feel bad about hunting. No matter how I looked at it, I felt regret about killing that pig. The animal is at once different from me and yet as a living creature it is in some ways the same. Maybe this is an important part of hunting too. Hunters ought to be aware of the seriousness of what they are doing and never treat it lightly.

THINGS AS THEY ARE

I went hunting to kill a pig and turn it into meat. But I realized I was looking for more than that. When I started my journey down the food chains of our society, I wanted to look at things as they really are. I did not want to look away from the reality. The hardest thing had been looking at where our meat comes from. Now I had seen it as up close and personal as you can get. There was no industrial or organic food chain here. It was just me and my food.

There was one other picture Angelo sent me. I didn't look at it until some time later. This was the picture I took of Angelo cleaning my pig when I needed to break away. It's a simple snapshot of the pig hanging from the tree. You can see in that one frame the animal and the butcher and the oak tree against the sun-filled sky and the pig-plowed earth. In that single picture you could see an entire food chain. There is the oak tree standing in the sun. On the ground are the acorns the tree made with the sunlight. There is the pig that ate the acorns, and the man preparing the pig to be eaten.

I had started out to see exactly where our food came from and now I had. The man in that photo did not create that food chain, he is just a part of it. Just as the tree took in the sunlight and the pig ate the acorns, the man is taking his nourishment from that natural cycle. In the end, whatever we think or feel, triumph or shame, that is the way it is.

21
Gathering

THE FUNGI

To make my hunter-gatherer meal, I needed not only hunting skills, but gathering skills as well. Since my menu included mushrooms, I would need to learn yet another set of skills and join yet another club, the semi-secret society of wild mushroomers. I found that club even more difficult to join than the club of hunters. Luckily, Angelo was once again going to be my guide.

At first glance, mushroom hunting looks easy. You just go through the forest happily picking mushrooms, kind of like picking tomatoes in the garden. The only difference is you didn't have to plant, water, fertilize, and weed the mushrooms. They just grew all by themselves. Easy, right?

Not so easy, as I was about to discover. For starters, I've

never gotten lost in a garden. It is surprisingly easy to get lost when you're deep in the woods with your head down, looking for wild mushrooms. Also in the garden, you know where the vegetables are growing. Mushrooms hide from you.

And of course, there's the whole poison thing. I have never once worried that a cucumber I grew from seed would kill me if I ate it. But picking and eating the wrong mushroom can get you killed. Mushrooms, you soon discover, are wild things in every way. That's why people who go looking for them call it mushroom *hunting*—not harvesting.

THE MUSHROOM HUNTER

It was a Sunday morning in late January when I got the call from Angelo.

"The chanterelles are up," he announced.

"How do you know? Have you been out looking?"

FUNGI FACTS

There are two basic types of fungi that produce mushrooms:

Saprophytic fungi live by consuming dead plants, like rotting roots and trees.

Mycorrhizal fungi live on or in the roots of living plants.

The kind of mushrooms grown on farms (often in caves) are saprophytic. That includes common white button mushrooms, shiitakes, cremini, portobellos, and oyster mushrooms.

The chanterelle and morel are mycorrhizal fungi.

The study of fungi is called mycology and a scientist who studies fungi is called a mycologist. Someone who hunts and eats and thinks about wild mushrooms a lot is called a mycophile. Someone afraid of mushrooms is a mycophobe.

"No, not yet. But it's been three weeks since the big rains. They're up now, I'm sure of that. We should go tomorrow."

At the time I barely knew Angelo (we had yet to go pig hunting), so I was very grateful for the invitation. To a mushroom hunter, a good chanterelle spot is a closely guarded secret. Before Angelo agreed to take me I'd asked a bunch of other mushroom hunters to take me along. Some of them acted like I had asked to borrow their credit card. Others promised to call me back, but never did. A few used the same old joke: "I could show you where I get my mushrooms, but then I'd have to kill you."

Even Angelo wasn't really giving away a secret. The place he took me was on private and gated land owned by an old friend of his. No one could get to it without permission from the owner.

© Michael Pollan

Looking for chanterelles at an undisclosed location in Sonoma County, California.

The chanterelle lives on the roots of oak trees, usually very old ones. There must have been hundreds of ancient oaks on the property, but Angelo seemed to know every one of them. "That one there is a producer," he'd tell me, pointing across the meadow to a tree. "But the one next to it, I never once found a mushroom there."

I set off across the meadow to hunt beneath the tree. I looked around for a few minutes, lifting the dead leaves with my stick, but I saw nothing. Then Angelo came over and pointed to a spot no more than a yard from where I stood. I looked, I stared, but still saw nothing but a mess of tan leaves. Angelo got down on his knees and brushed the leaves away to reveal a bright squash-colored mushroom the size of his fist. He cut it at the base with a knife and handed it to me. The mushroom was heavy, and cool to the touch.

How in the world had he spotted it? The trick, he explained, was to look for signs of something pushing up the leaves. Then you had to look at the ground sideways to see if you could catch a glimpse of the gold stems of the chanterelle. Yet when Angelo pointed to another spot under the same tree, a spot where he had seen another mushroom, I was still blind. Not until he had moved the leaves with his stick did the golden nugget of fungus flash at me. I became convinced that Angelo must be smelling the chanterelles before he saw them.

But that wasn't the case. I just had to learn how to look.

The way the mushroom hunters put it is to get your eyes on. And after following Angelo around for a while, I did begin to get my eyes on, a little. Before the morning was out I'd begun to find a few chanterelles on my own. The mushrooms started to pop out of the landscape, one and then another.

FIVE CHANTERELLES

But after a brief run of luck I promptly went blind again— and failed to find another mushroom all day. I would say there were no more mushrooms left to find, except that Angelo was still finding them in spots I had just visited. I had managed to find just five, though several of them weighed close to a pound each. My five chanterelles were tremendous, beautiful things I couldn't wait to taste.

That night I washed off the dirt, patted them dry, and then sliced the chanterelles into creamy white slabs. They smelled faintly of apricots. I knew at once that this was the same mushroom I had found near my house, the one I had been afraid to taste. The orange color matched, and these had the same shallow ridges running up the stalk. I cooked them as Angelo had recommended, first in a dry frying pan to sweat out their water, and then with butter and shallots. The mushrooms were delicious, with a light flavor—fruity with a hint of pepper—and a firm but silky texture.

And I wasn't the least bit concerned about waking up dead.

What had happened to resolve my omnivore's dilemma? Even after reading guidebooks or looking at photographs on my own, I still wasn't sure I'd had a true chanterelle. But when Angelo handed one to me, my doubts vanished. I knew that the next time I found a chanterelle anywhere, I would recognize it and not hesitate to eat it.

I spoke with other mushroom hunters who had the same experience. It seems we need to learn this information in person, from another human being. Maybe that's part of our omnivore's instinct. It's certainly an advantage we have over the omnivore rat, which cannot share its hard-won knowledge of food with other rats.

MUSHROOMS ARE MYSTERIOUS

Mushrooms each have their seasons. Once the rains stopped in April the chanterelles were done for the year. The next important mushroom hunt would be for the morels, in May. I used the time in between to read about mushrooms and talk to mycologists. I had a lot of questions, like: What made mushrooms come up when and where they did? Why do chanterelles live on oaks and morels on pines? Why under some trees and not others?

I learned that there aren't a lot of answers to even the most basic questions. Scientists know very little about the fungi, which are the third kingdom of life on earth. Part of the problem is simply that fungi are very difficult to observe. What we call a mushroom is only a small part of a fungus. Most of it is underground, consisting of a network of microscopic cells called mycelium. These thin, threadlike cells form a web buried in the soil. You can't dig up a mushroom to study it because the mycelium is too tiny and delicate. If you try to separate them from the soil they just fall apart.

We know the basic parts of a plant—roots, stem, leaves, flowers. But we don't even know for sure if fungi have parts, aside from mushrooms. We don't know exactly why or when the fungus produces a mushroom either. It can go years or even centuries without producing one.

Thanks to chlorophyll, plants are able to transform sunlight, water, and minerals into carbohydrates. Fungi work sort of in reverse. They recycle organic matter with powerful enzymes that can break down organic molecules into simple molecules and minerals.

A mycorrhizal fungus has cells that surround or even go into the roots of a plant. The fungus and the plant have a deal. The fungus gives the plant simple elements and minerals it has taken from the soil. In return, the plant gives the fungus a drop of the simple sugars (carbohydrates) it has made. The fungus cells reach far underground and so act as a second root system for the plant. Trees need these fungal networks to thrive. It is also possible that the fungus gives the tree protection from bacteria or other fungi.

Fungi are an essential part of the life cycle on earth. They are the masters of decay and recycling. Without fungi to break things down, the earth would soon be covered with a blanket of dead plants and animals.

That might be why some people just don't like mushrooms. Even the ones that don't poison us are closely linked to death and decay. Their job is to break the dead down into food for the living. That's much less appetizing than a plant that creates food from sunlight. Cemeteries are usually good places to hunt for mushrooms. (Mexicans call mushrooms *carne de los muertos*—"flesh of the dead.")

FANTASTIC FUNGI

About those poisons. Scientists aren't sure why some mushrooms produce them. The poison might be a defense against being eaten, or it might just be one of the chemicals the fungus needs to do its work that happens to be toxic to humans.

As a food, fungi (or mushrooms, which are the part we eat) don't have much nutritional value. They contain some vitamins, minerals, and some amino acids (the building blocks of protein) but few calories. So mushrooms are not a good source of energy for us. Yet they have enough energy to do some amazing things.

Consider:

SHAGGY MANE

(Coprinus comatus) can push their soft fleshy tissue through asphalt.

INKY CAPS

(Coprinus atramentarius) can mushroom in a matter of hours and then, over the course of a day, dissolve themselves into a puddle of blackish ink.

OYSTER MUSHROOMS

(Pleurotus ostreatus) can digest a pile of petrochemical sludge in a fortnight, transforming the toxic waste into edible protein.

JACK O'LANTERN

(Omphalotus olivascens) can glow in the dark, giving off an eerie blue light for reasons unknown

PSILOCYBIN

The psilocybes are a whole group of mushrooms that are hallucinogenic. They alter consciousness and produce hallucinations, or visions.

MUSHROOMING IS NO PICNIC

Through Angelo's friend Jean-Pierre I met another mushroom hunter named Anthony Tassinello. Anthony said he'd be willing to take me morel hunting. He wasn't too worried about keeping the spot secret since we would be hunting "burn morels." These are morels that come up in the spring following a pine forest fire. The fire had been big news and every mushroom hunter in California would be out looking for morels there. Plus, whatever spots we found would only be good for a couple of weeks.

Anthony e-mailed that I should meet him in front of his house Friday morning at six o'clock sharp. He warned me to come prepared for any weather. "We'll go rain, snow, or shine." He wasn't kidding. The weather up where we were going was extreme. It could snow in May or be very hot or both in the same day.

He also described the ground we would be covering. "It is very steep and rocky with huge, burned fallen trees and ground that is thoroughly soaked. Bring a hat, the sun is stronger at this elevation, plus it keeps cedar needles and spider-

GIANT FUNGUS EATS DETROIT?

A single fungus recently found in Michigan covers an area of forty acres underground and is thought to be a few centuries old.

webs out of your face and can double as a mushroom sack when your basket is full." Anthony also advised me to bring sunscreen and bug spray (for mosquitoes), at least a gallon of water, ChapStick, and, if I owned one, a walkie-talkie.

Suddenly, morel hunting didn't sound like much fun. In fact it sounded more like survival training than a walk in the woods. I crossed my fingers that Anthony was just trying to scare me, and set my alarm for 4:30 a.m. I wondered why it is all these hunting-gathering expeditions had to begin at such ungodly hours in the morning. I understood why you had to hunt pigs early in the day when they were active. But it's not as though these morels were going to disappear after lunch. Perhaps the idea is to use as much daylight as possible. Or maybe we wanted the early start to beat other mushroomers to the best spots.

WORKING THE BURN

I pulled up to Anthony's curb a little before six to find two thirtyish-looking men in rain slickers loading an SUV. They were packing enough equipment for an expedition down the Amazon. Anthony was a rail-thin six-footer with a goatee; his friend Ben Baily was a somewhat rounder and softer man with an easy laugh. I learned on the long ride that Anthony and Ben were childhood friends from Piscataway, New Jersey. After college they'd both moved to the Bay Area to become chefs. Anthony told me that we were going to be joined by someone they'd met at the burn the week before, a young guy known to them only by his mushrooming nickname: Paulie Porcini.

Paulie Porcini was part of the subculture of mushroom hunters who travel up and down the West Coast. They follow the mushrooms as they appear: porcinis in the fall, chanterelles in winter, morels in the spring. "These are people living out of vans," Ben explained. They make a living selling their mushrooms to brokers who set up shop in motel rooms near the forests. The brokers put up signs to let the mushroomers know where they are and they pay cash. Then they resell the mushrooms to restaurants and food stores.

We drove for several hours and gradually climbed into the mountains of the Eldorado National Forest. The forest is a twelve-hundred-square-mile swath of pine and cedar stretched between Lake Tahoe and Yosemite. As we rose, the temperature dropped down into the thirties and

© Michael Pollan

A burned-out pine forest in El Dorado National Forest, south of Lake Tahoe, California.

a frozen rain began to pelt the windshield. Snow covered the ground. It was early May, but we had driven back into winter.

We were looking for the edge between the snow and bare ground. That's where the morels would be growing. At an elevation of about forty-five hundred feet we found it. We parked the SUV and looked around. Soon after, Paulie Porcini appeared. He was a bearded, quiet fellow in his twenties who carried a walking stick and had a bandanna wrapped around his head. He seemed like someone who was very comfortable in the woods.

The forest was beautiful and it was ghastly. As far as you could see, it was a graveyard of black, soaring trunks. For five days the previous October the "power fire," as it was called, had roared across these mountains, consuming seventeen thousand acres of pine and cedar. The fire had been so fierce in places that it had eaten trees down to the roots. This left blackened holes where the trees had stood. Not much lived in this landscape. We heard owls and saw a few squirrels.

DOWN IN THE MUD

That was basically the last time all day I lifted my gaze to take in the view. As soon as Ben announced he'd spotted his first morel, I began looking down. The ground was covered with a thick carpet of pine needles and the charred trunks of pine. A morel resembles a tanned finger wearing a dark and deeply honeycombed dunce cap. They'd be easy to spot if they weren't brown and black. As it was, they seem to disappear against the forest floor.

To help me get my eyes on, Ben began leaving in place patches of morels he'd found, so I could study them where they grew. I found that if I actually got down on the ground I could see the little hats popping up here and there. From above they were invisible. Of course, the ground was thick black mud, but that seemed to be the price you paid for burn morels.

The morning was spent wandering across the steep hillside with our heads down, my gaze locked on a point about six steps in front of me. Wandering around that way, I completely lost track of where I was. To regain my bearings I'd have to stop and look up. The air was foggy and the hills were cut with deep ravines. I often had no idea in which direction the road was or where the others had wandered. Every now and then a burst of static would come over my walkie-talkie: "I've hit a mother lode down here by the creek" or "Where the hell are you guys?"

When I did see morels, it didn't feel like I had found them. It felt more like they had decided to show themselves. There's something mushroomers call the "pop-out effect." Here's how it works: When searching for something, you fix its visual pattern in your mind. Then it seems to "pop out" of the background.

FOREST VS. GARDEN

You don't need to play these tricks when looking for fruits and vegetables. They depend on animals to eat them and spread their seeds, so they have evolved to be noticed. In the garden nobody hides; nobody means you harm. Everything in the garden (or almost everything) is there because the gardener wants it there.

Gathering in the forest is a very different thing. We didn't create the forest. It does not exist for us. The morels would just as soon I pass them by. Even the bright berries aren't growing there for us. We didn't work to make the forest happen. It's more like we are stealing from it. Alone in the woods, out of earshot of my fellow mushroom hunters, I found myself, idiotically, talking to the morels. Whenever a bunch of them suddenly popped out, I would cry, "Gotcha!" You would never feel like that with an apple tree in an orchard. *Of course* the apples are there—a farmer planted them.

© Michael Pollan

Morels popping up through a bed of pine needles.

MORELS AND FIRE

I'd completely lost track of time and space when my walkie-talkie blurted, "Break for lunch—meet back at the car." I had wandered nearly a mile from the car, mostly downhill. By the time I worked my way back up to the road, the others were standing around munching trail mix. They all had pretty impressive hauls. "You couldn't have picked a better day," Ben gushed when I wandered over with my own bag full of morels. "The mushrooms are so on today, I've never seen it like this—we're killing them!"

We sat on a charred log (by now we all looked charred ourselves) and ate our lunch, talking about the mushrooms and the people who made their living as mushroom hunters. People have been gathering morels in burned forests forever; Ben mentioned that in Germany long ago people would set forest fires just so they could harvest morels.

Scientists think that morels are a mycorrhizal species that live on the roots of the pine trees. When the pines die in a fire, the fungi face a crisis. Suddenly there are no more roots supplying them with food. So the fungus fruits, sending up morels to release trillions of spores. It is up to the wind to spread the spores far from the blasted forest.

The morels are trying to escape the dying forest. Yet at the same time they also help it grow back. The slightly meaty odor of morels attracts flies, which lay eggs in the safety of the mushroom's hollow stalk. Larvae hatch and feed on the flesh of the morels. Birds then return to the forest to feed on the larvae. The birds drop seeds that sprout on the forest floor, beginning the process of regeneration.

MUSHROOM TREASURE

After lunch we wandered off on our separate ways again for a few more hours. I worked my way downhill, slip-sliding in the mud and following a stream that led to Beaver Creek. I had no idea where I was or where I was going. I was following the trail of mushrooms. Along Beaver Creek that afternoon the morels were totally on, as Ben would say. Almost everywhere I looked the dunce caps appeared, and I filled a bag in less than an hour. I had no idea how deep into the woods I'd wandered, and I was more than a little lost, but not to the morels, who weren't hiding from me any longer.

I felt, again, the gratitude I'd felt in that other forest, the moment that wild pig first appeared to me on the top of that ridge. It can be hard work, hunting and gathering, but if you come away with something, it's almost by chance. You don't feel your hard work has been rewarded. You feel more like you're getting something for nothing. A gift.

By the end of the afternoon we'd all ended up down by Beaver Creek. Around four we made our way back to the car. We changed our soaking socks on the tailgate and filled the entire cargo area of the SUV with morels. We tried as best we could to hide them from view. No reason, really, but a big haul of mushrooms just isn't something you want to advertise. (Earlier that afternoon a couple of mushroom hunters in an old van stopped to ask if I was having any luck. For no good reason I had lied through my teeth.)

We'd found sixty pounds of morels, it turned out—a personal best for Anthony and Ben. Before we climbed into the car to head home, we asked a hiker to take a picture of the four of us holding a crate loaded with morels, a huge one propped up on top of the pile. We were filthy and exhausted, but felt rich as kings.

Before we climbed into the car to head home, a passing hiker took a picture of the four of us holding a crate loaded w morels. From left: me, Paulie, Ben, and Anthony.

22
The Perfect Meal

Perfect?! A dangerous boast, you must be thinking. And, in truth, my do-it-yourself meal did not come out exactly as I hoped. The dessert, a cherry tart, was slightly burned. The morels were a little gritty. The salt I had gathered in San Francisco Bay was too toxic to serve. But for me it was still the perfect meal.

I set the date for the dinner—Saturday, June 18—as soon as my animal was in the bag. Wild California pig would be the main course. That gave me a couple of weeks to plan and gather the rest of the menu. I made myself some rules for what I would include.

1. Everything on the menu must have been hunted, gathered, or grown by me.
2. The menu should include at least one animal, vegetable, and fungus, as well as an edible mineral (the salt).
3. Everything served must be in season and fresh.

4. I would spend no money on the meal, but I could use items I already had in my pantry.

5. The guest list was limited to those people who helped me in my foraging and their partners. This included Angelo, Anthony, Richard, and a friend named Sue who took me chanterelle hunting. Plus, of course, my wife, Judith, and son, Isaac. Unfortunately, Jean-Pierre was in France. There would be ten of us in all.

6. I would cook the meal myself.

SALT OF THE EARTH

As with any set of rules, I soon found I needed to break one. The problem was the salt. I had learned that there are still a few salt ponds at the bottom of San Francisco Bay. On the Saturday before my dinner a very good-natured friend and I drove down to a lonely stretch of shoreline beneath the San Mateo Bridge. After an endless trek through trash-strewn wetlands, we found the salt ponds: rectangular fields of shallow water. The water was the color of strong tea. The shores were littered with garbage. There were soda cans and bottles, car parts and tires, and hundreds of tennis balls abandoned by dogs. There was everything . . . except salt.

There had been heavy rains all spring, making the ponds deeper than usual. There were no white salt crystals on the rocks, as I'd expected. We ended up filling a couple of soda bottles with the cloudy brown brine. That night, I evaporated the liquid in a pan over a low flame. The kitchen filled with a smelly chemical steam, but after a few hours there was a layer of brown crystals in the bottom of the pan. Once it cooled I managed to scrape out a few tablespoons.

The salt I wound up with was greasy and tasted so much like chemicals that it actually made me gag. Here was a good example of how disgust can save your life. No doubt professional salt gatherers have better ways to purify their salt, but I had no clue what these might be. So I abandoned plans to cook with or serve my own salt, and counted myself lucky to have survived.

Salt ponds occur naturally in the San Francisco Bay, and are also man-made and controlled by levees in order to make commercial salt. Because they are so shallow, algae often grows in them in various bright colors, which you can see from above.

PLANNING THE MENU

Perhaps the hardest rule to obey was the one about freshness. I was trying to bring to the table wild pig, wild mushrooms, fresh local fruit, and garden-picked vegetables all at the same time. Once again I had to bend the rules since there are no good local mushrooms in the Bay Area in June. Luckily I had dried a pound of the morels that I'd gathered the previous month. I decided to use those. (At least I had gathered them myself.)

For the appetizer I turned to the garden, where there were fava beans ready to pick. I'd planted them back in November, and by May I had scores of fat glossy pods. The fava is a broad, flat, bright green shelling bean. If picked young and quickly boiled, it has a starchy sweet taste that reminds me of spring-time just as much as fresh peas or asparagus. But by June many of my beans were not so young anymore, so I decided to make fava bean toasts. I'd mash the beans with roasted garlic and sage and serve them on toasted rounds of homemade sourdough bread. (The younger, sweeter beans I'd reserve for the pasta.) For a second appetizer, I asked Angelo to bring a block of the pâté he'd made from the liver of my pig.

So yes, okay, here was another exception to the rules: Angelo made the pâté. I also asked him to make the pasta for the first course: morels sautéed in butter with thyme and, for color, the tiny fava beans, over fresh egg fettuccine.

Wild California pig was the main course, but which cut and how to prepare it? Angelo recommended slowly braising the leg, in his opinion the most flavorful cut. (To braise it, I'd first sear it in a frying pan and then slow roast it in liquid.) I was curious to try the loin, and grilling outdoors over a fire seemed to me more in keeping with the hunter-gatherer theme. Unable to choose between the two approaches, I decided to try both. I would braise the leg in red wine (Angelo's) and homemade stock. The loin I would brine overnight, to keep the lean meat from drying out on the grill, cover it with crushed peppercorns, and then grill it fairly quickly over olive wood.

I wanted to bake my own bread and decided it would be fitting to use wild yeast. That would introduce a second type of fungus to the menu. Yeast is what makes bread dough rise. The yeast eats the sugars in bread dough and, as a by-product, gives off carbon dioxide. The bubbles of gas create little pockets in the dough. That's what gives bread its light and spongy texture. Bakers buy yeast in packets to add to their dough, but there is also wild yeast in the air. I found a recipe that gave instructions for gathering wild yeast, in a process that took several days but didn't sound too difficult.

After the main course there would be a salad. I had originally hoped to make it with foraged wild greens. Earlier in the spring I had found a lush patch of miner's lettuce and wild rapini in the Berkeley Hills, but by June the greens had begun to yellow. I decided to go instead with a simple salad of lettuces from my garden.

That left dessert, and for a while that posed a problem. My plan was to forage fruit, for a tart, from one of the many fruit trees lining the streets in Berkeley. I see no reason why foraging for food should be restricted to the countryside. In the weeks before the dinner I went on several urban scouting expeditions. In other words, I strolled around the neighborhood with a plastic bag. Since moving to Berkeley I've located a handful of excellent fruit trees—plum, apple, apricot, and fig. They all had branches I could reach from public land, but none of them had quite ripened yet.

It was my sister-in-law, Dena, who saved my dessert. She reported that her neighbor's bing cherry tree was so heavy with ripe fruit that several of its branches were at that very moment bending low over her backyard. I checked to make sure it was legal to pick fruit from someone else's tree that is hanging over your yard. It is and I did. Bingo! Bing cherries for my tart.

With dessert I would serve an herbal tea, made from wild chamomile. I'd picked the chamomile flowers in the Berkeley hills earlier in the spring and dried them. Then I mixed them with mint and lemon balm from the garden. I also had a jar of honey made by a friend in town. You could say the honey was foraged too, by the bees who made it.

CHEZ POLLAN

Now I had my menu and I wrote it out on a card. Being in Berkeley, home to many fine restaurants, I felt compelled to add a few over-the-top menu flourishes:

Tonight's Specials

Fava Bean Toasts and Sonoma Boar Pâté

Egg Fettuccine with Power Fire Morels

Braised Leg and Grilled Loin of Wild Sonoma Pig

Wild East Bay Yeast Levain

Very Local Garden Salad

Fulton Street Bing Cherry Tart

Claremont Canyon Chamomile Tea

2003 Angelo Garro Petite Syrah

The last item was one of Angelo's homemade wines.

I started cooking Saturday's meal on Tuesday morning, when I made the stock and started the wild yeast culture for the bread. For the stock I used bones from both my pig and from a grass-fed steer. After roasting the bones in the oven for an hour, I simmered them for the rest of the day in a stockpot with the vegetables and some herbs.

Gathering wild yeast turns out to be no big deal. The spores of various yeasts are floating in the air just about everywhere. Collecting them is a matter of giving them a moist place to rest and something to eat. Some species of yeast taste better than others, however, and this is where geography and luck enter in. The Bay Area has a reputation for its sourdough bread, so I figured the air outside my house would be an excellent hunting ground for wild yeast. I made a thick soup of organic flour and spring water. I briefly exposed the mixture to the air on a windowsill, then sealed it in an airtight container. By the following morning the surface of the chef, as it's called, was bubbling like pancake batter on a hot griddle. That was a good sign, because it meant the yeasts were already at work and growing.

Wednesday morning I drove into San Francisco to pick up the meat from Angelo. By the end of the week I had all my ingredients. I'd picked a gallon of cherries, harvested my fava beans, prepared the brine for the pig loin, made the stock, and soaked the dried morels in warm water. On Friday night, when I made a to-do list and schedule for Saturday, it hit me just how much I had to do. What was really scary was how much of it I had never done before. That included baking a wild yeast bread and cooking a wild pig two different ways.

I also hadn't added up how many total hours of oven time the meal would require. Braising the pig leg at 250 degrees would take half the day. I didn't see how exactly I could fit in the bread and the tart. For some reason it hadn't dawned on me earlier that I was cooking a very difficult meal for a group of very picky food experts. Now dawn on me it did.

OVER MY HEAD

To give you an idea of exactly what I'd gotten myself into, here's the schedule I wrote out Friday evening on both sides of an index card:

MY MEAL SCHEDULE

8:00 brine the loin; shell and blanch the fava beans*.	**12:00** knead bread dough; second rise.
9:00 make the bread dough. First rise.	**12:30** clean morels; harvest and chop herbs, sauté morels.
10:00 brown the leg; prepare liquid for braise.	**1:00** harvest and wash lettuce. Make vinaigrette dressing.
10:30 pit the cherries. Make pastry crust; refrigerate. Preheat oven for pig, 250°.	**2:00** knead dough again; make loaves. Prepare grill, teapot, cut flowers, set table.
11:00 pig in oven. Shell and skin fava beans. Roast garlic, puree favas.	

*Blanching is a very quick dunk in boiling water, followed by cold water.

3:00 roll piecrust, make tart. Remove pig and heat oven for bread (450°). Score loaves and bake.	**6:15** remove leg from oven; prepare loin (cover with garlic and herbs; roll in crushed pepper). Put loin on grill.
3:40 remove bread; bake tart (400°).	**7:00** guests arrive. Remove loin from grill.
4:00 remove tart from oven; put pig back in (250°).	
5:00 build fire. Crush peppercorns.	

GIVING THANKS

That was my plan for Saturday in the kitchen. Of course in reality the day unfolded nothing like that neat and orderly schedule. Instead it was a blizzard of rushed work, missing ingredients, unscheduled spills and dropped pots, unscheduled trips to the store, unscheduled pangs of doubt, and second-guessing. There were moments when I sorely wished for another pair of hands, but Judith and Isaac were away all day.

Did I really need to cook the pig two different ways? For dessert, why not just serve the cherries in a bowl? Or open a packet of fast-acting yeast?! Why in the world was I going to quite this much trouble?

When I thought about it, there seemed to be several reasons. This meal was my way of thanking all the people who had helped me with my hunting and gathering adventure. The effort I put into the meal would be a way of showing how much I appreciated what they had done. A bowl of fresh bing cherries is nice, but to turn them into a pastry is surely a more thoughtful gesture. (As long as I didn't blow the crust.) It's the difference between a Hallmark e-card and a hand-written letter.

The work was also a way of honoring the food. All these plants and animals and fungi were being sacrificed to our needs and desires. I wanted to do right by them. I guess I could have made wild boar hamburgers, but that wouldn't have felt like the right thing. Maybe that is one way a cook celebrates the ingredients, by wasting as little as possible and making the most of whatever the food has to offer.

AT THE TABLE

It remained to be seen whether my cooking would honor my ingredients or just embarrass me. In any case, by the hour set for the dinner, everything was more or less ready, except me. I raced upstairs to change and, before I had my shoes tied, heard the doorbell ring. The guests were arriving. They came bearing gifts: Angelo with his wine and pâté, and Sue with a bouquet picked from her garden. Anthony brought a bottle of homemade nocino, a jet-black Italian liquor he'd made from green walnuts—yet another gift from the forest for our feast.

Most of the guests were strangers to one another. All they had in common was foraging—and me. But as we settled into the living room with our glasses of wine, it didn't take long for the conversation to start flowing. The fava bean toasts and boar pâté went over well and that led to a discussion about boar hunting.

I disappeared into the kitchen to ready the pasta course. Within minutes Angelo appeared at my side, with an offer of help. I think he was a little worried I was in over my head. While we waited for the pasta water to come to a boil, I asked him to taste the morels. "It's good, but maybe it needs a little more butter." I handed him a stick and he dropped the whole thing in the pan. (So that's how the professionals do it!)

We dished out the pasta and I called everyone to the table for dinner. Candles were lit, wine was poured, the perfume of thyme and morels filled the room, and I raised my glass for a toast. I'd actually meant to write out something earlier, but the day had gotten away from me. So I kept it simple. I went around the table and spoke of each person's contribution to my foraging education and to this meal. I talked about Sue's generosity in sharing three of her choicest chanterelle spots. I talked about Anthony's allowing a complete—and completely green—stranger to accompany him hunting morels in the Sierra. I talked about hunting with Richard in Sonoma during that first failed outing. And lastly I talked about all the many things I'd learned from Angelo—things about mushrooms and pigs, about nature and the arts of cooking and eating well, and so much else besides. Then, worried I was in danger of melting down into sentiment, I raised my glass again and urged everyone to start.

I had actually wanted to say something more, to express a wider gratitude for the meal we were about to eat. I guess I chickened out, afraid that to offer words of thanks for the pig and the mushrooms and the forests and the garden would come off sounding corny. The words I was reaching for, of course, were the words of grace.

THE PERFECT MEAL

As you might expect, the talk at the table was mainly about food. Yet this was not the usual food talk of recipes and restaurants. These foragers talked about the plants and animals and fungi they had seen and met. They told stories of an oak forest in Sonoma, a pine burn in the Sierras, and a backyard in Berkeley. The stories brought all these places and the creatures in them to our table. Every item on our plates had a story—and not the kind of story printed on a milk carton about "organic" cows. These were stories the people at the table had lived.

The food, the places it came from, and the eaters at the table were all linked together. How different this was from the typical meal, in which we never even think about where the chicken or cherries come from. How completely differ-ent from a fast-food hamburger wolfed down without a moment's thought in a speeding car.

I don't want to make too much of it; it was just a meal, after all. A very tasty meal too, I don't mind saying. The wild pig was delicious both ways, with a nutty sweetness to it that tasted nothing like store-bought pork. The sauce for the leg was almost joltingly rich and earthy, powerfully reminis-cent of the forest. So were the morels and butter (or perhaps I should say butter and morels), which had a deep, smoky, almost meaty flavor. I could have done a better job cleaning the grit from the morels, and the tart was a shade overcooked. But the cherries themselves tasted like little bursts of summer on the tongue, and no one seemed to have any trouble polish-ing it off.

In the end, I did feel it was a perfect meal. It wasn't my cooking that made it perfect, but the connection we felt with the food, with the place we live and with each other. Wasn't that exactly the feeling of connection I had been looking for when I began my journeys along the food chains of the U.S.? This food had never worn a label or bar code or price tag, and yet I knew almost everything there was to know about it. I knew and could picture the very oaks and pines that had nourished the pigs and the mushrooms that were nourishing us. And I knew the true cost of this food, the precise amount of time and work it had taken to get it and prepare it.

If I had to give this dinner a name, it would have to be the Omnivore's Thanksgiving. I certainly felt thankful to be eating those plants, animals, and fungi. I was thankful to have experienced them in full, as living creatures and not as items shrink-wrapped in the supermarket. And I was thankful to be in the company of friends who appreciated the miracle of it all.

Of course, it was just one meal. The day after, I would go back to shopping at the supermarket or farmers' market. It's just not realistic for me to find and prepare meals like this more than once in a while. Most people will never be able to do it. Does that mean we are doomed to eating at the end of a long industrial food chain and never know where our food comes from, or what its true nature is? I hope not. Eating with awareness is one of the basic joys of life, and one that everyone can experience even without hunting and gathering your food.

ALL OUR MEALS

One of the wonders of my do-it-yourself meal was how little it had damaged the world. My pig's place in the forest would soon be taken by another pig. The morels would come up again when they needed to. The cherry tree would bear fruit again next year. The meal was fully paid for in every sense; there was no pollution or packaging left over. There were no hidden costs or waste to be disposed of.

The fast-food meal seems cheap, but as we have seen, the costs are actually enormous. The industrial food chain costs each and every one of us: in government spending, in pollution, in global warming, and in our health. You can say that my forager's meal is unrealistic, but I would answer that the fast-food meal is unrealistic also. It is not realistic to rely on a food system that poisons the planet. It is not realistic to call something a food system when it replaces food with an industrial product that does not nourish us—and in fact makes us sick.

Imagine if we had a food system that actually produced wholesome food. Imagine if it produced that food in a way that restored the land. Imagine if we could eat every meal knowing these few simple things: What it is we're eating. Where it came from. How it found its way to our table. And what it really cost.

If that was the reality, then every meal would have the potential to be a perfect meal. We would not need to go hunting for our connection to our food and the web of life that produces it. We would no longer need any reminding that we eat by the grace of nature, not industry, and that what we're eating is never anything more or less than the body of the world.

I don't want to have to forage every meal. Most people don't want to learn to garden or hunt. But we can change the way we make and get our food so that it becomes food again—something that feeds our bodies and our souls. Imagine it: Every meal would connect us to the joy of living and the wonder of nature. Every meal would be like saying grace.

AFTERWORD:
Vote with Your Fork

I suspect that reading this book will complicate your eating life. Writing it certainly complicated mine. And we're not alone. Sometimes I meet people who tell me that they liked my book, but they couldn't finish it. That's not what a writer ever wants to hear, so I always ask them, why not?

"Because in every chapter I learn about something I shouldn't eat anymore. I'm afraid if I get to the end, there won't be anything left to eat, and I'll starve."

Hearing this kind of thing from readers makes me appreciate that, in some ways, *The Omnivore's Dilemma* has deepened people's dilemmas about food. Do I feel bad about that? Not really. It's always better to know more rather than less, even when that knowledge complicates your life. Luckily, there are still plenty of things out there that are good to eat—and by good I mean not only delicious and healthy (good for us) but also good for the world: for the environment, for the workers who produce the food, and, in the case of meat or dairy, for the animals involved.

One of the strongest reactions to the book is from people who tell me they became vegetarians after reading it. *The*

Omnivore's Dilemma definitely created a lot of vegetarians. But what's more surprising has been to hear from former vegetarians who tell me that, after reading about Joel Salatin's farm, they started eating meat again. Why? Because they didn't realize that there were farms where the animals got to live good lives, eat the foods they were meant to eat, and then suffer only that one bad day right at the end of their lives. It was possible, they discovered, to eat meat with a clear conscience.

So I'm guessing that the number of new vegetarians inspired by the book has been balanced out by the number of new carnivores. But whichever conclusion readers come to, they are more thoughtful about their choices—they act now out of knowledge rather than ignorance, and that's the most important thing. Ignorance is not bliss, at least not if you're a person who cares about the health of your body and your world.

Since I wrote this book, my family has changed the way we eat in many ways. I've lost my appetite for feedlot meat and so have they. We used to enjoy a fast-food meal now and then, and even today my sixteen-year-old son, Isaac (when you met him in the book, at the McDonald's meal, he was only eleven), likes an occasional chicken nugget. But what he's learned from me about how the animals live on feedlots, and about what's in those chicken nuggets, has made him think twice about eating fast food on a regular basis. He's completely lost his appetite for Big Macs and Whoppers, and he has stopped drinking soda except on special occasions.

My family also eats much less meat than we used to, and when we do eat it, we get it from farms or ranches or companies we know enough about to trust. We only buy grass-fed beef, which we can find in local markets (it's becoming increasingly common); and sometimes we buy it directly from a rancher. (You can find farmers selling pastured meat and milk in your area at eatwild.com.) In the case of plant-based foods, we usually buy organic or local (and ideally both—I think organic fruits and vegetables taste better, and I also like the idea that my food dollars are supporting farmers who care about the land). We also try to shop at the farmers market as often as possible. The food there is picked fresh, which means it is at the peak of its taste and nutritional quality, and every dollar goes directly to the farmers.

If this all sounds like a lot more trouble than buying whatever's on sale at the supermarket, you're right. It also costs a little more. But I think it's worth it. It's amazing how knowing the story behind your food can make it taste better. (Or, if it's a bad story, worse.) But I also enjoy meeting farmers at the farmers market, and seeing how my food dollars can help build a new food chain in America, one devoted to health at every step: to the health of the land, the health of the plants and animals, the health of my family, and the health of my community.

I call shopping and eating this way "voting with your fork." How you and your family choose to spend your food dollars represents one of the most powerful votes you have. You can vote to support the kind of feedlot where steer number 534 spent his miserable life, or you can vote for farms like Polyface, where animals live the lives they were meant to, the land is healed in the process, and the farmers make a decent living. That kind of alternative farm was created not only by visionary farmers like Joel Salatin, but by visionary consumers—like you.

I've never liked to think of myself as a mere "consumer"—the word sounds like someone who uses things up and diminishes the world, and very often that's exactly what a consumer does. But a consumer can be a creator too, by using his or her eating choices to help build a new food chain. That is a potent vote, and you get three of them every day. But perhaps best of all, when it comes to food, you don't have to wait till you're eighteen to start voting. You can start today, at your next meal.

That doesn't mean we're going to get that vote right every time or at every meal. We won't. Sometimes there are no good alternatives to vote for. Sometimes you're just going to want a Big Mac. There will be those special occasions when you crave that tall, cold cup of high-fructose corn syrup—I mean, a soda. But there's a big difference between the special splurge and the everyday habit, and the problem these days is that fast food has, for many of us, become everyday food. You don't have to go cold turkey—just put fast food back in its place, as special occasion food. And, when you are eating it, think about what you now know about your meal. How's it taste now?

If you cast your food vote consciously just once or twice a day, you will be doing a lot—for the farmers, for the animals, for the environment, and for your own health. I know: You don't make all the food decisions in your household. But you have more influence than you realize. Ever since you were little, pestering your mom to buy the cool new cereal you saw on TV—or tossing it in the shopping cart when she wasn't looking—you've had a major impact on how your family's food dollars get spent. So what about using that influence in a new way—say, by encouraging your parents to shop at the farmers market or to join a CSA? ("CSA" stands for Community Supported Agriculture. These are local farms that families "join" for a few hundred dollars a year. In return, they get a weekly box of fresh produce. It's often cheaper than shopping at the farmers market, and can even be cheaper than your local supermarket.) And then offer to help your parents cook a couple of nights a week—or take over one whole night yourself. Cooking for your family is a great way to influence how they eat.

Voting with your fork at school can be a challenge, but it's worth trying to do. How a school spends its food dollars can have a tremendous impact on the whole food system. In many schools today, students and parents are working together to improve the food service: to take away the soda machines (why should those companies be allowed to tempt you at school?); to encourage cafeterias to serve real food made from scratch (rather than just microwave chicken nuggets and Tater Tots); and even to teach classes on how to grow and cook food yourself. Physical education is already a mandatory part of your school day, after all, so why not eating education? It's just as important to your health. Is your school teaching you how to be a lifelong fast-food junkie? Or is it teaching you the importance, and the pleasure, of eating real food at real meals?

It's an exciting time to be an eater in America. You have choices today that your parents couldn't have dreamed of: organic, local, CSAs, humanely raised milk and meat. When they were your age, there was basically only one way to feed yourself: from the industrial food chain. You have the option of eating from a very different food chain—you can vote with your fork for a better world, one delicious bite at a time.

THE OMNIVORE'S SOLUTION:

Some Tips for Eating

I'll bet I know your last burning question: "What now?" Now that you know all that you know about the food chains we depend on, how exactly should you fill up your plate? Most of my readers have the same question, so I've developed a handful of everyday rules to guide you through the new-found challenges (and possibilities!) of mealtime. (You can find more of them in the books I wrote after *The Omnivore's Dilemma*, called *In Defense of Food* and *Food Rules*.)

My advice comes in three parts:

EAT REAL FOOD.

That sounds pretty simple, but you now know it's not so easy to do. There are many things disguised as food in our supermarkets and fast-food restaurants; I call them "edible food-like substances" (EFLS for short) and suggest you avoid them. But how do you tell the difference between real food and EFLS? Here are a few rules of thumb:

1. **Don't eat anything your great-grandmother wouldn't recognize as food.** Imagine she's by your side when you're picking up something to eat. Does she have any idea what that Go-Gurt portable yogurt tube is or how you're supposed to eat it? (She might think it's toothpaste.) The same goes for that Honey-Nut Cheerios, cereal bar, the one with the layer of fake milk running through the middle, or the (even weirder) cereal "straw."

2. **Don't eat anything with more than five ingredients, or with ingredients you don't recognize or can't pronounce.** As with the Twinkie, that long ingredient list means you're looking at a highly processed product—an edible food-like substance likely to contain more sugar, salt, and fat than your body needs, and very few real nutrients.

3. **Don't eat anything containing high-fructose corn syrup (HFCS).** Think about it: only corporations ever "cook" with the stuff. Avoid it and you will automatically avoid many of the worst kinds of EFLS, including soda.

BUY REAL FOOD.

To make sure you're buying real food:

1. Get your food from the outside perimeter of the su-

permarket and try to avoid the middle aisles. In the cafeteria, go for the salad bar or the fruit basket. These places are where you still find fresh plant and animal foods that have only been been minimally processed. In the middle aisles of the store—and in the school vending machines—are where most of the EFLS lurk.

2. **Don't buy, or eat, anything that doesn't eventually rot.** A food engineered to live forever is usually full of chemicals. Food should be alive, and that means it should eventually die.

3. **Shop at the farmers' market, through a CSA, or at a farmstand whenever you can.** Get out of the supermarket, the corner deli, and the gas station, and you won't find those flashy fake foods.

4. **Be your own food detective.** Pay attention to where your food comes from (were those berries picked in your state or halfway around the world?) and how it is grown (Organic? Grass-fed? Humanely raised?). Read labels and ask questions. What's the story behind your food? And how do you feel about that story?

EAT REAL MEALS.

How you prepare and eat food is often just as important as what you eat. So:

1. **Cook.** The best way to take control of your meals is to cook whenever you can. As soon as you start cooking, you begin to learn about ingredients, to care about their quality, and to develop your sense of taste. You'll find over time that, when you prepare and eat real food, fast food gets boring—more of the same old taste of salt, fat, and sugar in every Chips Ahoy! or microwave pizza. There are so many more interesting tastes to experiment with in the kitchen and to experience at the table.

2. **Garden.** The freshest, best-tasting food you can eat is freshly picked food from the garden. Nothing is more satisfying than to cook and eat food you grew yourself.

3. **Try not to eat alone.** When we eat alone we eat without thinking, and we usually eat too much. Just think about how thoughtlessly you can put away a bag of chips or cookies in front of the television or computer, or while doing your homework. Eating should be social; food is more fun when you share it.

4. **Eat slowly and stop when you're full.** The food industry makes money by getting you to eat more than you need or even want to. Just because they offer a supersized 64-ounce Big Gulp and 1,250-calorie, 5-cup restaurant plate of spaghetti and meatballs doesn't mean that's the amount you should eat. Take back control of your

portions (a normal-size serving of spaghetti is about a cup and a half).

5. **Eat at the table.** I know, it sounds obvious. But we snack more than we dine these days; 19 percent of the meals consumed in America today are eaten in the car. The deepest joys of eating come when we slow down to savor our food and share it with people we love. The ***real*** meal—family and friends gathered around a table—is in danger of extinction. For the sake of your family's health and happiness, and for your own, do what you can to save it. You might be surprised how much enjoyment it can bring.

Q & A
with Michael Pollan

DID YOU EVER EAT PART OF STEER 534?

My plan was to eat a steak from my steer, but it never happened. I published an article about No. 534 before he was slaughtered, and the people at the feedlot and processing plant were so angry about it that they refused to give me my meat. They thought I had portrayed their business in an unfavorable light, which was true. This happens sometimes when you publish controversial articles.

So I did the next best thing: the night before No. 534 was scheduled to be slaughtered, I went to a steakhouse, ordered a ribeye cooked medium rare, and thought about my steer as I ate it.

The Blair Brothers did send me a check for my steer after he was processed and sold. I made a small profit of $30 on my $600 investment in No. 534.

WHY DIDN'T YOU NAME STEER #534?

I thought about it. In fact my son, Isaac, suggested I name him "Night," since he was black. But I decided that was a bad idea. He wasn't a pet and I didn't want to bond with him.

I also didn't want my readers to bond with him, because if they did they might be angry with me when I allow him to be slaughtered.

WOULD YOU EVER GO HUNTING AGAIN?

I haven't been hunting since my adventure with Angelo and I'm not sure I will do it again. It was a very emotional experience for me, and while I'm happy I did it, and learned a lot from hunting a boar, I don't feel like I need to do it again. Hunting is one of those experiences that it is important to do once—a rite of passage. But, like my bar mitzvah, once is probably enough for me. For one thing, I'm such a klutz that if I spent enough time in the woods with a gun, sooner or later someone would probably get hurt.

I have, however, gone mushroom hunting many times since writing the book, and find that I really enjoy it. It's still incredibly hard, but also incredibly rewarding when you find a nice fat porcini or chanterelle.

WHAT WAS THE WORST PART OF KILLING A CHICKEN?

The worst part of killing a chicken is discovering how quickly you can get used to it, especially when you're on an assembly (or disassembly) lines with other people for whom the work is routine. After the fifth or sixth chicken, it felt like a job, and I lost my sensitivity to what was at stake. That scared me.

WHAT'S YOUR FAVORITE FOOD?

My favorite food is probably paella, a one-pot dish from Spain that consists of clams, lobster, chicken, and chorizo sausage cooked on a bed of saffron rice. My mother, who makes the best paella anywhere, prepares it once every summer, when the family is together at the beach, so it's a special occasion meal.

LEAST FAVORITE FOOD?

My least favorite food would probably be organ meats, though I don't mind the occasional taste of pâté. I believe you should really eat the whole animal if you're going to eat meat, but most of the organs still gross me out.

HOW ABOUT WHEN YOU WERE A KID?

As a kid, I loved fast food and could eat three or four McDonald's hamburgers at a meal—not Big Macs, which hadn't been invented yet, but the single-patty ones. I loved the french fries too. I loved eating it all in the car, how the beefy french-fry smell would fill the station wagon! Now the very thought of that makes me a little nauseous.

DID YOU GARDEN WHEN YOU WERE GROWING UP?

Yes! I loved to garden when I was a kid. I learned how to do it from my grandfather, who had a big vegetable garden that he loved working in every spare moment. Starting around age ten, I planted a vegetable garden of my own behind our house on Long Island, though I didn't call it a garden—I called it a farm. And every time I had five or six ripe strawberries, I'd put them in a paper cup and sell them to my mom.

WHAT'S YOUR FAVORITE THING THAT YOU GROW IN YOUR GARDEN NOW?

These days I have a little vegetable garden in my front yard, where the lawn used to be. The best thing growing in it? These yellow cherry tomatoes called "Sun Gold"—they're so sweet that they hardly ever make it to the kitchen. We eat them before they get there.

WHERE, AND HOW, DO YOU SHOP FOR FOOD?

I live in Berkeley, a food-obsessed city, and that makes eating fresh organic food and grass-fed meat easier than in some other places. Also, our farmers' market operates fifty weeks of the year, because the weather is so good. (I know, we're very lucky.) I shop at the farmers market every Thursday, and get most of my produce there; I also buy my eggs and some of my meat and fish there. But we also go to the super-market every week. There, I try to buy organic, which is increasingly common (even Walmart now sells organic), and I look for local produce too, which shows up in the summer. Some supermarkets now sell grass-fed meat, but I ask for it even when they don't, as a way to encourage them to stock it.

But I think eating vegetables and fruit is so important that I buy them even when they're not organic—and even when they're not fresh. There's nothing wrong with frozen vegeta-bles, and they're usually a bargain. Some canned vegetables are a great deal too, though they often have too much salt. The key thing? Eat plants (including grains), animals, and fungi as lightly processed as you can find them at the prices you can afford.

HOW DID YOU LEARN TO COOK? HOW CAN I?

I'm still learning how to cook. But I started out by helping my mother in the kitchen. She's a great cook and doesn't think of cooking as a chore. I especially loved frying chicken, scram-bling eggs, and baking brownies—all magic transformations.

Later on, I bought a few simple cookbooks and learned by trying out recipes that sound appealing—this is something worth trying if your mom isn't much of a cook. Sometimes I'll try to figure out how to make something I've liked in a restaurant, which can be an interesting challenge when you don't have a recipe. But I've learned you can't go too far wrong in the kitchen, and people are more intimidated than they should be, probably because we watch cooking shows on TV that make cooking look like rocket science. As long as you start with good ingredients, don't get too fancy, and taste things along the way, it'll probably come out all right. Baking is different: You really need to follow recipes or you'll end up with stuff you don't want to eat.

WHAT'S YOUR FAVORITE RECIPE?

At the moment, it's a trick I learned from Angelo Garro for making poached eggs, which is my favorite breakfast. The challenge of poaching a perfect egg is keeping the thing together—the white part tends to wander off. Here's the trick: Boil water in a shallow pan. Before you crack the egg, sink the whole egg in the boiling water for exactly ten seconds. Then crack the egg into a big kitchen spoon and gently slide it into the water. The egg will hold together, and in three minutes you'll have a perfectly poached egg that you can remove with a slotted spoon. If you want to get fancy, put a few drops of balsamic vinegar on the egg. That's the way they serve poached eggs in Sicily, and it's delicious.

Further Resources

INTERNET

Active Kids Get Cooking (www.activekidsgetcooking.org.uk) is a program which promotes healthy cooking and eating in schools throughout the UK.

BBC Good Food: Get Kids Cooking! (www.bbcgoodfood.com/howto/guide/collection/family-kids) wants to get kids into cooking. Recipes and tips galore!

Chefsters (http://chefsters.com/) is an online club based on the TV show *Chefsters*. Members share recipes and other ideas for healthy eating.

Eat Local Challenge (www.eatlocalchallenge.com) offers resources and encouragement for people trying to eat locally.

Eat Well (www.eatwellguide.com) is an online source of sustainably raised meat, poultry, dairy, and eggs. Enter your zip code to find healthful, humane, and eco-friendly products from farms, stores, and restaurants in your area.

Eat Wild (www.eatwild.com) lists local suppliers for grass-fed meat and dairy products.

The Edible Schoolyard (www.edibleschoolyard.org) started as a one-acre garden and kitchen classroom at Martin Luther King, Jr. Middle School in Berkeley, California, and now has a small network of affiliate schools.

Food Routes (www.foodroutes.org) is a national nonprofit dedicated to "reintroducing Americans to their food—the seeds it grows from, the farmers who produce it, and the routes that carry it from the fields to our tables."

Jamie Oliver: School Dinners (www.jamieoliver.com/school-dinners.php) is the chef's website devoted to his campaign for better and healthier school meals.

The Leopold Center for Sustainable Agriculture (www.leopold.iastate.edu) "explores and cultivates alternatives that secure healthier people and landscapes in Iowa and the nation."

Local Harvest (www.localharvest.com) helps you connect with local farmers, CSAs, and farmers' markets.

Mycolog (www.mycolog.com) includes a variety of fascinating mushroom facts.

National Family Farm Coalition (www.nffc.net) is an organization to help support the livelihood of food producers, and feed the world's people within their own borders.

Pesticide Action Network (www.panna.org) promotes the elimination of dangerous pesticides and offers solutions that protect people and the environment.

Sky Vegetables (www.skyvegetables.com) builds and maintains sustainable gardens on rooftops.

Slow Food USA (www.slowfood.com) supports good, clean, and fair food while preserving traditional methods of preparation and farming.

Spoons Across America (www.spoonsacrossamerica.org) is a national nonprofit that promotes and organizes children's culinary education.

Sustainable Table (www.sustainabletable.org) offers a variety of excellent resources on local, sustainable, and community-based food, including special features for teachers and educators.

The Vertical Farm Project (www.verticalfarm.com) promotes indoor farming in urban settings.

Weston A. Price Foundation (www.westonaprice.org) is an archive of information on the sorts of traditional whole-food diets advocated by Weston A. Price. Local chapters are good resources for finding some of the best pastured animal foods.

W.K. Kellogg Foundation (www.wkkf.org) helps fund some great initiatives surrounding food attitudes and food policy—look at "What We Support: Healthy Kids."

VIDEO

Nourish is a public television program, aimed at high school students and narrated by Cameron Diaz, that looks at our relationship to food from a global perspective, connecting our food choices to the environment and to our health.

Fresh by Ana Jones is an inspiring look at the burgeoning movement to reform our food system.

Food Inc. is an investigative documentary by filmmaker Robert Kenner about industrial farming and its effect on our health.

What's on Your Plate is a documentary by Catherine Gund that follows two girls from New York City as they explore their place in the food chain.

King Corn is a documentary featuring two East Coast college grads who move to the Midwest to plant an acre of corn and follow it all the way to the dinner plate.

Acknowledgments

I had a lot of help in the kitchen preparing *The Omnivore's Dilemma*.

First to Gerry Marzorati, my longtime friend and editor at the *New York Times Magazine*, who first suggested five years ago that I spend some time writing about food for the magazine. Unbeknownst to either of us, he was pointing me down the path that led to this book.

I am especially grateful to the farmers and the foragers I write about here. George Naylor in Iowa, Joel Salatin in Virginia, and Angelo Garro in California were my food-chain Virgils, helping me to follow the food from earth to plate and to navigate the omnivore's dilemma. All three gave unstintingly of their time, their wisdom, and their always excellent company. Thanks, too, to the hunters and gatherers who graciously welcomed so rank an amateur on their expeditions: Anthony Tassinello, Ben Baily, Bob Carrou, Richard Hylton, Jean-Pierre Moulle, Sue Moore, and David Evans.

In educating myself on food and agriculture, I've incurred a great many debts. Among my most generous and influential teachers have been: Joan Gussow, Marion Nestle, Fred Kirschenmann, Alice Waters, Todd Dawson, Paul Rozin, Wes Jackson, and Wendell Berry. Thanks also, for information and insight, to Bob Scowcroft, Allan Nation, Kelly Brownell, Ricardo Salvador, Carlo Petrini, Jo Robinson, David Arora, Ignacio Chapela, Miguel Altieri, Peter Hoffman, Dan Barber, Drew and Myra Goodman, Bill Niman, Gene Kahn, and Eliot Coleman.

Many people supported the writing of this book in other ways. In California, Michael Schwarz generously read the manuscript and offered timely encouragement and helpful suggestions, reminding me what a good editor he was before he forsook print for television. In Berkeley, the faculty, staff, and students of the Graduate School of Journalism, and in particular Dean Orville Schell, have created a stimulating and supportive community in which to do this work. Mark Danner, an old friend and once again a colleague, has, as ever, provided a valuable sounding board. The students in my food chain class have taught me more than they probably realize about these issues over the past few years. Mesa Refuge, in Point Reyes Station, provided the perfect setting in which to write and research a key chapter. And the John S. and James L. Knight Foundation has supported my research in crucial ways.

I'm especially grateful to Chad Heeter, for his dogged research and fact-checking, not to mention his willingness to accompany me on a futile quest to gather salt in San Francisco Bay. Nathanael Johnson, Felicia Mello, and Elena Conis nailed down several elusive facts just when it looked like they might get away. My assistant,

Jaime Gross, contributed to this project in many ways, but I'm particularly grateful for her superb research and fact-checking.

In New York, I'm grateful for the excellent work and good cheer of Liza Darnton, Kate Griggs, Sarah Hutson, and Tracy Locke at the Penguin Press, my publishing home. Thanks to Liz Farrell at ICM. At the *New York Times Magazine*, where some of the material in this book first appeared, I've profited handsomely from the superb editing of Paul Tough and Alex Star and (before they moved on to other magazines) Adam Moss and Dan Zalewski.

In a publishing industry not known for loyalty or continuity, I've been blessed by the constancy of both my editor and agent. This is the fourth book of mine that Ann Godoff has edited, albeit at three different houses. At this point I can't imagine doing a book with anyone else, which is probably why I keep following her around Manhattan. Her moral, intellectual, emotional, and financial support is a critical ingredient in the making of this book. This is also the fourth book of mine represented by Amanda Urban, a verb that doesn't come close to capturing everything she does to keep me whole and on the proper path.

Speaking of constancy, this is also the fourth time I've relied on Mark Edmundson to read and comment on a book manuscript; as ever, his editorial and reading suggestions, as well as his literary judgment, have been invaluable. This time around, he (and his family) contributed in another way as well, by joining me for one of the meals chronicled in these pages. Thanks to Liz, Willie, and Matthew for their gameness, good appetite, and hospitality.

But the prize for gameness in the pursuit of a book chapter must go to Judith, who shared the two meals that bookend the book—the McDonald's cheeseburger at one end and the wild boar at the other—and so much more. A book becomes a sometimes disagreeable member of the family for a period of years, but Judith treated this one with patience, understanding, and good humor. Far more crucial to the book, though, has been her editing. Since I first began publishing, Judith has been my indispensable first reader, and there's no one whose instincts about writing I trust more.

Last but no longer least is Isaac. This is the first book Isaac has been old enough and sufficiently interested in to actually help me with. His own approach to food—Isaac is the pickiest eater I know—has taught me a great deal about the omnivore's dilemma. Though he declined to taste the boar, Isaac's contribution to this book—coming in the form of smart suggestions, stimulating conversations at the dinner table, and, on the bad days, the best comfort a father could wish for—has been more precious than he can know. Thank you.

I had further help creating this young reader's edition of *The Omnivore's Dilemma*. Richie Chevat did a masterful job of adapting the book for a new generation of readers, streamlining a complex narrative without ever over-simplifying it—not an easy feat. Malia Wollan, my research assistant, contributed to the project in so many ways: gathering and researching all the new visual material, reading and commenting on each draft, and working tirelessly to insure the book's accuracy. Alisha Niehaus, the book's editor, somehow managed to keep the project, with its many chefs and moving parts, right on track. I'm grateful for her skillful editing, unwavering enthusiasm, and faith in both the book and its audience. Thanks also to Shanta Newlin, for getting the word out so skillfully, and to Jasmin Rubero, for her design, and her imagination in giving visual expression to all this information.

SOURCES

Listed below, by chapter, are the main works referred to in the text, as well as others that supplied me with facts or influenced my thinking. Web site URLs are current as of March 2009. All cited articles by me are available at www.michaelpollan.com.

INTRODUCTION

Pollan, Michael. *The Botany of Desire* (New York: Random House, 2001). See the chapter on potatoes, as well as the bibliography on control.

———. "Power Steer," *New York Times Magazine*, March 31, 2002.

PART I
CHAPTER 1: HOW CORN TOOK OVER AMERICA

In addition to the printed sources below, I learned a great deal about the natural and social history of *Zea mays* from my conversations with Ricardo Salvador at Iowa State (www.foodandsocietyfellows.org/fellows.cfm?id=80342) and Ignacio Chapela at the University of California at Berkeley. Ignacio introduced me to his colleague Todd Dawson, who not only helped me understand what a C-4 plant is, but generously tested various foods and hair samples for corn content using his department's mass spectrometer.

The two indispensable books on the history of corn are:

Fussell, Betty. *The Story of Corn* (New York: Knopf, 1994). The statistics on wheat versus corn consumption are on page 215.

Warman, Arturo. *Corn & Capitalism: How a Botanical Bastard Grew to Global Dominance*. Trans. Nancy L. Westrate (Chapel Hill: University of North Carolina Press, 2003).

Other helpful works touching on the history of corn include:

Anderson, Edgar. *Plants, Man and Life* (Berkeley: University of California Press, 1952).

Crosby, Alfred W. *Germs, Seeds & Animals: Studies in Ecological History* (Armonk, NY: M. E. Sharpe, 1994).

————. *Ecological Imperialism: The Biological Expansion of Europe, 900–1900* (Cambridge, U.K.: Cambridge University Press, 1986).

Diamond, Jared. *Guns, Germs, and Steel* (New York: W. W. Norton, 1997).

Eisenberg, Evan. *The Ecology of Eden* (New York: Alfred A. Knopf, 1998). Very good on the coevolutionary relationship of grasses and humankind.

Iltis, Hugh H. "From Teosinte to Maize: The Catastrophic Sexual Mutation," *Science* 222, no. 4626 (November 25, 1983).

Mann, Charles C. *1491: New Revelations of the Americas Before Columbus* (New York: Alfred A. Knopf, 2005). Excellent on the evolutionary origins of the plant and pre-Columbian maize agriculture.

Nabhan, G. P. *Enduring Seeds: Native American Agriculture and Wild Plant Conservation* (San Francisco: North Point Press, 1989).

Rifkin, Jeremy. *Beyond Beef: The Rise and Fall of the Cattle Culture* (New York: Plume, 1993).

Sargent, Frederick. *Corn Plants: Their Uses and Ways of Life* (Boston: Houghton Mifflin, 1901).

Smith, C. Wayne (Ed.). *Corn: Origin, History, Technology and Production* (New Jersey: John Wiley & Sons, 2004, figure 1.4.5).

Wallace, H. A., and E. N. Bressman. *Corn and Corn Growing* (New York: John Wiley & Sons, 1949).

Weatherford, Jack. *Indian Givers: How the Indians of the Americas Transformed the World* (New York: Crown, 1988).

Will, George F., and George E. Hyde. *Corn Among the Indians of the Upper Missouri* (Lincoln: University of Nebraska Press, 1917).

CHAPTER 2: THE FARM, AND CHAPTER 3: FROM FARM TO FACTORY

The best accounts of the history and workings of the commodity corn complex in the United States are a series of studies by Richard Manning and C. Ford Runge commissioned by the Midwest Commodities and Conservation Initiative, a joint project of the World Wildlife Fund, the American Farmland Trust, and the Henry A. Wallace Center for Agricultural & Environmental Policy.

Manning, Richard. *Commodities, Consensus, and Conservation: A Search for Opportunities* and *The Framework of a Commodities System* (April 2001).
Runge, C. Ford. *King Corn: The History, Trade, and Environmental Consequences of Corn (Maize) Production in the United States* (September 2002).

In writing about the rise of industrial agriculture I also drew on the following works:

Kimbrell, Andrew. *The Fatal Harvest Reader: The Tragedy of Industrial Agriculture* (Washington, D.C.: Island Press, 2002).
Manning, Richard. *Against the Grain* (New York: North Point Press, 2004).
Morgan, Dan. *Merchants of Grain* (New York: Viking, 1979).
Russell, Edmund. *War and Nature: Fighting Humans and Insects with Chemicals from World War I to Silent Spring* (Cambridge, U.K.: Cambridge University Press, 2001).
Schwab, Jim. *Raising Less Corn and More Hell: Midwestern Farmers Speak Out* (Urbana: University of Illinois Press, 1988). See the interview with George Naylor beginning on page 111.
Scott, James. *Seeing Like a State: How Certain Schemes to Improve the Human Condition Have Failed* (New Haven: Yale University Press, 1998). Scott, an anthropologist and political scientist, puts industrial agriculture in the illuminating context of other modernist schemes, including architecture and Soviet collectivization.
Smil, Vaclav. *Enriching the Earth: Fritz Haber, Carl Bosch, and the Transformation of World Food Production* (Cambridge, MA: M.I.T. Press, 2001). This indispensable book tells the story of Fritz Haber's life and work, explains the technology of synthesizing nitrogen, and explores its impact on the environment and world population.
———. *Feeding the World* (Cambridge, MA: M.I.T. Press, 2000).
Wargo, John. *Our Children's Toxic Legacy* (New Haven: Yale University Press, 1996). An important work on the regulation and biology of pesticides.

For detailed information on individual pesticides, see the Web site of the Pesticide Action Network (www.panna.org). On atrazine, the herbicide most widely applied to U.S. cornfields, see Hayes, Tyrone, et al. "Atrazine-Induced Hermaphroditism at 0.1 PPB in American Frogs *(Rana pipiens)*: Laboratory and Field Evidence," *Environmental Health Perspectives* 3, no. 4 (April 2003), and Hayes, Tyrone B. "There Is No Denying This: Defusing the Confusion about Atrazine," *BioScience* 54, no. 12 (December 2004).

On the question of industrial agriculture's dependence on fossil fuel, there is a rich and somewhat daunting literature. The late Marty Bender, at the Land Institute, helped me to navigate a great many complexities, as did David Pimentel at Cornell. The figure of 0.25 gallons of oil per bushel of corn comes from unpublished research by Ricardo Salvador (see his Web site, cited earlier); David Pimentel, et al., offers a figure of 0.33 gallons in "Environmental, Energetic, and Economic Comparisons of Organic and Conventional Farming Systems," *BioScience* 55, no. 7 (July 2005). For more on the general subject of energy use in agriculture, see chapter 10.

On the equally vexing topic of federal agriculture policy, I have had many fine tutors, foremost among them George Naylor himself, as well as the staff of the National Family Farms Coalition (www.nffc.net), of which he is president. The subsidy facts on page 47 come from the Environmental Working Group's Farm Subsidy Database (farm.ewg.org/farm/summary. php). Other sources for this material (which figures in chapter 3 as well) included:

Michael Duffy, Iowa State (www.sust.ag.iastate.edu/gpsa/faculty/duffy.html).
Dan McGuire, American Corngrower's Association (www.acga.org). McGuire generously shared his archive of documents on the history of U.S. agricultural policy since the 1930s.
Daryll Ray, University of Tennessee Institute of Agriculture (www.agpolicy. org). See especially his report "Rethinking U.S. Agricultural Policy: Changing Course to Secure Farmer Livelihoods Worldwide" (issued by the Institute's Agricultural Policy Analysis Center in September 2003 and available at www.agpolicy.org/blueprint.html).
Mark Ritchie, Institute for Agriculture and Trade Policy (www.iatp.org).
Other sources on the history of farm policy:
Critser, Greg. *Fat Land: How Americans Became the Fattest People in the World* (Boston: Houghton Mifflin, 2003). Critser summarizes the history of farm policy since the 1970s, linking it to the current surplus of food and the consequent epidemic of obesity.

Duscha, Julius. "Up, Up, Up: Butz Makes Hay Down on the Farm," *New York Times Magazine,* April 16, 1972.

Rasmussen, Wayne D., and Gladys L. Baker. *Price Support and Adjustment Programs from 1933 through 1978: A Short History* (Washington, D.C.: USDA Economics, Statistics and Cooperatives Service, 1978).

Ritchie, Mark. *The Loss of Our Family Farms: Inevitable Results or Conscious Policies? A Look at the Origins of Government Policies for Agriculture* (Minneapolis: League of Rural Voters, 1979). Ritchie also shared with me his archive of policy statements by the Committee for Economic Development. The CED, an influential business group from the 1950s through the 1970s, led the campaign to dismantle New Deal farm policy. See their "Toward a Realistic Farm Program" (1967) and "A New U.S. Farm Policy for Changing World Food Needs" (1974).

————, et al. *United States Dumping on World Agricultural Markets* (Minneapolis: Institute for Agriculture and Trade Policy, 2003).

Chapter 4: The Grain Elevator

My estimate of the portion of the U.S. corn crop that passes through the corporate hands of Cargill and ADM is based on Richard Manning's reporting in *Against the Grain* (New York: North Point Press, 2004, p. 128) that ADM buys 12 percent of the nation's corn crop, and on a 1999 estimate by Alexander Cockburn and Jeffrey St. Clair (*Counterpunch*, November 20, 1999) that Cargill buys 23 percent of the corn crop.

Cronon, William. *Nature's Metropolis: Chicago and the Great West* (New York: W. W. Norton, 1991).

Kneen, Brewster. *Invisible Giant: Cargill and Its Transnational Strategies* (London: Pluto Press, 2002).

Manning, Richard. *Against the Grain* (New York: North Point Press, 2004). Manning uses the metaphor of biomass to describe the surplus of commodity grain on page 137.

Sahagún, B. de *(Historia general de las cosas de Nueva España, 1558–69) Florentine Codex: A General History of the Things of New Spain.* 12 vols. Trans. A. J. O. Anderson and C. E. Dibble (Santa Fe, NM: School of American Research and University of Utah, 1950–69).

Michael Duffy and George Naylor helped me to sort out exactly what a farmer receives for a bushel of corn from the market and the government.

That said, the various formulae and contingencies involved, not to mention the nomenclature, are dauntingly complex, and neither Naylor nor Duffy bears responsibility for any oversimplifications or errors in my computations. What I call the county "target price" is technically a "marketing loan rate," but since the program is structured in such a way as to make taking out loans unattractive (unlike the old nonrecourse loan program), the wording is confusing. However, it's important to understand that this price level is not a target price in the sense that it once was, when the USDA set a floor for commodity prices that it then supported by offering farmers nonrecourse loans.

Chapter 5: The Feedlot—Turning Corn into Meat

This chapter had its origins in a piece I wrote for the *New York Times* called "Power Steer" (March 31, 2002). In researching cattle and the U.S. cattle industry, I learned a great deal from Bill Niman of Niman Ranch in Oakland; Kansas feedlot operator Mike Callicrate; Colorado rancher Dale Lassiter; animal-handling expert Temple Grandin (www.grandin.com); South Dakota bison rancher and writer Dan O'Brien; Cornell microbiologist James Russell; and Rich and Ed Blair, the South Dakota ranchers profiled in this chapter. Valuable published sources include:

Carlson, Laurie Winn. *Cattle: An Informal Social History* (Chicago: Ivan R. Dee, 2001).

Durning, Alan B., and Holly B. Brough. *Taking Stock: Animal Farming and the Environment* (Washington, D.C.: World Watch Institute, 1991).

Engel, Cindy. *Wild Health: How Animals Keep Themselves Well and What We Can Learn from Them* (Boston: Houghton Mifflin, 2002).

Frazier, Ian. *Great Plains* (New York: Picador, 1989).

Grandin, Temple. *Animal Handling in Meat Plants* (video: Grandin Livestock Handling System, www.grandin.com, undated).

Hamilton, Doug. *Modern Meat* (a documentary for *Frontline;* aired on PBS, April 18, 2002).

Johnson, James R., and Gary E. Larson. *Grassland Plants of South Dakota and the Northern Great Plains* (Brookings, SD: South Dakota State University, 1999).

Lappé, Frances Moore. *Diet for a Small Planet* (New York: Ballantine Books, 1991). Still the strongest case against eating beef, though in making it Lappé assumes a production system based on grain.

Luttwak, Edward. "Sane Cows, or BSE Isn't the Worst of It," *London Review of Books* 23, no. 3 (February 8, 2001).

Manning, Richard. *Grassland: The History, Biology, and Promise of the American Prairie* (New York: Penguin, 1997).

Nierenberg, Danielle. *Happier Meals: Rethinking the Global Meat Industry* (Washington, D.C.: Worldwatch Institute, 2005).

O'Brien, Dan. *Buffalo for the Broken Heart: Restoring Life to a Black Hills Ranch* (New York: Random House, 2001). This is a rancher's account of the cattle business and a promising alternative to it. O'Brien's ranch happens to share a fence with the Blairs.

Ozeki, Ruth L. *My Year of Meats* (New York: Penguin, 1999). Very funny, well-researched novel about the U.S. meat industry.

Rampton, Sheldon, and John Stauber. *Mad Cow U.S.A.: Could the Nightmare Happen Here?* (Monroe, ME: Common Courage Press, 1997).

Rifkin, Jeremy. *Beyond Beef* (New York: Plume, 1993).

Robinson, Jo. *Why Grassfed is Best!: The Surprising Benefits of Grassfed Meats, Eggs, and Dairy Products* (Vashon, WA: Vashon Island Press, 2000). The list of possible ingredients in cattle feed from page 69 comes from page 10 of this book.

Russell, James B. *Rumen Microbiology and Its Role in Ruminant Nutrition* (Ithaca, NY: self-published, 2002).

Schell, Orville. *Modern Meat: Antibiotics, Hormones, and the Pharmaceutical Farm* (New York: Vintage, 1985).

Schlosser, Eric. *Fast Food Nation* (Boston: Houghton Mifflin, 2001).

Sinclair, Upton. *The Jungle* (London: Penguin, 1985).

Smil, Vaclav. *Feeding the World: A Challenge for the Twenty-First Century* (Cambridge, MA: M.I.T. Press, 2001).

CHAPTER 6: PROCESSED FOOD

I've written about the imperatives behind the processing of food on several occasions (the articles are listed below), and on that subject have profited enormously from my conversations with nutritionists Marion Nestle and Joan Gussow, and my readings of industry trade magazines, especially *Food Technology* (Institute of Food Technologists, Chicago). Larry Johnson at the Center for Crops Utilization Research at Iowa State was generous with his time and expertise, showing and telling me all I wanted to know about the wet-milling of corn and soybeans. The Corn Refiners Association (www.corn.org) is an invaluable resource on the history, technology, and products of corn refining; see especially their annual reports, a trove of interesting statistics and history. Their new campaign offering the "facts" about high fructose corn syrup, which I refer to in the next chapter, may also be of interest (www.sweetsurprise.com).

Ettlinger, Steve. *Twinkie, Deconstructed* (New York: Hudson Street Press, 2007).

Ford, Brian J. *The Future of Food* (New York: Thames & Hudson, 2000).

Goodman, Michael, and Michael Redclift. *Refashioning Nature: Food, Ecology, and Culture* (London: Routledge, 1991).

Gussow, Joan Dye, ed. *The Feeding Web: Issues in Nutritional Ecology* (Palo Alto, CA: Bull Publishing, 1978). This remains an invaluable anthology (unfortunately out of print) on the entire range of food issues, and serves as a reminder that much of the discussion our culture is having about the politics and ecology of food today is a reprise of a discussion that took place in the 1970s. The quote about the relationship between a food's identity and its raw materials and the excerpt from the IFF annual report appear in an essay by Gussow titled "Whatever Happened to Food? Or Does It Pay to Fool with Mother Nature?" pp. 200–4.

Levenstein, Harvey. *Paradox of Plenty* (Berkeley: University of California Press, 2003).

———. *Revolution at the Table: The Transformation of the American Diet* (Berkeley: University of California Press, 2003).

Nestle, Marion. *Food Politics* (Berkeley: University of California Press, 2002).

Pollan, Michael. "Naturally," *New York Times Magazine,* May 13, 2001.

———. "The Futures of Food," *New York Times Magazine,* May 4, 2003.

———. "The (Agri)cultural Contradictions of Obesity," *New York Times Magazine,* October 12, 2003.

Schlosser, Eric. *Fast Food Nation* (Boston: Houghton Mifflin, 2001).

Tannahill, Reay. *Food in History* (New York: Stein and Day, 1973).

Tisdale, Sally. *The Best Thing I Ever Tasted: The Secret of Food* (New York: Riverhead, 2001).

CHAPTER 7: FAT FROM CORN

Bray, George, et al. "Consumption of High-fructose Corn Syrup in Beverages May Play a Role in Epidemic of Obesity," *American Journal of Clinical Nutrition* 79 (2004), 537–43.

Brownell, Kelly D., and Katherine Battle Horgen. *Food Fight: The Inside Story of the Food Industry, America's Obesity Crisis, and What We Can Do About It* (Chicago: Contemporary Books, 2004).

Critser, Greg. *Fat Land: How Americans Became the Fattest People in the World* (Boston: Houghton Mifflin, 2003). His research into calories in servings of McDonald's fries over the years appears in Chapter 5, in the sidebar on page 97.

Drewnowski, Adam, and S. E. Specter. "Poverty and Obesity: The Role of Energy Density and Energy Costs in the American," *American Journal of Clinical Nutrition* 79 (January 2004), 6–16. For this important article, Drewnowski and Specter studied how many and what kind of calories a dollar can buy in various parts of the supermarket.

Kroc, Ray. *Grinding It Out: The Making of McDonald's* (Chicago: Contemporary Books, 1977).

Lender, Mark E., and James Kirby Martin. *Drinking in America: A History* (New York: The Free Press, 1982).

Logsdon, Gene. *Good Spirits: A New Look at Ol' Demon Alcohol* (White River Junction, VT: Chelsea Green, 1999).

Love, John F. *McDonald's: Behind the Arches* (New York: Bantam, 1986). Love tells the story of David Wallerstein, pages 296–97.

Narayan, K. M. Venkat, et al. "Lifetime Risk for Diabetes Mellitus in the United States," *Journal of the American Medical Association* 290 (2003), 1884–90.

Nestle, Marion. *Food Politics* (Berkeley: University of California Press, 2002).

Pollan, Michael. "The (Agri)cultural Contradictions of Obesity," *New York Times Magazine,* October 12, 2003. This chapter extends and elaborates the argument I made in this article.

———. *The Botany of Desire* (New York: Random House, 2001). See the material on sweetness in the chapter on apples, as well as the bibliography on sweetness.

———. "Farmer in Chief," *New York Times Magazine,* October 12, 2008.

Rorabaugh, W. J. *The Alcoholic Republic: An American Tradition* (Oxford: Oxford University Press, 1979). An eye-opening account of American drinking habits from the Revolution through the temperance movement.

Satcher, David. "The Surgeon General's Call to Action to Prevent and Decrease Overweight and Obesity," (Washington, D.C.: U.S. Department of Health and Human Services, 2001); available on the Web at www.surgeongeneral.gov.

Winson, Anthony. "Bringing Political Economy into the Debate on the Obesity Epidemic," *Agriculture and Human Values* 21 (2004), 299–312.

Chapter 8: The Omnivore's Dilemma

Allport, Susan. *The Primal Feast: Food, Sex, Foraging, and Love* (Lincoln, NE: Writers Club Press, 2003).

Berry, Wendell. "The Pleasures of Eating," in *What Are People For?* (New York: North Point Press, 1990), pp.145–52.

Fernández-Armesto, Felipe. *Near a Thousand Tables: A History of Food* (New York: The Free Press, 2002).

Harris, Marvin. *The Sacred Cow and the Abominable Pig: Riddles of Food and Culture* (New York: Simon & Schuster, 1987).

Kass, Leon. *The Hungry Soul* (New York: The Free Press, 1994). I found a William Ralph Inge quote in this endlessly suggestive philosophical inquiry into how the particular nature of human eating defines us.

Katz, Solomon H. "Food and Biocultural Evolution: A Model for the Investigation of Modern Nutritional Problems," *Nutritional Anthropology,* ed. Francis E. Johnston (New York: Alan R. Liss, 1987), 41–63.

Lévi-Strauss, Claude. *The Origin of Table Manners: Introduction to a Science of Mythology,* Volume 3. Trans. John and Doreen Weightman (New York: Harper & Row, 1978).

———. *The Raw and the Cooked: Introduction to a Science of Mythology,* Volume 1. Trans. John and Doreen Weightman (Chicago: University of Chicago Press, 1983).

Levy, Ariel. "Carb Panic," *New York,* December 12, 2002.

Nestle, Marion. *Food Politics* (Berkeley: University of California Press, 2002).

Mooallem, Jon. "The Last Supper: Living by One-handed Food Alone," *Harper's* (July 2005). My source for the statistic that 19 percent of American meals are eaten in the car.

O'Connor, Anahad. "The Claim: The Tongue is Mapped Into Four Areas of Taste," *New York Times*, November 11, 2008.

Pinker, Steven. *How the Mind Works* (New York: W. W. Norton, 1997). Valuable on hunting and gathering; visual perception; the cognitive niche; and the evolution of disgust.

Pollan, Michael. "Our National Eating Disorder," *New York Times Magazine,* October 17, 2004.

Rozin, Paul. "The Selection of Foods by Rats, Humans, and Other Animals" in *Advances in the Study of Behavior,* Volume 6, eds. J. Rosenblatt, R. A. Hide, C. Beer, and E. Shaw (New York: Academic Press, 1976), pp. 21–76.

———. "Food Is Fundamental, Fun, Frightening, and Far-Reaching," *Social Research* 66, no. 1 (Spring 1999). This is a special issue on food with many excellent essays.

————, et al. "Attitudes to Food and the Role of Food in Life: Comparisons of Flemish Belgian, France, Japan and the United States," *Appetite* (1999).

————, et al. "The Borders of the Self: Contamination Sensitivity and Potency of the Mouth, Other Apertures and Body Parts," *Journal of Research in Personality* 29 (1995), 318–40.

————, et al. "The Cultural Evolution of Disgust," in *Food Preferences and Taste: Continuity and Change,* ed. H. M. Macbeth (Oxford: Berghahn, 1997).

————, et al. "Disgust," in *Handbook of Emotions,* 2nd ed., eds. Lewis M. and J. Haviland (New York: Guilford, 1999).

————, et al. "Lay American Conceptions of Nutrition: Dose Insensitivity, Categorical Thinking, Contagion, and the Monotonic Mind," *Health Psychology* 15 (1996), 438–47.

————, and A. E. Fallon. "A Perspective on Disgust," *Psychological Review* 94, no. 1 (1987), 23–41.

————, and J. Schulkin. "Food Selection," in *Handbook of Behavioral Neurobiology, Food and Water Intake,* Volume 10, ed. E. M. Stricker (New York: Plenum, 1990), 297–328.

Taubes, Gary. "What If Fat Doesn't Make You Fat?" *New York Times Magazine,* July 7, 2002.

Wrangham, Richard, et al. "The Raw and the Stolen: Cooking and the Ecology of Human Origins," *Current Anthropology* 40, no. 5 (December 1999). Wrangham argues persuasively here and elsewhere that it is cooking that made us human.

CHAPTER 9: MY FAST-FOOD MEAL

"A Full Serving of Nutrition Facts," pamphlet published by McDonald's (2003).

Horovitz, Bruce. "Marketers Feed Kids' Craving for Dippable Food," *USA Today*, posted online April 8, 2004.

Schlosser, Eric. *Fast Food Nation* (Boston: Houghton Mifflin, 2001).

On ethanol and air pollution see Libecap, Gary D. "Environmental Phantasm: Political Forces Keep Dreams of Ethanol Alive," Property and Environment Research Center (PERC) (June 2003); http://www.perc.org/articles/article230.php and the Web site of the Sierra Club, www.sierraclub.org.

PART II
CHAPTER 10: BIG ORGANIC

On the pastoral tradition, Leo Marx is invaluable. I learned a great deal about farming, grass, animals, and Joel Salatin from Salatin's books, all of which are worth reading, even if you aren't planning to raise chickens; he's a consistently entertaining writer. *Stockman Grass Farmer,* Allan Nation's monthly tabloid for grass farmers, is the indispensable media outlet for the movement. The USDA National Organic Program website includes their producer and labeling guidelines (www.ams.usda.gov/nop).

Klinkenborg, Verlyn. *Making Hay* (Guilford, CT: Lyons Press, 1997).
Marx, Leo. *The Machine in the Garden* (Oxford: Oxford University Press, 2000).
Pollan, Michael. "Sustaining Vision," *Gourmet* (September 2002).
Salatin, Joel. *Family Friendly Farming* (Swoope, VA: Polyface, 2001).
———. *Holy Cows & Hog Heaven: The Food Buyer's Guide to Farm Friendly Food* (Swoope, VA: Polyface, 2004).
———. *Pastured Poultry Profit$: Net $25,000 in 6 Months on 20 Acres* (Swoope, VA: Polyface, 1996).
———. *Polyface Farm* (video: Moonstar Films, www.moonstarfilms.com, undated).
———. *$alad Bar Beef* (Swoope, VA: Polyface, 1995).
———. *You Can Farm: The Entrepreneur's Guide to Start and $ucceed in a Farming Enterprise* (Swoope, VA: Polyface, 1998).
Virgil. *Eclogues, Georgics, Aeneid 1–6,* Volume 1. Trans. H. Rushton Fairclough (Cambridge, MA: Harvard University Press, 1986).
Williams, Raymond. *The Country and the City* (New York: Oxford University Press, 1973).

CHAPTER 11: MORE BIG ORGANIC

Parts of this chapter are based on an article on the industrialization of organic food I published in the *New York Times Magazine* (May 13, 2001). Among the sources in the organic movement who have done the most to educate me are: Joan Gussow; Fred Kirschenmann at the Leopold Center at Iowa State (www.leopold.iastate.edu); Bob Scowcroft at the Organic Farming Research Foundation; Michael Sligh and Hope Shand at ETC (www.etcgroup.org); the late Betsy Lydon; farmer and author Eliot Coleman; farmer Woody Derycks; farmers Tom and Denesse Willy;

farmer Warren Weber; farmer and author Michael Ableman; Drew and Myra Goodman and Mark Merino at Earthbound Farm; George Siemens at Organic Valley; John Diener at Greenways Organic; Gene Kahn at General Mills; Miguel Altieri; Julie Guthman; Peter Rosset; Charles Benbrook; Roger Blobaum; and Maria Rodale. Several of the scientific articles comparing organic and conventional produce are included in the list of printed sources following; others are available at the Organic Center (www .organic-center.org).

Altieri, Miguel. *Agroecology: The Science of Sustainable Agriculture* (Boulder, CO: Westview Press, 1995).

———. "The Ecological Role of Biodiversity in Agroecosystems," *Agric. Ecosyst. and Env.* 74 (1999), 19–31.

Barron, R. C. ed. *The Garden and Farm Books of Thomas Jefferson* (Golden, CO: Fulcrum, 1987). In a letter to his daughter, Jefferson suggests that the problems she's having with insects could be the result of exhausted soil; see page 156. Eliot Coleman first told me about this passage.

Belasco, Warren. *Appetite for Change: How the Counterculture Took on the Food Industry 1966–1988* (New York: Pantheon, 1989). Belasco persuasively traces organic food's roots to the sixties counterculture.

Benbrook, Charles M. *Elevating Antioxidant Levels in Food Through Organic Farming and Food Processing: An Organic Center State of Science Review* (Foster, RI: Organic Center, 2005).

Berry, Wendell. *The Gift of Good Land* (San Francisco: North Point Press, 1981).

———. *Home Economics* (San Francisco: North Point Press, 1987).

———. *The Unsettling of America: Culture and Agriculture* (San Francisco: Sierra Club Books, 1977).

Carbonaro, Marina, and Maria Mattera. "Polyphenoloxidase Activity and Polyphenol Levels in Organically and Conventionally Grown Peaches," *Food Chemistry* 72 (2001), 419–24.

Chassy, A. W., et al. "A Three-Year Comparison of the Content of Antioxidant Microconstituents and Several Quality Characteristics in Organic and Conventionally Managed Tomatoes and Bell Peppers," *Journal of Agricultural and Food Chemistry* 54 (2006), 8244–52.

Coleman, Eliot. "Can Organics Save the Family Farm?" *The Rake* (September 2004).

Curl, Cynthia L., et al. "Organophosphorus Pesticide Exposure of Urban and Suburban Pre-school Children with Organic and Conventional Diets," *Environmental Health Perspectives* 3, no. 3 (March 2003).

Davis, Donald R., et al. "Changes in USDA Food Composition Data for 43 Garden Crops, 1950 to 1999," *Journal of the American College of Nutrition* 23, no. 6 (2004), 669–82.

———. "Trade-Offs in Agriculture and Nutrition," *Food Technology* 59, no. 3, 120.

Dewhurst, R. J., et al. "Comparison of Grass and Legume Silages for Milk Production," *Journal of Dairy Science* 86, no. 8 (2003), 2598–2611.

Diamond, Jared. *Collapse: How Societies Choose to Fail or Succeed* (New York: Viking, 2005).

Freyfogle, Eric T., ed. *The New Agrarianism: Land, Culture, and the Community of Life* (Washington, D.C.: Island Press, 2001).

Guthman, Julie. *Agrarian Dreams* (Berkeley: University of California Press, 2004).

Harvey, Graham. *The Forgiveness of Nature: The Story of Grass* (London: Jonathan Cape/Random House, 2001). For the great humus controversy, see chapter 17, pages 300–19.

Hayes, Tyrone, et al. "Atrazine-Induced Hermaphroditism at 0.1 PPB in American Frogs *(Rana pipiens):* Laboratory and Field Evidence," *Environmental Health Perspectives* 3, no. 4 (April 2003).

———. "There Is No Denying This: Defusing the Confusion about Atrazine," *BioScience* 54, no. 12 (December 2004).

Howard, Sir Albert. *An Agricultural Testament* (New York: Oxford University Press, 1943).

———. *The Soil and Health* (New York: Schocken, 1972).

Lang, Tim. "Food Safety and Public Health: Will the Crisis Ever End?" Cardiff Law School Public Lecture Series: 4, Thames Valley University, 2001.

Lewis, W. J., et al. "A Total System Approach to Sustainable Pest Management," *The Proceedings of the National Academy of Sciences* 84 (1997).

Manning, Richard. *Commodities, Consensus and Conservation* (April 2001). In his study of commodity agriculture, Manning quotes Plato on agriculture's impact on the environment, and the importance of healthy soils (page 2):

What now remains of the formerly rich land is like the skeleton of a sick man . . . Formerly, many of the mountains were arable. The plains that were full of rich soil are now marshes. Hills that were once covered with forests and produced abundant pasture now produce only food for bees. Once the land was enriched by yearly rains, which were not lost, as they are now, by flowing from the bare land into the sea. The soil was deep, it absorbed and kept the water in loamy soil, and the water that soaked into the hills fed springs and running streams everywhere. Now the abandoned shrines at spots where formerly there were springs attest that our description of the land is true.

Marx, Leo. *The Machine in the Garden* (Oxford: Oxford University Press, 2000).

Mitchell, A. E., et al. "Comparison of the Total Phenolic and Ascorbic Acid Content of Freeze-Dried and Air-Dried Marionberry, Strawberry, and Corn Grown Using Conventional, Organic, and Sustainable Agricultural Practices," *Journal of Agricultural and Food Chemistry* 51 (2003),1237–41.

Pirog, Rich, and Andrew Benjamin. "Checking the Food Odometer: Comparing Food Miles for Local Versus Conventional Produce Sales in Iowa Institutions," Leopold Center, July 2003. Data for sidebar on page 158 came from here.

Rosset, Peter M. *The Multiple Functions and Benefits of Small Farm Agriculture* (Oakland: Food First, 1999). Rosset documents the ways in which small diversified farms are actually more efficient than large ones.

Sligh, Michael, and Carolyn Christman. *Who Owns Organic?* (Pittsboro, NC: RAFI-USA, 2003).

Stoll, Steven. *The Fruits of Natural Advantage: Making the Industrial Countryside in California* (Berkeley: University of California Press, 1998).

Tilman, David. "The Greening of the Green Revolution," *Nature,* 396 (November 19, 1998).

Wargo, John. *Our Children's Toxic Legacy* (New Haven: Yale University Press, 1996).

Wirzba, Norman, ed. *The Essential Agrarian Reader* (Lexington, KY: University Press of Kentucky, 2003).

Wolfe, M. S. "Crop Strength Through Diversity," *Nature* 406, no. 17 (August 2000).

On the complex and contentious subject of energy use in conventional and organic agriculture, I relied on many sources, including David Pimentel, Rich Pirog at the Leopold Center, the late Marty Bender at the Land Institute, and Karen Klonsky and Peter Livingston at the University of California at Davis, as well as the indefatigable work of researchers Chad Heeter and Malia Wollan. Pimental helped us calculate the energy required to grow, pack, wash, cool, and ship across country a pound of organic lettuce, using his data and additional information graciously provided by Earthbound Farm. Pimentel's numbers are sometimes criticized as high because he includes "embodied energy," i.e., the fossil fuel required to manufacture things like tractors. His numbers remain the most comprehensive, however, and whenever a specific figure is in dispute I've used the more conservative number or stated the range. On energetics in agriculture see also:

Carlsson-Kanyama, Annika, and Mireille Faist. *Energy Use in the Food Sector: A Data Survey. AFN-report 291* (Swedish Environmental Protection Agency: Stockholm, Sweden, 2000).

Heller, Martin C., and Gregory A. Keoleian. *Life Cycle-Based Sustainability Indicators for Assessment of the U.S. Food System,* Report No. CSS00-04. (Center for Sustainable Systems, University of Michigan, 2000). This study is the source for my figures on the portion of U.S. energy consumption devoted to the food system (one-fifth) and the portion of that amount (one-fifth) accounted for by farming (as opposed to packing, cooling, or shipping).

Livingston, Peter. "A Comparison of Economic Viability and Measured Energy Required for Conventional, Low Input, and Organic Farming Systems over a Rotational Period." Unpublished thesis. California State University, Chico, CA, 1995.

Lovins, Amory, L. Hunter Lovins, and Marty Bender. "Agriculture and Energy," *Encyclopedia of Energy Technology and the Environment* (New York: John Wiley & Sons, 1995).

Pimentel, David, ed. *Handbook of Energy Utilization in Agriculture* (Boca Raton, FL: CRC Press, 1980).

Pimentel, David, and Marcia Pimentel, eds. *Food, Energy, and Society* (Niwot, CO: University Press of Colorado, 1996).

Pimentel, David, et al. "Environmental, Energetic, and Economic Comparisons of Organic and Conventional Farming Systems," *BioScience* 55, no. 7 (July 2005), 573–82. The statistic on the energy savings of organic production (30 percent) comes from this study, though as Pimentel acknowledges, if the farm's fertility is not generated on the farm or nearby, this savings quickly disappears.

Tourte, Laura, et al. "Sample Costs to Produce Organic Leaf Lettuce." University of California Cooperative Extension, 2004.

PART III
CHAPTER 12: POLYFACE FARM, AND CHAPTER 13: GRASS

Benyus, Janine M. *Biomimicry: Innovation Inspired by Nature* (New York: Perennial, 2002). Offers a fine account of the Land Institute's project to perennialize agriculture.

Eisenberg, Evan. *The Ecology of Eden* (New York: Knopf, 1998).

Farb, Peter. *Living Earth* (New York: Pyramid Publications, 1959).

Harvey, Graham. *The Forgiveness of Nature: The Story of Grass* (London: Jonathan Cape/Random House, 2001).

Hawken, Paul, Amory Lovins, and L. Hunter Lovins. *Natural Capitalism* (New York: Bay Books, 2000). Another good account of the Land Institute's work.

Jackson, Wes, et al., eds. *Meeting the Expectations of the Land: Essays in Sustainable Agriculture and Stewardship* (San Francisco: North Point Press, 1984).

———. *New Roots for Agriculture* (Lincoln, NE: University of Nebraska Press, 1985).

Judy, Greg. *No Risk Ranching: Custom Grazing on Leased Land* (Ridgeland, MS: Green Park Press, 2003).

Logsdon, Gene. *All Flesh Is Grass: The Pleasures and Promises of Pasture Farming* (Athens, OH: Swallow Press/Ohio University, 2004).

Nation, Allan. *Knowledge Rich Ranching* (Ridgeland, MS: Green Park Press, 2002).

Savory, Allan. *Holistic Management: A New Framework for Decision Making* (Washington, D.C.: Island Press, 1999). Savory is a pioneer in using intensive grazing to restore arid grasslands, and is changing the way environmentalists regard the role of grazing in ecosystem health.

The Stockman Grass Farmer, published monthly.

Voisin, André. *Grass Productivity* (Washington, D.C.: Island Press, 1989).

CHAPTER 14: THE ANIMALS

For further reading on the advantages of polyculture, see *Permaculture* magazine (www.permaculture.co.uk); *Permaculture Activist* (www.permacultureactivist.net); and the works of Bill Mollison. Also see:

Furuno, Takao. *The Power of Duck: Integrated Rice and Duck Farming* (Tasmania, Australia: Tagari Publications, 2001). This is another example from another tradition of a polyculture farm. Furuno is the Joel Salatin of Japan.

Imhoff, Dan. *Farming with the Wild: Enhancing Biodiversity on Farms and Ranches* (San Francisco: Sierra Club Books, 2003).

Rosset, Peter. *The Multiple Functions and Benefits of Small Farm Agriculture* (Oakland: Food First, 1999).

CHAPTER 15: THE SLAUGHTERHOUSE

Joel explains exactly how to kill a chicken and compost slaughter waste in chapters 15 and 16 of *Pastured Poultry Profit$* (Swoope, VA: Polyface, 1996).

On slaughter practices, humane and otherwise, see Temple Grandin's Web site (www.grandin.com).

CHAPTER 16: THE MARKET

Berry, Wendell. *Citizenship Papers* (Washington, D.C.: Shoemaker & Hoard, 2003). See especially the essays "The Total Economy" (pp. 63–76) and "The Whole Horse" (pp. 113–26), where the Berry quotes in this chapter are found.

Blank, Steven. *The End of Agriculture in the American Portfolio* (Westport, CT: Quorum Books, 1998).

Fallon, Sally. *Nourishing Traditions* (Washington, D.C.: New Trends Publishing, 2001). Fallon is the president of the Weston A. Price Foundation: www.westonaprice.org.

Fernald, Anya, et al. *A World of Presidia: Food, Culture, and Community* (Bra, Italy: Slow Food Editore, 2004).

Gussow, Joan Dye. *This Organic Life: Confessions of a Suburban Homesteader* (White River Junction, VT: Chelsea Green Publishing, 2001).

Halweil, Brian. *Eat Here: Reclaiming Homegrown Pleasures in a Global Supermarket* (New York: W. W. Norton & Company, 2004).

———. *Home Grown: The Case for Local Food in a Global Market* (Washington, D.C.: Worldwatch Institute, 2002).

Kloppenberg, J., Jr., et al. "Coming into the Foodshed," *Agriculture and Human Values* 13, no. 3 (1996), 33–41. This article appears to be the first use of the term "foodshed": "The concept of a 'foodshed' (a term that elicits images of food flowing into a place) has been developed to promote discussion and action about the disempowerment and destructive nature of this current system with regards to the community and the environment."

Lyson, Thomas A. *Civic Agriculture: Reconnecting Farm, Food, and Community* (Medford, MA: Tufts University Press, 2004).

McKibben, Bill. "Small World: Why One Town Stays Unplugged," *Harper's* 307, no. 1843 (December 2003), 46–54.

Nabhan, Gary Paul. *Coming Home to Eat: The Pleasures and Politics of Local Foods* (New York: W. W. Norton, 2001).

Norberg-Hodge, Helena, et al. *Bringing the Food Economy Home: Local Alternatives to Global Agribusiness* (London: Zed Books, 2002).

Petrini, Carlo, ed. *Slow Food: Collected Thoughts on Taste, Tradition, and the Honest Pleasures of Food* (White River Junction, VT: Chelsea Green Publishing, 2001). See also Petrini's speeches on the Slow Food Web site.

Pollan, Michael. "Cruising on the Ark of Taste," *Mother Jones* (May 2003). An essay on the politics of Slow Food.

Porter, Michael E. *The Competitive Advantage of Nations* (New York: The Free Press, 1990).

Revkin, Andrew C. "Energy, an Ingredient in Local Food and Global Food," The *New York Times* Dot Earth Blog, December 11, 2007.

Rosenthal, Elisabeth. "Environmental Cost of Shipping Groceries Around the World," *New York Times,* April 26, 2008.

Yeong, Choy Leng. "NW Salmon Sent to China Before Reaching U.S. Tables," Bloomberg News, July 16, 2005.

CHAPTER 17: MY GRASS-FED MEAL

For a digest of research on the health benefits of grass-fed meat, milk, and eggs, see www.eatwild.com.

Brillat-Savarin, Jean-Anthelme. *The Physiology of Taste.* Trans. Anne Drayton (London: Penguin, 1994).

Child, Julia. *Mastering the Art of French Cooking* (New York: Alfred A. Knopf, 2001).

McGee, Harold. *On Food and Cooking: The Science and Lore of the Kitchen* (New York: Charles Scribner, 2004).

Robinson, Jo. *Pasture Perfect: The Far-Reaching Benefits of Choosing Meat, Eggs, and Dairy from Grass-Fed Animals* (Vashon, WA: Vashon Island Press, 2004).

———. *Why Grassfed Is Best! The Surprising Benefits of Grassfed Meat, Eggs, and Dairy Products* (Vashon, WA: Vashon Island Press, 2000).

For recent research on the role of omega-3s and other fats in the diet, see the proceedings of the 2004 meeting of the International Society for the Study of Fatty Acids and Lipids (www.issfal.org.uk). The research on the benefits of omega-3s cited in my chapter came from the following articles:

de Groot, R. H. M., et al. *Correlation Between Plasma (N-3) Fatty Acid Levels and Cognitive Performance in Women*. Report. Department of Psychiatry and Neuropsychology, Nutrition and Toxicology Research Institute Maastricht (Maastricht University, The Netherlands, 2004).

Kelley, R. L., et al. *Effect of Dietary Fish Oil on Puppy Trainability*. Report. The Iams Company Technical Centre (Lewisburg, OH: 2004).

Smuts, C. M., et al. *The Effect of Omega-3 Rich Spread on the Cognitive Function of Learners 6–9 Years Old from a Low Socio-Economic Community*. Nutritional Intervention Research Unit, MRC. Report (Parow Valley, Stellenbosch, South Africa, 2004).

PART IV
CHAPTER 18: THE FOREST

Fascinating mushroom facts can be found at www.mycolog.com

Allport, Susan. *The Primal Feast: Food, Sex, Foraging, and Love* (Lincoln, NE: Writers Club Press, 2003).

Budiansky, Stephen. *The Covenant of the Wild: Why Animals Chose Domestication* (New Haven: Yale University Press, 1999). Thoreau's quote on hunting is on page 157.

Leopold, Aldo. *A Sand County Almanac* (New York: Ballantine, 1986).

Nelson, Davia, and Nikki Silva. *Hidden Kitchens: Stories, Recipes, and More from NPR's The Kitchen Sisters* (New York: Rodale, 2005). See especially the chapter on Angelo Garro, pages 172–89.

CHAPTER 19: EATING ANIMALS

Berger, John. *About Looking* (New York: Vintage International, 1991).

Budiansky, Stephen. *The Covenant of the Wild: Why Animals Choose Domestication* (New York: William Morrow & Co., 1992). A valuable book on the evolution of domestication in animals.

———. *If a Lion Could Talk: Animal Intelligence and the Evolution of Consciousness* (New York: The Free Press, 1998).

Coetzee, J. M. *The Lives of Animals* (Princeton: Princeton University Press, 1999).

Dennett, Daniel C. *Kinds of Minds: Toward an Understanding of Consciousness* (New York: Basic Books, 1996).

Ehrenfeld, David. *Beginning Again: People and Nature in the New Millenium* (New York: Oxford University Press, 1995).

Ovid. *Metamorphoses*. Trans. A. D. Melville. (Oxford: Oxford University Press, 1998).

Flannery, Tim. *The Eternal Frontier: An Ecological History of North America and Its Peoples* (New York: Atlantic Monthly Press, 2001). Flannery's account of how the Plains bison evolved under the pressure of hunting by Indians is on pages 223–29.

Regan, Tom. *The Case for Animal Rights* (Berkeley: University of California Press, 1983).

———, and Peter Singer, eds. *Animal Rights and Human Obligations* (Englewood Cliffs, NJ: Prentice Hall, 1989).

Scully, Matthew. *Dominion: The Power of Man, the Suffering of Animals, and the Call to Mercy* (New York: St. Martin's Press, 2002). An eloquent defense of animals, and an indictment of factory farming, from the right.

Singer, Peter. *Animal Liberation* (New York: Ecco, 2002).

———. *Practical Ethics* (Cambridge, U.K.: Cambridge University Press, 1999).

———, ed. *In Defense of Animals* (New York: Basil Blackwell, 1985).

Thomas, Keith. *Man and the Natural World: A History of the Modern Sensibility* (New York: Pantheon, 1983).

Williams, Joy. *Ill Nature: Rants and Reflections on Humanity and Other Animals* (New York: Vintage, 2001).

Wise, Steven M. *Drawing the Line: Science and the Case for Animal Rights* (Cambridge, MA: Perseus, 2002).

CHAPTER 20: HUNTING

Nelson, Richard. *The Island Within* (New York: Vintage, 1991). "The Gifts of the Deer" is one of the great accounts of hunting.

Ortega y Gasset, José. *Meditations on Hunting*. Trans. Howard B. Westcott (New York: Scribner's, 1972). A remarkable book, brilliant and more than a little mad. My own meditations on hunting owe a large debt to Ortega's.

Shepard, Paul. *Coming Home to the Pleistocene* (Washington, D.C.: Island Press, 1998).

———. *Nature and Madness* (Athens, GA: University of Georgia Press, 1998). Writing in the tradition of Ortega, Shepard offers a bracing reevaluation of Paleolithic culture and psychology.

———. *The Tender Carnivore and the Sacred Game* (Athens, GA: University of Georgia Press, 1998).

Chapter 21: Gathering

My education in the mysteries of the fungal kingdom profited from time spent in the field with Ignacio Chapela and David Arora, as well as with mushroom hunters Anthony Tassinello, Ben Baily, Sue Moore, and Angelo Garro. The following books and articles were also valuable:

Arora, David. *Mushrooms Demystified* (Berkeley: Ten Speed Press, 1986).

Hudler, George W. *Magical Mushrooms, Mischievous Molds* (Princeton: Princeton University Press, 2000).

Krieger, Louis C. C. *The Mushroom Handbook* (New York: Dover Publications, 1967).

Lincoff, Gary H. *National Audubon Society Field Guide to North American Mushrooms* (New York: Alfred A. Knopf, 2003).

McKenna, Terence. *Food of the Gods: The Search for the Original Tree of Knowledge* (New York: Bantam, 1993).

Rommelmann, Nancy. "The Great Alaskan Morel Rush of '05," *Los Angeles Times Magazine,* July 10, 2005.

Schaechter, Elio. *In the Company of Mushrooms: A Biologist's Tale* (Cambridge, MA: Harvard University Press, 1998).

Stamets, Paul. *Growing Gourmet and Medicinal Mushrooms* (Berkeley: Ten Speed Press, 2000).

———. *Mycelium Running: How Mushrooms Can Help Save the World* (Berkeley: Ten Speed Press, 2005).

Treisman, Ann. "Features and Objects in Visual Processing," *Scientific American* 254, no. 11 (November 1986), 114–25. Treisman, a research psychologist, developed the concept of the "pop-out effect" in human visual processing.

Weil, Andrew. *The Marriage of the Sun and Moon: Dispatches from the Frontiers of Consciousness* (Boston: Houghton Mifflin, 2004). See chapters 7 to 9.

Chapter 22: The Perfect Meal

Brillat-Savarin, Jean-Anthelme. *The Physiology of Taste.* Trans. Anne Drayton (London: Penguin, 1994).

Leader, Daniel, and Judith Blahnik. *Bread Alone: Bold Fresh Loaves from Your Own Hands* (New York: Morrow, 1993). See chapter 13 on gathering wild yeast for the chef and baking a levain. I also learned about baking with wild yeasts from Robbie Barnett.

McGee, Harold. *On Food and Cooking: The Science and Lore of the Kitchen* (New York: Charles Scribner, 2004).

THE OMNIVORE'S SOLUTION

Pollan, Michael. *In Defense of Food: An Eater's Manifesto* (New York: Penguin Press, 2008).

INDEX